FINDING HOME AGAIN

Hope survives the war in Ukraine

a memoir

SHARON T. MARKEY

foreword by JEREMY CAMP

Copyright © 2026 by Sharon T. Markey

Published by Pensive Scriptorium

All rights reserved. No part of this book may be reproduced or transmitted in any form or by any means, electronic or mechanical, including photocopying, recording, or by any information storage and retrieval system, without written permission from the author, except as permitted by U.S. copyright law.

For permission requests, contact sharon@MommyJoys.com.

Scripture quotations are taken from the Holy Bible, New Living Translation, copyright ©1996, 2004, 2015 by Tyndale House Foundation. Used by permission of Tyndale House Publishers, Carol Stream, Illinois 60188. All rights reserved.

Trademark Notice: This book may contain references to brand names and products, including Airbnb, Booking.com, Delta, Duplo, IKEA, KLM, and LEGO. All such names and trademarks are the property of their respective owners and are used solely for descriptive and identification purposes. Their use does not imply endorsement, sponsorship, or affiliation.

This work depicts actual events in the life of the author as truthfully as recollection permits and/or can be verified by research. Some names have been changed, some events have been compressed, and some dialogue has been recreated.

Front cover art by Sarah Janisse Brown. Author photo by Viktoria Mokra.

ISBN: 978-1-971012-01-8

Praise for this Book

This book shows a side of Russia's war against Ukraine that we have not been told. The war has been politicized, it's been moralized, but until now, it's not been personalized.

~ Leonard Lee, author of *Leading from the Middle*

FINDING HOME AGAIN *is a rare gem. This memoir reads like a novel yet carries the spiritual weight of a testimony. Sharon T. Markey's story is not only a chronicle of war and displacement, but also a profound testament to the resilience of faith when the world collapses.*

As the war began, Sharon evacuated from Ukraine to Hungary with her six sons—alone—demonstrating extraordinary courage and maternal strength. Her honesty, bravery, and unwavering trust in God moved me profoundly. This powerful account will stir your heart, strengthen your faith, and remind you that home is not just a place: it's a promise.

~ Dr. Russell Chun, creator of Interlinkt.org, a mobile resource for refugee resettlement

Gripping and important story of one family's escape from war, their faith in God and each other. A powerful true story. I loved it.

~ Joe Bunting, *Wall Street Journal* bestselling writer

This memoir is a poignant account of a family uprooted by war, forced to adapt to constant upheavals and uncertainty. Anyone who has ever yearned for home will be touched by the way this family discovered blessing in the midst of their trials and found a new home in an unexpected place. It is a timely story for our day, bringing the plight of refugees into sharp focus while extending hope for a better future.

~ Evelyn Puerto, award-winning author of *Through the Rapids*

As a therapist, supervisor, and educator, I read FINDING HOME AGAIN *through the lens of trauma, and what* Sharon T. Markey *offers in these pages is one of the most honest, accessible, and powerful lived experiences of trauma I've encountered in narrative form. Without clinical jargon, she brings us into the raw reality of displacement, loss of safety, and the weight of caregiving in crisis. What's remarkable is that she doesn't tie it up in a bow. Instead, she walks the reader through the ambiguity, the helplessness, the physical and emotional dysregulation . . . and the quiet, persistent presence of God in the middle of it all. It's beautiful!*

This is a deeply human book. It's an invaluable read not only for those who have experienced trauma but also for those of us who walk with the traumatized. It reminds us that trauma isn't always visible, and healing isn't always linear, but faith, connection, and telling the truth about our experience are essential pieces of the journey.

I recommend this book to anyone working in the fields of trauma, missions, or mental health. Sharon's story isn't just one of survival, it's one of soul-deep strength!

~ Dr. Casey Hall, assistant professor of counseling at Colorado Christian University

To George,
my kindred spirit,
life partner,
and biggest cheerleader.

This book exists because you believed in me
and pushed me to pursue my dreams.

Foreword

If you're holding this book, you're holding something special. *Finding Home Again* isn't just a story you'll read—it's one you'll carry with you. It's honest. It's raw. And it gives language to the questions and struggles that often sit unspoken in the heart.

My wife, Adrienne, and I have spent years working with refugee families in our city—listening to their stories, helping them settle in, and mourning their losses alongside them. We've also witnessed the Markey family live through seasons of heartbreak, beauty, displacement, and deep faith. Their journey mirrors much of what we've experienced in our own lives: grief that swallows you, questions that seemingly have no resolution, and the kind of faith that clings to God when nothing else makes sense.

This book tells the story of a family leaving everything behind because of war. But as you'll see, this isn't just about refugees or relocating. It's about what we all yearn for: a place to belong—a sense of home. And most importantly, the comfort of knowing God is still holding on, even when everything else changes.

Finding Home Again will stir something in you. If you've ever felt lost, uncertain, homesick, or overwhelmed, this book will remind you that you're not alone. You'll be inspired to open your arms a little wider to the people around you.

Jeremy Camp
Nashville, Tennessee, USA
August 2025

CONTENTS

1

Choosing a Home

"Where are you from?" For most of my life, I've struggled to answer this simple question. I was born in Hawaii to a Japanese mother and a Caucasian father, but I grew up in Southern California. For nine months of the year, I attended a predominantly white school. The other three months I spent in Hawaii with my mostly Asian family. I saw myself as an alien in California, but when I returned home to my island birthplace, the locals saw me as a visitor from the Mainland.

Few understood me, and I struggled to relate to my peers. But when I met my future husband, something clicked.

George grew up in the USA in the state of Indiana, but moved to Ukraine at the age of sixteen with his missionary parents. When we met at a church conference in California, he had been living abroad for nine years. No longer fully American but not quite Ukrainian, he got me, and I recognized something in him I'd never encountered. He was a kindred spirit who, like me, existed on a plane somewhere between two worlds.

When we married, I was excited to join his life in Ukraine. I had finally chosen a home. After the wedding, I moved to Kyiv—and immediately nosedived into four and a half years of depression.

Everything was unfamiliar. I couldn't understand anyone and could barely make myself understood. Tasks like seeing a doctor or shopping for a winter coat were overwhelming. I was terrified to leave our apartment alone, but I was determined to make it work. Ukraine was my home now, and I was going to push through until it felt that way.

Eventually, I made friends, learned the language, and became comfortable. We had children—six sons—and began raising them. Ukraine was home, and life overflowed with joy and wonder.

Then, on February 24, 2022, everything changed.

2

What Would You Do?

December 2021
Tbilisi, Republic of Georgia

Despite the Russian troops massing on the border of Ukraine, my husband George and I left our six sons at home in Kyiv to enjoy a get-away. Friends had agreed to take care of our kids for a few days as a birthday favor for George, and we were celebrating in Tbilisi, where Renée, his twin sister, lived with her family. The twins hadn't been together on their birthday in years. My husband's widowed mother also lived in Tbilisi. We were all Christian missionaries.

George and I relished the time away in a romantic new destination. We strolled arm-in-arm along sun-drenched cobblestone streets, laughing as we tried to decipher the letters of the curious Georgian script, a collection of curlicues lined up in neat rows. We dined out and bought fresh-squeezed pomegranate juice from a street vendor. It was a living red, like liquid rubies, and tasted like luxury and health and exotic, far-away places.

But the best part of the trip was simply spending time with George's family. His mother, Pam, had been like a mother to me ever since I married her eldest son and left my family in California to join his life two continents and an ocean away in Ukraine. I treasured every moment with her, and they didn't happen often enough, as far as I was concerned. Over the years, Renée and I also developed a bond, and I felt as close to her as to my own sister.

On our final day, we all gathered for dinner at the home of Renée and her husband, Jed. We ordered takeout, and Pam insisted I get extra food—her treat. She was always worried I was too skinny or wasn't getting enough iron, and she'd made it her mission to ensure I was well fed during the entirety of our stay in Tbilisi. I enjoyed her mothering.

After the meal, we hung out late into the evening playing board games under the direction of Josh, Jed and Renée's sixteen-year-old son. Once the games were put away and we were on the verge of leaving, our fourteen-year-old niece treated us to an unplanned cello performance. Her fingers danced gracefully across the strings as she coaxed beautiful music from the instrument. As we stood listening, I leaned against George and slipped my arm around his waist. He kissed the top of my head.

People often tell us we're an adorable couple. I love how fit and trim George is and how he makes me feel so petite. At six-foot-two, he's almost a whole head taller than I. With his gentle blue eyes, wavy dark hair, and rugged beard and mustache, he's always the most handsome man in the room.

I also have wavy dark hair, but it hangs past my waist, and my eyes are brown and ever-so-slightly Asian. They don't go with my strong German nose, and I can often tell that new acquaintances are trying to figure out my ethnicity. I always chuckle inside when they finally work up the courage to ask. I smile and explain I'm half Japanese. George likes my enigmatic face and frequently tells me how beautiful I am. After over two decades of marriage, spending time together is still our favorite activity.

Our niece ended her recital with a flourish, and we all applauded. My thoughts wandered to our upcoming morning flight and all the items waiting on my to-do list at home. George, Pam, and I prepared to leave, but then Jed asked a question that would shred my to-do list and replace it with tasks I had never imagined.

"So, what do you guys plan to do if Russia invades?"

George and I had a well-established life in Kyiv, the capital of Ukraine, where we lived with our sons, two pet rats, and a German shepherd mix, named Jack, that we had adopted as a stray puppy five years earlier. Ukraine was home. I'd lived there nineteen years, George, twenty-nine. Our kids, ages three through fourteen, had never lived anywhere else.

By that point, we had seen two revolutions, the Russian invasion and takeover of Ukraine's Crimea in 2014, and eight years of fighting in the eastern part of the country. Initially, this unofficial war with Russian-backed separatists was terrifying, but as the years dragged on and the violence remained confined to the east, eventually what was once unthinkable became simply another fact of life.

Since October, I had heard scattered rumors of Russian troops gathering on Ukraine's eastern border, but I hadn't given them much thought. Even if Russia officially stepped in to take over the two regions where separatists were fighting Ukrainian forces, I didn't foresee any tangible effect on us. For eight years, the conflict had left us unmolested, and I assumed it always would. Kyiv and Western Ukraine were untouchable. Nobody there wanted Russian rule.

Jed's question caught me completely off-guard. Jed was a veteran missionary and all-around savvy, knowledgeable person. I swallowed hard and took a deep breath, trying to slow my heart and calm the rising anxiety attack I could feel constricting my chest. If Jed was asking this question, it could only mean there was a real risk to our family and our way of life.

"What would you do?" I asked, feeling cornered.

"Well, you'd need to have your documents, cash, and valuables packed and ready to go. And you'd need to have an evacuation plan."

"Right." I nodded, keeping my face calm, trying not to show my inner turmoil. Jed sounded serious. George and I hadn't even talked about the threat of a Russian invasion. Maybe that needed to change.

3

Go or Stay?

December 8, 2021
Kyiv, Ukraine

The next morning, George and I rose before dawn and caught our flight back to Ukraine. The main airport that services Kyiv is located outside the capital in the town of Boryspil. The USSR was responsible for this awkward arrangement. Placing the airport so far from Kyiv made it easy to control the access regular citizens had to foreigners. And vice versa.

As George and I rode home in a taxi, I contemplated the irony: even after thirty years of Ukrainian independence, Russia was still trying to limit Ukraine's access to non-Russian influences. In 2014, pro-European protests in Kyiv ousted Ukraine's then pro-Russian president. The Kremlin responded by invading Ukraine's Crimea and backing separatist fighters in eastern Ukraine. Eight years later, Crimea was still occupied, and Russia was poised to invade eastern Ukraine in response to Kyiv seeking closer ties with the West.

Our route home took us across the Dnipro River, a broad waterway that cuts Kyiv in half. High hills overlook the western side, forming the backbone of the city. Many of Kyiv's most famous landmarks line the ridge. Two were easily visible from the bridge. The Motherland Monument, a gargantuan steel woman with a stern face and masculine arms, towered over the river, holding a shield and sword aloft. Erected by the Soviets, she stands taller than the Statue of Liberty. I'd always found her particularly ugly. Farther up the river we could see the graceful domed buildings of the Kyiv-Pechersk Lavra, an Orthodox monastery complex and UNESCO World Heritage Site.

Our driver turned right off the bridge, following the bank of the Dnipro, between the hills and the river. We were almost home. Rising above the trees along the top of the ridge, the silver crown of a huge metal arch came into view. It had been built by the Soviets to commemorate the 1654 reunification of Ukraine with Russia. After Ukraine's independence in 1991, it had been renamed the People's Friendship Arch, supposedly to celebrate the friendship between Ukraine and Russia. That seemed ludicrous now. I often wondered why they didn't just tear the thing down.[1]

Our driver turned left, away from the river, entering the district of Podil, where we lived—an old neighborhood where every building had either historic or architectural significance. In stark contrast to other parts of the city, where many of the structures were dismal Communist-era apartment complexes, Podil had a quaint, European feel.

The older buildings were brick, many with plaster facades and elaborate ornamentation framing the windows and running below the rooflines. Some of these buildings had been recently restored and painted bright colors. The ground floors often housed shops, cafes, and restaurants, with walk-up apartments on the upper stories.

Living in Podil was one of my favorite things about our life. But if asked to choose the best aspect, I would have said the many friends within walking distance, who were regularly in and out of our home. Our apartment also played a major role in our happiness. Six months earlier, we had relocated to a three-story mansion dating back to the 1890s. It had fallen into disrepair, and a developer acquired it in the 1990s. He reconstructed it and divided it into two units, each with three stories and a basement.

Our unit had four bedrooms—five if you counted the one we created in the basement—and several other rooms, including a

---

1. *On May 14, 2022, the Kyiv City Council renamed the People's Friendship Arch the Arch of Freedom of the Ukrainian People. Some have called for its complete dismantling, but as of this writing, it still stands.*

large one on the first floor filled with beanbag chairs we used for movie nights and Sunday services for our fledgling church.

Our driver stopped beside an arch between two buildings. We thanked him, retrieved our bags, and walked through into a small courtyard. Our three-story building formed one side. It was covered in grapevines that looked lovely in the spring, summer, and early fall. The vines had no leaves in December, but they still bore the shriveled remnants of the last summer's fruit. The grapes were already ripe when we moved, but with the hecticness of unpacking and settling in, I never harvested them.

We crossed the courtyard to our building entrance. Our dog, Jack, was the first member of the family to notice our arrival. He came running to meet us, his tail wagging wildly, his feet unable to stay still as he pranced around us in excitement. Soon all six kids joined us, as well as our apartment mate, Olya, a strikingly beautiful and talented Ukrainian woman, a graduate of the prestigious Kyiv Conservatory of Music. We all exchanged warm hugs and excited greetings.

Olya had been renting half of the duplex where we had lived previously and had moved with us into the mansion. She was a dear friend and a member of the team of people helping us start our church. After living with us throughout most of COVID, she practically felt like family. She was poised to release her first album of original songs in February 2022, and we were excited to see her launch her music career.

As soon as we unpacked from our trip, I created evacuation bags. I filled two rolling carry-on suitcases with our important documents, valuables, and items that had sentimental value. Along with the expected things like cash and jewelry and photographs, I included our extensive collection of essential oils. If we had them, I knew I could treat everything from bug bites and insect stings to fever, fungal infections, and food poisoning. I also slipped in a professional hair dryer that a group of friends had recently given me for my birthday. Though it felt frivolous, I knew we couldn't afford to replace it, and if we did evacuate, I would regret leaving it behind.

When I was done, I stacked the two suitcases next to my desk, ready to go at a moment's notice. George seemed amused, but after almost two decades of marriage, he was accustomed to my extreme fixation on safety.

Suspecting he didn't take the threat of invasion seriously, I was pleased when he thoughtfully discussed our family evacuation plan with me. He'd already figured it out. It was simple: pull our five-seat sedan out of the car-sharing fleet where it was generating passive income, pack our six kids and three pets inside, and head west. Olya could squeeze in too, if she wanted.

I was reassured that he had a plan. In retrospect, it was surprisingly short-sighted, especially for such an intelligent man. George has two master's degrees—one of them in applied mathematics—and a knack for generating ideas. Some of them are great. Time would prove this one wasn't.

We celebrated Christmas and the New Year while the buildup of Russian troops continued. They were now positioned on three sides of Ukraine. Those in Belarus were especially alarming. Unlike the soldiers on Ukraine's eastern and southern borders, those directly north of us in Belarus could quickly reach Kyiv. But surely they were only there to intimidate. Putin wouldn't dare attack Kyiv, would he?

As we progressed into January 2022, concern over what Russia was planning continued to mount. We began to receive emails from the US Embassy advising us to leave Ukraine, and my family in the United States started to contact me frequently. They refrained from telling us what to do, but it was obvious they were terribly worried and wanted us out of the country.

Their fear was contagious.

One morning, craving relief from the suspense, I asked God for guidance. With trembling fingers, I opened the Bible app on my phone to the daily reading. I was stunned when I saw these verses from Psalm 27:

The Lord is my light and my salvation—
So why should I be afraid?
The Lord is my fortress, protecting me from danger,

So why should I tremble?
When evil people come to devour me,
When my enemies and foes attack me,
They will stumble and fall.
Though a mighty army surrounds me,
My heart will not be afraid.
Even if I am attacked,
I will remain confident.[2]

I reread the words again and again, my breath coming fast in excitement. These verses were talking about our specific situation. Although they'd been penned thousands of years ago, they were fresh and alive. It was no coincidence that I was scheduled to read them on the exact day I sought guidance from God. This was his answer. I interpreted them to mean that, no matter what happened, we were to stay where we were and trust God to protect us.

Profound calm filled me, instantly neutralizing my anxiety and questions. The all-powerful Creator of the universe had told me he would protect us. The situation hadn't changed, but everything felt different, as if I had stepped into a parallel reality. I recognized this as the supernatural peace Jesus had promised to his followers.

However, as the days passed, I struggled to remain in this new reality. I desperately wanted to trust God, remain calm, and live one day at a time, but it was hard. Sometimes I experienced again the bliss of feeling God's perfect care enveloping me, but it was a daily—sometimes an hourly—struggle. And each time I received a new text message from one of my worried relatives, my fragile sense of peace would shatter into a million razor-sharp fragments.

George didn't share my anxiety. He has always been a wonderful balance to my hyperactive sense of danger.

"It'll be alright. Nothing's going to happen," he'd often say.

Over the years, I learned to lean into his reassurances. They kept me grounded. But though I longed to be persuaded by his calm confidence, this time I wondered if he was falling victim to wishful thinking.

---

2. *Bible quotation taken from the* New Living Translation

Despite George's conviction that nothing would happen, we talked about theoretical resettlement options. Western Ukraine and Tbilisi were at the top of our list, but we had no desire to leave Kyiv. Our whole life was there—our work, our kids' schools, most of our friends. How much do you disrupt your family over fear of a what-if? Without knowing the cost of staying, the cost of leaving felt too high.

Plus, I believed God had told us to stay.

Even though I didn't think Russia would actually launch a full-scale invasion, as the weeks passed, I experienced mounting suspense. The greatest challenge was not fear of the what-ifs, but uncertainty about the here-and-now. What were we supposed to do? Doubts formed in my mind about what that psalm meant. Did God really want us to stay? Were we being obedient to him? Or were we just being irresponsible parents by not evacuating our children?

I told George if I knew none of us would die as a result of our decision to stay, I would be at peace, no matter what happened. But without that foreknowledge, I was tormented. Should we go or should we stay? How long did we have to decide?

It became hard to breathe, as if the weight of indecision was crushing my chest. During the day, I longed for the oblivion of sleep, but when I went to bed, I lay awake in the darkness, my mind and heart racing.

4

Just In Case

January–February 2022
Kyiv, Ukraine

Despite the uncertainty, life continued normally. One morning in late January, I looked out our kitchen window and noticed a strange man in our private courtyard. At first, I thought he was lost. It wasn't uncommon for people to wander into our courtyard and leave when they realized there was no outlet. But unlike them, he wasn't consulting a smartphone. He was just standing there, chewing. It was an odd place for a snack.

Then I noticed his shoes. Though the weather was below freezing, he wore open-toed rubber house slippers without socks. His pants were too short, and the sight of his ankle skin exposed to the frigid air made me cringe.

He approached our building and ripped one of our beautiful grapevines loose. What in the world did he think he was doing? He yanked off a cluster of old grapes—they looked more like raisins—and crammed a fistful in his mouth. Shock replaced my anger as I realized how hungry he had to be to resort to eating them.

What could I give him? I assumed he was homeless, so I couldn't offer him packages of uncooked rice or buckwheat, but it was still early in the day, and I hadn't prepared any meals yet. All I had were two loaves of freshly baked bread. I grabbed a knife and cut one in half. It was still warm, and the aroma of cinnamon tickled my nostrils as I sliced through it, revealing a hearty loaf studded with raisins. It was a special gluten-free recipe, developed to help George manage his celiac disease. It was high in protein and iron and loaded with flavor. It would make a wonderful breakfast for the man outside. I put it in a bag and added four apples.

I glanced out the window and was dismayed to see that the man was already gone. He couldn't have gotten far. I could catch him if I hurried.

I was still wearing my pajamas, but I realized I didn't have time to get dressed. I quickly pulled on my knee-high winter boots and threw on my knee-length down coat. Satisfied no one would be able to tell I was wearing pajamas, I grabbed the bag of food and dashed out the door.

I raced through the arch and out onto the sidewalk. I stopped, surprised not to see the man anywhere. Which way had he gone? I stared up and down the street and finally spotted him half a block away, walking quickly. I ran as fast as I could in my tall boots, past old brick buildings covered in aging plaster that had fallen off in places to reveal the brickwork beneath. I finally caught up with the man a short distance before the first intersection.

"Excuse me," I said in Ukrainian, panting a little from exertion, my breath making puffs of steam in the winter air.

He stopped and faced me.

I shoved the bag of food toward him. "This is for you."

He accepted it, laid a hand on his chest, and said, "Thank you," in Ukrainian. His eyes were expressive and vulnerable and conveyed the depth of his gratitude.

I had so much I wanted to communicate, but in the awkwardness of the moment, I couldn't form a single coherent sentence. I just smiled, then turned and walked home. I watched for him in our courtyard and looked for him when I walked around our neighborhood, but I never saw him again.

There was no way I could foresee that soon I'd be the one without appropriate footwear, forced to accept the generosity of others.

In early February, two of George's brothers visited us. Jon and Aaron lived with their families in Western Ukraine in the city of Ternopil, a place we ourselves had once called home. Prompted by advice from my dad, George and I decided to send our three oldest sons back with George's brothers. That way, if we needed to evacuate, it would be easier for everyone to fit into our car.

Kyiv schools were shut due to COVID, so it was a perfect opportunity for the kids to get some coveted time with their cousins in Ternopil. Despite the short notice, I knew the boys would be excited about the trip.

I headed down to the basement, where we had our family room, a playroom, and a small bedroom with a triple bunk bed. Two of the boys sat on the family room couch, improvising a duet on ukuleles. They spent hours this way. The entire basement was their domain, a space for uninhibited creativity and play.

"Hey, boys," I said.

"Yeah, Mommy?" Kiyoshi stopped playing and looked up at me. Even though he was thirteen, he still called us "Mommy" and "Daddy." All the kids did, perhaps because that was what I still called my own parents.

Kiyoshi had looked so Asian as a baby that we used his Japanese middle name from birth. Even now, he still looked more Japanese than the rest of his brothers. While they all had light brown hair and eyes ranging from gray-blue to medium brown, Kiyoshi's hair was nearly black, his eyes dark and serious.

Sitting next to Kiyoshi, eleven-year-old Peter was a stark contrast in temperament and appearance. He continued to strum his ukulele, his curly, sandy-brown hair bouncing as he bobbed his head to his beat.

"Peter, are you listening?" I said.

"Yeah." He kept playing.

"You boys are going to Ternopil with Uncle Jon and Uncle Aaron today."

"What?" Kiyoshi's eyebrows rose.

"No way! We'll get to see Georgie!" Naming his favorite of his eight cousins in Ternopil, Peter finally stopped strumming and did a little, seated dance.

"They're leaving soon, so you need to pack your backpacks right now. Take clothes and anything that's really special to you. Make sure you take the ukuleles too."

"Wait, is this because there might be a war?" Kiyoshi looked sharply up at me, his dark eyes intense.

"I don't really think there will be, but just in case. The rest of us will come in a few weeks, and then we'll all come back home by train."

"Whoa! We get to be there that long?" Peter's gray-blue eyes were wide, and his mouth was hanging open.

From the basement, I took the stairs to the third floor, where our eldest son, Samuel, had his bedroom. He was lying on his stomach on his bed, reading a novel. His two passions were reading and running, and if he wasn't in his room with a book, he was likely out running laps around our block.

My lanky fifteen-year-old was almost as tall as I was. His hair was shaved in a buzz cut, except for a narrow strip down the center of his head that he had been growing out for years. He kept it pulled back in a rattail that hung down the back of his neck. He didn't look up when I entered.

"Samuel?"

"Yeah?" He glanced up at me with clear gray eyes.

"You and Kiyoshi and Peter are going to Ternopil."

"Really? When?"

"As soon as you can be ready."

"What about my birthday party? I still didn't get to have my friends over."

"We'll have to wait until you get back. We couldn't do it right now anyway, because of COVID."

"Yeah, I guess."

"Pack some clothes and anything that's really special to you, just in case something happens."

"In case what happens?"

"Like if Russia invades."

"No, that's not gonna happen."

In the midst of the preparations, I gathered the three younger boys, kneeling to get on their level. "Hey, guys. Samuel, Kiyoshi, and Peter are going to Ternopil with Uncle Jon and Uncle Aaron."

"What? Why can't we go?" Eight-year-old James had arresting hazel eyes, framed by luxurious lashes. They were glaring at me reproachfully.

"You little guys need to stay with me and Daddy, but we're going to go too."

"When?" asked five-year-old Andrew, his forehead furrowed and his eyebrows tilted up in the middle, communicating worry. I often joked it was his default facial expression, and that wasn't much of an exaggeration.

"In a few weeks. You'll get to see your cousins."

Three-year-old Isaac perked up. "Cousins?" His brown eyes were wide and dancing.

"Yes, your cousins!" I wrapped my arms around him. He snuggled into my embrace, and I kissed his downy hair.

"Come here," I said to the other two. They moved in, and we shared a group hug.

Before long we were all exchanging hugs with their older brothers and Jon and Aaron. George and I followed them out to Jon's van. Kiyoshi and Peter were taking our two pet rats, and Kiyoshi secured their cage with a seatbelt.

"Have a good time, boys!" I forced my lips into a smile and willed it not to wobble.

Kiyoshi stood beside the van with slumped shoulders, displaying none of the excitement he normally had before a trip to see his cousins.

"Kiyoshi, are you okay?" I asked.

"Yeah."

"Really?" I forced him to make eye contact and raised my eyebrows.

"I'm fine." He looked away.

Realizing I would not get him to talk, I gave him a tight hug instead, desperate to impart comfort and strength to my most serious son. Samuel and Peter were upbeat. They hugged me, then their dad, before jumping into the van.

"I love you, boys. Say hi to everyone!" I wanted to snatch them back, hold them close, and never let go.

"Have a great time!" George said as he slid the van door closed. The sound rumbled in my chest and bowed my shoulders. I locked my eyes on my boys as Jon pulled away from the curb.

George and I stood on the sidewalk holding hands, watching the van carrying half our children as it drove away. George headed back to our apartment before it was completely out of sight. My fingers entwined with his, I followed reluctantly, looking backwards over my shoulder as I walked.

5

Wave Goodbye to Daddy

February 2022
Kyiv & Ternopil, Ukraine

George and I decided to pull our sedan out of the car-sharing fleet to keep parked by our apartment, gassed and ready. But the same night George planned to retrieve it, a renter totaled it.

The timing was too precise to be coincidence. I had the bizarre impression of watching events unfold on a movie screen, our life a thriller where the hero constantly encountered ridiculous obstacles. The notion gave me unexpected comfort. If our misfortune was scripted, so was our ending, and I believed the writer would work things out for our good. Did God do this so I would trust him instead of relying on our carefully laid plans?

The US Embassy told all American citizens to leave Ukraine immediately by any means available. They sent us a schedule of chartered flights to the US and offered us tickets for purchase. Anyone who chose to remain in Ukraine was to understand the US Government would not evacuate them if Russia invaded.

One day I got a call on my cell phone from an unfamiliar US number. I was shocked when the voice on the line identified himself as a representative of the US State Department. He asked about our plans and emphasized that the US would take no responsibility for us if we ignored their recommendation to leave. I thanked him and hung up, shaken. It was one more complication in the script of our lives, and I worried our decision to remain in our home made us troublemakers in the eyes of the American government.

I went back and forth in my mind multiple times per day—should we go or should we stay? It was a near-constant mental refrain, a mantra that ensured I could never find tranquility.

Though nothing was wrong with my body, I felt physically ill much of the time. I remembered the powerful feelings of courage and peace that filled me when I read Psalm 27, but that experience felt increasingly distant and unreal. I knew if God told me he would protect us, he would be true to his word—but what if I had misinterpreted what he was saying because I wanted to stay in Kyiv so badly?

But it had seemed so vivid. I had been sure the Spirit of God spoke those words to my heart. However, when I reread them now, they were just pretty poetry, vaguely comforting, but not enough to carry me through. I longed for rock-solid faith in the face of danger, but I wanted God to give me a new sign each day to confirm we were supposed to stay. My resolve was disintegrating.

I told myself nothing was going to happen, but I stocked our apartment with drinking water and non-perishable foods. I kept our home running, but if someone had shadowed me, they would have noticed I often sighed. A heavy exhalation would precede a period of paralysis, as I stood with unfocused eyes, breathing shallowly through my mouth, trapped in a vision of bombs falling on our home and my children being crushed beneath the rubble.

Noting my turmoil, George called a friend who was a chaplain to the Ukrainian armed forces for her take on the situation. After the beginning of the unofficial war in 2014, she began traveling to serve soldiers on the front lines in her capacity as a psychologist. She had moved from Kyiv and now lived in a town much closer to the fighting. She was in constant contact with army personnel. Did she agree with the general consensus among Kyivans that nothing too awful was going to happen, because Russia's President Putin was too smart to launch a full-scale invasion?

She did not.

"George, if I were in your place, I would get Sharon and the kids out of Kyiv. *Listen to me*! Get...them...out!"

We didn't argue. It was a relief to have a definitive answer from someone we trusted. We bought four train tickets to Ternopil for the next day, Sunday, February 20. George decided to stay in Kyiv to continue our church planting work with our team. I packed several changes of clothes in the kids' backpacks and told them to add anything they would be really sad never to see again.

The next morning, we met with the small church that gathered each Sunday in our home. After the service, we said our goodbyes, unaware that some of us might never see each other again.[1] A friend gave me a large cake as a parting gift. Managing three little kids, four backpacks, the two small suitcases I had packed in December, and my musical instruments was stressful enough—and now I had a cake. It felt overwhelming. I wanted to refuse the gift, but I smiled and thanked her.

As we were about to walk out the door, five-year-old Andrew approached me with his trademark worried expression.

"I want to take my electric guitar."

"Oh. We don't have room for it." I couldn't wrap my mind around transporting one more item, especially a bulky toy. We could always buy him another one.

Andrew started to cry—huge, choking sobs. Surprised, I got down on one knee to look into his eyes. "What's wrong?"

"What if the Russians bomb our house and break my guitar?" he wailed.

My breath caught, and my pulse quickened. This couldn't be happening. How did he know? We had never spoken in his hearing about Kyiv being bombed. No child should ever have to worry about explosions destroying his home.

I looked at the tormented face of my little five-year-old, his innocence shattered. Something broke inside me, and I clasped him in a desperate hug, fighting back tears. "Of course you can take your guitar, buddy."

He wore his backpack and used the guitar strap to hang the bright-red, plastic toy across the front of his body. He attracted amused looks at the train station, but he was so pleased.

I too wore a backpack and had a musical instrument—my flute—slung across my front. I held three-year-old Isaac by the

---

1. *At the time of this writing, all of these friends are still alive, but there are several whom I haven't seen since the parting described here, and one has enlisted in the armed forces of Ukraine.*

hand, and with my other hand, carried Isaac's backpack and my violin. Andrew and James carried the cake between them, each holding one handle of its plastic shopping bag. George managed one of the wheeled carry-on suitcases. Eight-year-old James, always confident and independent, insisted on taking the other.

Our train was waiting on the tracks. Our goodbye was cheerful, as if we were just going away for a short time. The kids all hugged their dad, then George and I shared a warm embrace and a kiss. I hoisted our suitcases up the high steps into the old-fashioned train car. George had a congenital spinal condition that acted up anytime he carried more than fifteen pounds, so for years I had done all the heavy lifting.

We'd reserved all four berths in a sleeping compartment. We put our things inside, then crossed to the window outside our compartment for a last look at George. I hoisted little Isaac up so he could see. George stood smiling and waving until the train lurched into motion and slowly pulled away. To my surprise, George began to jog down the platform, keeping pace with our window, still smiling and waving.

"What? Look at Daddy!" James said.

As the train gained speed, George picked up his pace, a goofy expression on his face as he maintained eye contact. The kids were all giggling and waving. I waved and smiled too, but I was terrified he would trip and fall beneath the train car and be cut in half like the unfortunate Anna Karenina. I wanted to wave my arms and yell at him to stop. I held my breath, my eyes riveted to his progress.

Watch where you're going! I urged him silently.

Oh God, don't let him trip! I prayed.

Gradually, the train got too fast for him to keep up, and he stopped running. I started to breathe again. We all pressed our faces to the glass and watched him standing and waving until we couldn't see him anymore.

We returned to our compartment, and the kids made themselves comfortable on the two bottom berths. I passed out special snacks, then sat down and leaned back, exhaling and letting my shoulders relax. It was done. The decision was made. We were on our way to a safer place.

As Kyiv receded into the distance, the suspense and indecision of the past two months dissipated. The corners of my lips lifted in the barest of smiles. Despite the upheaval, I believed we would look back on this trip as nothing more than unexpected time with our relatives in Ternopil.

The ride took seven hours. When we arrived in Ternopil that night, fellow passengers helped me lift the kids and our stuff off the train. Jon and Aaron found us on the crowded platform. They had Samuel, Kiyoshi, and Peter with them. We all hugged, and the big boys took our bags.

Jon had brought his nine-seat van to the train station, and he drove us to the headquarters of a Christian organization in town. They had prepared two guest rooms for the seven of us. The three youngest kids and I had a beautiful, spacious room on the fourth floor, and the three older boys had a smaller room with two sets of bunk beds on the third floor. The boys were excited to be reunited. They talked and explored while I unpacked. It was late when I finally put everyone to bed.

The next day, I stocked up on grocery staples to use while we called this place home. When I was done, our food supplies filled a huge plastic tub on a shelf in the pantry area of the industrial kitchen. I smiled with satisfaction and a sense of accomplishment as I surveyed the results of my labor. I stretched and kneaded the muscles of my lower back with my knuckles.

I put my friend's cake in the fridge, and I served it to the kids and their cousins the first time we all got together. Those were happy days, because the cousins loved each other's company. We spent as much time together as we could.

We settled into a comfortable rhythm, learning which rooms in the extensive building were good for playing and when we needed to be quiet, to not disrupt classes or meetings. I was constantly busy either with meal preparation, or laundry, or overseeing the older boys' schoolwork, or monitoring little kids to make sure they didn't disturb anyone. I did not have a spare moment, but I was content. It was enough to be free of the suffocating suspense and tension that had blanketed my days for so long.

Two days after we arrived, on Tuesday, February 22, a relative in the US called me. There was concern in his voice.

"The media here is saying that in situations like this, Russia's usual next step is to destabilize things by sending in trained assassins to take out influential people. One of the categories of people is foreign religious workers." He stopped to let that sink in.

My mouth went dry. Both of us were well aware that George was more than just a missionary pastor. He was the Ukrainian overseer for Calvary Chapel, an international association of evangelical churches.

"Wow. Um, thanks for letting me know." I felt dizzy and nauseated.

"George needs to get out of Kyiv. He needs to be with his family."

"Yeah. I'll talk to him."

After I got the kids to bed that night, I called George and related the conversation. What ensued was the only real fight of our entire marriage.

"You need to get out of Kyiv," I said.

"I'll be fine."

"You don't know that."

"Nothing's going to happen."

"How can you say that? You have no idea what's going to happen!"

"I don't want to abandon our team."

"Our children need their father *alive*!"

"I'm more likely to be struck by lightning than end up on a Russian hit list!" he responded with uncharacteristic heat.

It was impossible to find a compromise, and we hung up. I was furious with him, dumbfounded by his stubbornness and shortsightedness—and terrified by what they might cost us.

The next morning he apologized and assured me that the boys and I were his top priority. Our team all insisted he rejoin us. He arranged to catch a ride on Monday with a friend and her son, who were planning to travel west by car. It was Wednesday, February 23. He wasn't jumping on the next train as I wanted, but I didn't push. We had made our peace, and I was satisfied knowing he would come as soon as the weekend was over . . . if a Russian hitman didn't find him first.

I tried not to dwell on that possibility.

I had been so busy since arriving in Ternopil, I hadn't managed to shower, and I was determined not to let another day go by. Though it was late when I finally got the kids to bed, I stayed up for a few minutes of self-care. I took my time, scrubbing and relaxing in the stream of hot water, using a special exfoliating mitt from Morocco. When I was done, I rinsed it out carefully, dwelling on fond memories of the dear friend who had given it to me, whom I hadn't seen for years. I hung it up to dry before heading back upstairs to my room.

It was after midnight when I finally slipped between the sheets. I was exhausted and looked forward to sleeping a solid seven or eight hours.

It was not to be.

6

Are You Okay?

February 24, 2022
Ternopil, Ukraine

I woke at 5:30 am on that Thursday morning with an urgent sense that I needed to pray. George came to mind, so I prayed for him. Then my thoughts turned to a friend who had recently moved to the city of Ivano-Frankivsk in Western Ukraine, and I prayed for him as well.[1]

The sound of hurried footsteps somewhere inside the building broke the silence of the early morning. It sounded like several people. Building doors banged shut, car doors slammed, and a vehicle drove away. It seemed odd before sunrise, but I didn't think much about it.

I prayed more. After about ten minutes, I rose and quietly left the room, taking my phone with me. I took a seat on the carpet outside our room to read the Bible before the kids awoke. When I turned on my phone, the first thing I saw was a text from Jon.

Jon: **Are you awake?**

Me: **Yes.**

Jon: **Are you okay?**

Fighting a panicky feeling in my throat and chest, I frantically tapped and swiped my phone to figure out why Jon would think I might not be okay.

---

1. *I later learned that explosions had rocked airfields outside both Kyiv and Ivano-Frankivsk in those early morning hours of February 24.*

Then I saw it—a message from George.

February 24, 2022, 5:03 am: **We are okay. But there were a couple of explosions near Kyiv. We are gathering at our apartment. Getting ready to leave.**

I crumpled over sideways. Soon I was face-down on the carpet, wordlessly pouring out my anguish, my shock, my utter consternation to God. It was a communion of spirits that bypassed language. My mind was at a loss for words.

I hadn't been in that posture long when an unfamiliar sound intruded. I had never heard an air-raid siren, but I immediately knew exactly what it was.

Surely it was just a test of the system. There was no way the insignificant town of Ternopil way off in Western Ukraine was a target, was there?

I rushed downstairs to find someone who knew. Few people were around, but I found a lady on the third floor. She explained the commotion I had heard earlier. It was an American family leaving for the Polish border as soon as they learned that Russia had attacked. However, she didn't know what the sirens meant.

We couldn't find any information online. The sirens stopped, and we discussed the various possibilities. A test of the system. A warning to be on the alert. A call to take immediate shelter. While we debated, the sirens started again.

This time I didn't hesitate. The system was clearly working. A second round of sirens could only mean one thing: Ternopil was in danger. Whether the threat was imminent or merely possible, I wasn't waiting to find out. I had six children in my care—I wasn't taking any chances.

I went into the older boys' bedroom and woke them up. As soon as they all had their eyes open, I explained the situation.

"Russia just attacked Ukraine. Do you hear that noise? That's an air-raid siren. We need to go to the basement right away. Get ready while I get your brothers, okay?"

I paused for a moment to satisfy myself that they were getting up, then I ran back to my room, taking the stairs two at a time in my house slippers.

The little boys were still sleeping. I quickly got them out of bed and grabbed everyone's coats. Quietly, I told them we needed to go to the basement. Seeming to sense my urgency, they followed me without question. We went to collect the big boys, and I was astonished to find that Samuel, my fifteen-year-old, had gone back to bed.

I pulled the covers off him.

"Samuel, get up!"

He snatched the comforter back, rolling away from me and pulling it over his head in one motion.

"Samuel, right now! You have to get up!" I tried to yank the covers off again, but his hold was too strong. I saw his rattail trailing out from under the blanket, and for a split second I contemplated using it to drag him out of bed.

"Go away! Leave me alone!" he whined loudly.

In the desperation of the moment, I was tempted to do exactly what he said—I could just leave him alone and take the rest of the kids to safety. But that was absurd. I had to save *everyone*. This man-child was too big for me to physically force down the stairs, but somehow I finally got him up and moving.[2]

Shoes were only allowed on the ground floor, and all of ours were on racks at the bottom of the stairs.

Quickly but calmly, I issued directions. "We don't have time to put on shoes or coats. Just grab your shoes, and we'll put them on in the basement."

I instinctively counted heads and realized I was missing a child. "Where's Samuel?" I asked, panicked.

"He went back upstairs because he forgot his coat." Thirteen-year-old Kiyoshi never missed anything.

I deliberated for a split-second and decided I couldn't waste more time dealing with my eldest son while risking the safety of the other five.

The basement entrance was outside. Right before we exited the building's glass door, five-year-old Andrew balked.

"We have to go outside without shoes?" His face had its characteristic worried expression, his forehead furrowed and his eyebrows tilted up in the middle.

---

2. *Samuel has no memory of this struggle, and we've concluded it was a sleep-walking episode.*

"Look," I said, pointing outside. "There's no snow, and it's dry. C'mon, we have to hurry."

"Okay . . ." He still looked anxious but allowed me to lead him outside.

The air-raid siren had stopped, and it was eerily quiet. The calm only intensified my sense of urgency.

"Brrr, it's cold," eight-year-old James said as we trooped down a short pathway in our socks and pajamas, shoes and coats filling our arms.

We descended a short flight of stairs into a covered well beside the building. There was a door with an electronic keypad. We'd never used it, but someone had told us the code when we arrived. Everyone was shivering while I figured out how to open it.

It was a nice basement, with couches, a foosball table, and even a restroom. It was unheated, however, so we were glad to have our coats. Once everyone was inside, I ran back into the building and sprinted upstairs to find Samuel. I met him coming back down with his coat. Finally, I got everyone safe in the basement.

"Mommy, I'm hungry." Andrew looked worried again.

"Okay, I'll go get breakfast. You kids stay here." I wanted to be confident the threat had actually passed before we all left our shelter.

"Is it safe to go out now?" Kiyoshi asked dubiously, examining my face with his dark eyes.

I wasn't surprised that my most safety-conscious son had already grasped the seriousness of the situation. "I think so. The sirens have been quiet for a while. I'll be really fast, and if I think it's not safe, I'll come back right away."

I felt dangerously exposed as I hurried aboveground to the kitchen. The building seemed deserted. I quickly grabbed rolled oats, honey, dried cranberries, bowls, and spoons. I breathed a sigh of relief once I was back with my kids again.

There was an electric tea kettle in the basement, and I made six bowls of oatmeal by pouring boiling water over the oats. The kids chattered happily as they enjoyed their food. For them, the meal restored a semblance of normalcy to that historically abnormal day.

I was relieved no one asked why I wasn't eating. I wasn't about to tell my children the truth—that anxiety had left me too nauseated to eat. They didn't need to know how frightened their mother was.

I was paralyzed with shock, and I had no idea what to do. I hadn't heard an all-clear. Did that mean we still needed to take cover? I didn't consider calling family or friends in Ternopil. What could they tell me? They had to be as confused and frightened as I was. They didn't need me calling and pestering them. So for the next few hours, the boys and I just sat in the basement.

Of the handful of people remaining in the building, only one joined us, the woman who had told me about the American family leaving early that morning. When she saw us sheltering in the basement, she brought us a stack of blankets and a five-liter bottle of drinking water. Her presence comforted me, but she couldn't stay long. She found friends heading for the border and hitched a ride. We wished her well and hugged her goodbye.

She's abandoning us, I thought to myself. I knew I was being illogical. That morning when everyone was in shock, scrambling to make plans, she noticed the overwhelmed mom with six kids and came to our rescue, but her powers were limited. She couldn't conjure up a vehicle or whisk us to safety, and that's what I wanted. What was I going to do?

For nineteen years, George and I had made every major decision together. Now I was facing some of the most momentous choices of my life, and he wasn't there to navigate them with me. I missed his calming presence and the easy way he could dream up unconventional solutions. In contrast, my mind was blank, and I felt trapped. I just needed to wait for George. Once we were together, he and I could figure out what to do next.

But what if the situation deteriorated, and I found we couldn't wait? How was I supposed to get everyone out of the country? Jon was the only relative in Ukraine with a vehicle, and he wouldn't have room for us. His own family would take up all but one seat.

Were trains still running? If they were, how long did we have before Russia bombed the tracks and left us stranded? And for that matter, did I want to risk getting on a train with my children? Wouldn't that make us easy targets for Russian fighter jets? And assuming we made it out safely, where should we go? Poland was closest, but where would we stay once we got there? I couldn't even speak Polish.

An American who had disregarded my government's warnings, I felt alone with six kids in a country at war, and I had no idea how to get us to safety.

7

Will I Ever See You Again?

February 24, 2022: Day 1 of War
Kyiv, Ukraine

George told me that the night before the war began, he and the seven members of our team decided if Russia invaded Ukraine, they would all evacuate from Kyiv. George didn't think that would be necessary.

Early the next morning, explosions jolted everyone from sleep. It was surreal. Not only had the invasion of Ukraine begun—Kyiv itself was under attack. George was in shock. Horror replaced his confidence that nothing bad was going to happen. The whole team quickly gathered at our apartment with its private basement and the stores of non-perishable food and water I had collected.

Our friend Yana, who had planned to drive George to Ternopil on Monday, said she was leaving immediately with her school-aged son. She had two free seats in her car. Everyone agreed that Olya should go with George. Everyone, except for Olya. She couldn't stand leaving the others behind, but it didn't make sense to waste the opportunity to get another person out of the city. Ultimately, the decision of the majority prevailed, and Olya frantically packed.

George had already prepared a carry-on suitcase for the Monday trip. Now he just threw a few things into his backpack in a panicked rush. The whole time, he was on his phone, trying to get a handle on the situation in the country and figure out how he could help.

Yana and her young son showed up by 7 am. Everyone gathered to see George and Olya off. No one knew if they would meet again, and their final, desperate embraces strove to communicate what throats choked with tears could not.

Oh God, what's going to happen?

Will I ever see you again?

I love you so much.

Goodbye . . .

Yana's car was crammed full. Somehow they repacked everything to fit George and Olya's luggage and clear the seats they were supposed to occupy. Olya squeezed into the back beside a cage containing a parrot, and George wedged himself into the front passenger seat with our dog, Jack, sitting on the floor between his legs. Guilt over leaving the team behind weighed heavy on him, but he knew he had to get to his wife and kids.

For weeks, Yana had been keeping her gas tank full in case she and her son had to evacuate, but as several dates proposed on social media for the supposed invasion came and went uneventfully, she had let her guard down. Now she had only a half tank of diesel and a half tank of propane in her car, which had been modified to run on both fuel sources. She stopped at the first gas station, not far from our apartment. There were fifteen cars in line. Impatient to get on the road, George wanted to keep going and stop outside the city, but Yana was insistent. They needed to buy fuel now—if they waited, the lines would be worse.

Consumed with guilt over leaving the others, Olya wanted to abandon the plan entirely and walk back to our apartment by herself.

"Don't you even think about it!" Yana snapped.

Olya stayed put.

There was no line by the propane tank, and an attendant served them. When Yana tipped him, he asked if they needed diesel, which he dispensed without making them wait in line. George gave him another big tip and a banana.

As they left the gas station, Yana, who had attended our church for the first time the previous Sunday, asked George to pray. For her, prayer meant voicing her requests to "the Universe," but that day, she wanted to pray to the God of the Bible.

They headed for Yana's mom's apartment on the city's western edge. Her mom was adamant about not leaving Kyiv. The stop was to eat breakfast and say goodbye. The GPS predicted it would take forty-five minutes, but as they drove, the estimate kept increasing, and the route kept changing.

People were pouring onto the roads, and traffic slowed practically to a standstill. In their panic, many drivers were getting into accidents. Cars abandoned by the side of the road became a common sight. Some had been ditched after an accident; others appeared simply to have run out of gas. Desperate families continued on foot.

It took over three hours to get to Yana's mom's apartment. By the time they arrived, they had abandoned the idea of leaving that day. All reports said the fighting around Kyiv was fierce. They'd be safer sheltering in the city than sitting for hours in traffic on an open highway. George, Olya, and Jack would return to our apartment to wait out the weekend. Hopefully by Monday, the roads would be clear. They prayed together again, and Yana joined in with a heartfelt, impassioned prayer to God.

George felt disappointed at the delay in rejoining his family but relieved to be rejoining the team. Using the app for the car-sharing fleet our car had been in, George easily found a rental nearby, which he unlocked by scanning the QR code on the driver's door. The drive back to our apartment took only fifteen minutes. The roads in that direction were deserted.

Even though George and Olya's return was a bad outcome, the others welcomed them back with happy exclamations and hugs. In the hours since George and Olya had left, more people had come to shelter in our basement. George was especially pleased to see our neighbors, an expatriate family from Ethiopia. The husband was an epidemiologist with the World Health Organization, and their two young daughters were great friends with our boys.

George contacted our chaplain friend to see what she thought of his plan to wait until Monday to leave the city. She insisted he do everything he could to get out of Kyiv the very next day. Her urgency dampened the optimism George had felt from being surrounded by so many friends.

Late that night, Yana decided she would leave her mom's apartment at 7 am the next morning and gave George a rendezvous point nearby. The government had declared martial law, and there was a curfew in effect until 7 am. George agreed to the plan, confident he could figure out a way to travel across the city during curfew.

When I found out, I was alarmed that George was planning to violate the curfew. What would happen if he were caught? People were saying he could be shot on sight as a Russian collaborator. I was terrified for him. Characteristically, George didn't share my concern. He said he'd read a government post that said the police would simply be checking the documents of anyone out during curfew.

I was so desperate for George to get to safety that I didn't have the emotional resources for another argument about what he should do. If he believed breaking the law to rendezvous with Yana was his best option, I was prepared to trust his judgment and pray, but not without taking a few precautions.

We were already hearing reports that Russia had placed agents in strategic Ukrainian cities ahead of time. The day before the invasion, Olya had noticed groups of Russian-speaking men loitering in our neighborhood. Many Kyivans speak Russian, but these men stood out because they carried themselves like thugs and seemed to be waiting for something. Thankfully, the police took them away before they caused any trouble. According to social media, they were Russian agitators.

Learning about these agents was chilling confirmation that my earlier concern for George's safety had not been completely misplaced. George apologized for not having taken me seriously. We switched to a secure messaging app and told everyone who knew of George's whereabouts not to share that information anywhere online.

8

Crushing Anxiety and Sheer Terror

February 24, 2022: Day 1 of War
Ternopil, Ukraine

The kids and I spent the first half of the day mostly alone in the cold basement. Then, shortly after noon, people came.

I looked up when they pushed open the basement door, and profound relief flooded me when I saw familiar faces. It was Jon and the Ukrainian pastor of the church that George and I had started in this city fourteen years earlier. Emotion choked my throat. Speech was impossible, but no words were necessary: we just held each other in turn, tears in our eyes, drawing comfort from each other's presence.

Jon took the boys and me to his apartment, where we joined his wife Stephanie and their six kids. George's other brother, Aaron, and his wife, Dara, and their two children also came, making a total of fourteen cousins.

Given the large number of children in George's extended family and how many of us are missionaries, I've been asked if we are Mormons. We aren't. We're simple followers of Jesus. We study the Bible carefully and try to do what it says. We have no affiliation with a specific denomination, and our missionary work is supported by non-denominational churches across the US and Europe.

The large number of children is due to the unique culture of the Markey family. George's family of origin has nine children, eight biological and one adopted in Ukraine. When George and his siblings started their own families, it felt natural to have more than two or three children, because they knew firsthand the joys and benefits of a large family. At the time of this writing, there are forty grandkids in the Markey family.

While the fourteen cousins played in Jon and Stephanie's apartment that first day of the war, the adults talked. In some ways, it felt like a normal family gathering, except we were painfully aware of the tragedy happening elsewhere in the country. But for those few hours, we were able to assume a facade of normalcy, as if we were just hanging out and talking over cups of tea. Of course, the only thing we talked about was the unthinkable reality to which we had awoken that morning.

None of us had decided if we would stay or evacuate. Jon floated the idea of driving his family to Poland and then coming back for me and my kids. The plan made me uneasy, but I didn't explore why. Oddly uncertain without George and keenly aware of my dependence on others, I simply nodded and said, "Okay." Who was I to object? Beggars can't be choosers.

As evening lengthened into night, Jon drove us back to our accommodations. Instead of the dark, deserted building I expected, the place was filled with many other guests. They had fled their homes that day and made their way west.

Once all my boys were ready for bed, I called a meeting in my room. The only adult responsible for six kids, I had to make sure we would function as a team if there was an emergency.

"Kids, I want to talk about what to do if we hear air-raid sirens." Everyone locked their eyes on me as I continued. "Do you know what they mean?"

"There could be bombs," Kiyoshi said.

"Yeah, so that's why it's really important that we get to the basement quickly if we hear them. Do you understand?"

They all nodded solemnly.

"We're going to pack all our shoes and coats into bags so we won't have to waste any time finding them. Kiyoshi, I want you to keep those bags in your room. It'll be your responsibility to make sure they get to the basement with us, okay?"

Kiyoshi gave a curt nod.

"Peter, I want you to help Andrew get down the stairs quickly. I'll carry Isaac."

"Okay, Mommy!" Peter said, almost cheerfully. The somber atmosphere only slightly dampened his carefree nature.

Instead of a physical drill, I asked the four older boys to explain the plan until I was satisfied each knew his part. Then we prayed together and said goodnight. I tucked the three youngest into bed in my room. They fell asleep in under a minute. Exhausted from my early morning and the strain of the day, I couldn't wait to surrender to sleep myself. However, I barely had time to notice the boys' deep, even breathing before the peace was broken by the now familiar wail of the air-raid siren.

Groaning inwardly, I moved to James's bed.

"James!" I said softly but urgently, putting gentle pressure on his shoulder. He didn't respond. The sustained wailing of the siren made my pulse quicken.

"James!" I shook him. His body was completely limp. He might as well have been comatose. I felt panic rising. We were way too exposed up here on the top floor.

I spoke louder. "James, we have to get up! There's an air-raid siren!"

Finally, his eyes cracked open a sliver.

"James, get up!"

His eyes flew wide open. Shaking himself, he threw the covers off and jumped out of bed as I moved to wake Andrew. He was just as hard to rouse as James. I grabbed his shoulders and sat him up to help him come around. Once he was on his feet, I scooped up three-year-old Isaac, and the four of us headed downstairs to the older boys' room.

They were standing just inside their door, waiting for us. Kiyoshi was holding the bags with our coats and shoes. In an orderly fashion, we quickly walked down the remaining two flights of stairs, outside, and down the exterior stairs to the basement. We punched in the code on the electronic keypad.

The basement was dark and empty. I realized my six boys and I were the first ones to make it to the bomb shelter, despite being housed on the two top floors of the building. I was so proud of them. We put on our shoes and coats while we waited for people to arrive. Before long, the other evacuees joined us. Soon the basement felt crowded.

Using the stack of blankets the kind lady had brought us while we sheltered in the basement that morning, I tried to make the boys comfortable on the floor next to a wall—as far as possible from the small ventilation windows just below the ceiling along one side of the room. Someone produced a guitar, and someone else grabbed a cajon drum, and soon there was a lively concert of Christian worship music drowning out the sirens, completely changing the atmosphere.

After a while, the musicians stopped, and someone said, "It's probably safe to go back to bed." Isaac, Andrew, and James were already asleep again. I hated to wake them, and I realized we would probably get more rest in the basement, especially if the sirens started again. I announced I was staying put with my kids. Several of the men offered to move a couch to us, away from the wall with the little windows, and in the meantime, other people rethought their plans. Ultimately, everyone spent the night in the basement. The men moved all the couches to the inner wall, and someone passed out blankets and pillows. Before long, a chorus of snores filled the air.

Despite my exhaustion, sleep was elusive. I was lying crossways on an uncomfortable couch bed that I shared with three other women whose names I didn't know. We were strangers thrown together by the events of this horrific day. My kids were asleep, and now that I didn't have the care of the children to distract me, I was face-to-face with my profound worry for George's safety. He was planning to break curfew at 6 am and somehow traverse half the city to catch his ride to safety.

I lay rigid in the darkness, afraid to move lest I disturb the stranger lying so close I could feel her warmth. I struggled against the coils of fear slowly crushing what remained of my faith and hope. What if George were shot or detained for breaking curfew? Or what if he never made it out of our neighborhood? Would he survive if our apartment suffered a direct hit, or would the whole building collapse into the basement?

What if the Russians succeeded in taking Kyiv? What would happen to Americans still left in the capital? Was George's name on a hit list? Did they know our address? Would he be able to lie low and avoid detection until . . . until what? If the city fell, the new Russian authorities would certainly be watching all the ways out, wouldn't they? What if George did escape the city, only to become a war casualty on the open highway?

It was impossible to sleep. Around 1:30 am, I texted George.

Me: **I love you. If I never see you again, I just want you to know that you've been a better husband than I could ever have imagined.**

George responded right away: **I love you too! You have been an amazing wife too. But I'm sure we will see each other again!**

Me: **I hope you're right.**

If we lost communication, we had agreed to meet at the home of Anna, a friend in Budapest, Hungary, who had offered to put us up if war broke out.

As usual, I was convinced the worst could happen, and George was certain it wouldn't. Throughout the watches of that night, I peered into a future where I was a widow, and I tried to develop a plan of action for my worst-case scenario. Over and over, I faced down the possibility that I would have to raise our six children by myself.

As a single mom, I'd be practically useless as a missionary. Should I move us back to the United States? Could we live with my parents while I got back on my feet? But Southern California was so expensive . . . maybe we should settle near George's relatives in Indiana. I threw myself into prayer, knowing there alone would I find the peace I so desperately craved.

Jesus, you know what the future holds. No matter what happens, I know you'll be there with me. I know I can get through this with you.

I had tears of premature heartbreak in my eyes, both for my widowed self and my fatherless kids, but as I focused on Jesus and his goodness, power, and love for me, my pain and anxiety lessened, and I could breathe. But when I thought of all the dangers facing George, the grief and fear would overwhelm me again, squeezing my chest and clamping my throat.

It was an exhausting battle that I waged through every moment of the darkness.

Time slowed almost to a standstill.

Seconds slowly ticked by to form minutes.

Minutes gradually added up to hours.

That night was an entire month of stress and anxiety. I had never longed so intensely for the dawn.

Separated from my husband and consumed by worry for his safety, I questioned Jon's idea of taking Stephanie and their kids to Poland and then returning for me. Would he even be allowed to come back into Ukraine? And if he was, what about his wife? I didn't want Stephanie to experience this agony, wondering if her husband would make it back alive. Lying in the darkness, surrounded by people snoring loudly, I contemplated asking Jon to take us with them. Under normal circumstances, I wouldn't have considered cramming fifteen people into a nine-seat van, but I was sure Jon would agree these weren't normal circumstances.

And then, over the snoring, I heard it—the descending whistle of an incoming bomb.

I froze. My breath lodged in my throat.

It couldn't be.

What should I do?

Should I awaken everyone? But what was the point? We were already in the bomb shelter. We would either survive or not. No use disturbing everyone's sleep.

Every sense on high-alert, I awaited the blast, praying it would not be a direct hit on our building. It never came. I relaxed slightly and started breathing again. Maybe that one had been a dud. Then I heard another bomb incoming.

This couldn't be happening.

I waited, holding my breath, but again, there was no explosion.

I exhaled and relaxed. *Thank you, Jesus.* Then I heard another whistle begin. *Oh no, not again.* I lay frozen in the darkness, praying for protection. The whistle reached the bottom of its arc, and I tensed, anticipating impact, but again, there was nothing.

What were the odds of three bombs in a row not exploding? It was strange that the sound wasn't disturbing anyone else. I listened intently to the snoring around me. As another whistling descent began, a doubt formed in my mind. The whistle had started right at the end of a snorting inhalation. The whistle reached the end of its descent, and this time, I wasn't surprised when it failed to detonate. The snorting began anew, and again, right on its heels, came the whistle.

There were no bombs falling out of the skies above Ternopil, just someone whose snoring included an unfortunate whistling sound.

Relieved, I returned to praying for George. I believed Ternopil was unlikely to be targeted, and my worry was mainly for his safety. But then I heard another sound. Almost buried under the layers of snoring, though faint, it was familiar. Straining my ears, I could hear the staccato popping of distant gunfire, a sound I remembered hearing from my childhood home on the edge of gang territory in Southern California.

How could the insignificant town of Ternopil be under attack? What could Putin possibly want here? Were they fighting in the streets already? Would the Ukrainian defense hold out? If not, how soon would Russian soldiers make it to our location? I held my breath, listening, trying to gauge how far away the gunshots were. Should I awaken everyone so we could barricade the basement door?

My eyes were wide open, staring into the darkness as I tried to isolate the gunshots from the cacophony of snores and the frantic hammering of my heart. Was I interpreting the sounds right? I was the only one awake to sound the alarm. If I was right and did nothing, I could kill us all. But if I was wrong and disturbed everyone, I would inflict needless terror, steal necessary sleep, and be painfully embarrassed.

I had to be sure. The gunshots were still far away. There was time to think. I closed my eyes and focused my whole being on analyzing everything I could hear. I strained my ears to catch the minutest detail, any hint of what was happening outside. I forgot to breathe. As I listened, gradually the popping sounds coalesced in my mind, and I realized they were the snoring inhalations of one sleeper. We were not in imminent danger.

The night crawled by. After hours of crushing anxiety broken up by moments of sheer terror, I was utterly exhausted on every level. As sunrise approached, light finally dawned in my disordered mind. My children's safety and future rested solely on my shoulders. It was foolish to wait for George if it might put them at risk.

Around 5:30 am I texted Jon: **If you decide to leave, will you please take us with you?**

Jon later confided that he and Stephanie also had a difficult night. When they returned to their apartment after the air-raid alert, they could not sleep. At home in their own bed—the one place that should have felt safe—they felt exposed and threatened. By morning, they were at a breaking point.

Jon still had not fallen asleep when my message came through. He responded immediately: **How soon can you be ready to go?**

9

What We Left Behind

February 25, 2022: Day 2 of War
Ternopil, Ukraine

Jon's words provided relief from the torment of the night. I welcomed the chance for action and something to distract me from my worries. How quickly could I gather our few belongings and dress the kids to leave the scene of my waking nightmare?

I texted back: **Give us 30 minutes.**

Everyone was still sleeping in the basement. I didn't want to leave my kids without at least one of them knowing my whereabouts. I knelt beside Kiyoshi, my thirteen-year-old. As soon as I whispered in his ear, he sat up and listened closely as I explained my plans.

"Do you want me to come help you?" he asked.

Realizing his help would be invaluable, I crawled to Peter, my eleven-year-old. It took a few tries to rouse him. Once he was awake, he pushed himself up on one elbow and made a sleepy smacking noise with his mouth while blinking his eyes. His curly, sandy-brown hair looked exactly the same as when he had lain down to sleep. Though always unruly, it was a convenient, low-maintenance hairstyle, perfect for a fun-loving, easygoing boy.

I explained the plan. "If one of your brothers wakes up, tell them where I am, okay?"

"Okay, Mommy," Peter said, yawning. He lay back down, unperturbed.

Kiyoshi and I split up. He went to the older boys' room on the third floor, and I took the stairs two at a time to my room on the fourth floor. I was still busy packing when Kiyoshi rejoined me.

"You're done already? That was fast!" I was putting covers on toothbrushes and placing them in the toiletry bag.

"Should I go pack up our stuff in the kitchen?" Kiyoshi asked.

I had forgotten about the large stock of grocery staples I purchased in anticipation of staying for two or three weeks. Abandoning them distressed me, but it didn't make sense to haul them along. Jon's van would already be overloaded.

"Just get the things that would be useful as snacks on the road," I answered.

Kiyoshi hurried downstairs to the kitchen and soon returned to help me finish. While we were working, my phone rang. It was a video call from George. It was 5:37 am, and he was getting ready to violate curfew to rendezvous with Yana, but he had a problem.

"Yana just called," George said. "Her son had a bad allergic reaction to Jack. I guess he got really sick last night after we left."

"Oh no!"

"She said she was really sorry, but I can't bring Jack. She's worried her son wouldn't survive a whole day in the car with him. What do I do?"

With the Russian army advancing on Kyiv, I had only one thought: George had to leave while he still could. "You have to get out of Kyiv," I said matter-of-factly.

"And leave Jack?" he asked plaintively.

"If that's the only option, yes." The fate of our dog was insignificant compared to the life of the father of my children. "Is anyone still staying at our apartment?"

"Yeah."

"Could they take care of Jack?"

"Yeah, I can ask."

I glanced at Kiyoshi. He'd heard everything. Jack was more his dog than anyone else's. They shared a special bond. Kiyoshi was sensitive and emotional, and Jack helped him balance his sometimes violent feelings. When Kiyoshi was having a bad day, he would snuggle with Jack, petting the dog's velvety ears and talking to him.

Right then, Kiyoshi's face looked pale against his dark hair. His brown eyes were intense, and I wondered how to handle the coming outburst. But he was calm. Displaying maturity beyond his years, he immediately grasped why George had to leave without Jack. Later we learned there were evacuation trains and buses George could have taken with our dog, but at the time, it felt like catching a ride with Yana and her son was George's only hope.

"Daddy, can I see Jack?"

George turned his phone to face the dog so that Kiyoshi and Jack could see each other.

"Jack! Jack! Hey, Jack! Look at me! Hi, boy!" The dog didn't seem to recognize Kiyoshi over the phone, and Kiyoshi gave up trying to get him to make eye contact.

"I love you, boy! Bye, buddy!" Kiyoshi used the same cheerful tone he always used with Jack, even though I could see his eyes were wet with unshed tears.

George turned the phone back to himself. "Kiyoshi, I'm sorry."

Kiyoshi gave a tight-lipped nod.

"Okay, I've gotta go," George said.

"Yeah, we do too," I said. "We're going to leave with Jon and Stephanie." Things were happening so quickly, I hadn't written George about our plans, but I knew he would understand.

"Oh, where are you going?"

"We'll probably cross into Poland then go to Hungary. We'll be in touch. I love you. Be safe!"

"I love you too—I will!"

"Bye, Daddy!" Kiyoshi said.

"Bye, Kiyoshi. I love you! I'm so sorry about Jack."

I hung up the phone and gave Kiyoshi a long, tight hug. I felt physically ill with worry and grief for both Jack and my son, but there was no time to sit and cry. I took a deep breath and moved on to the next thing.

Kiyoshi and I carried our belongings downstairs and put them near the exit. I woke the other boys and got them ready to leave. They had mixed reactions to the plan.

"What about Daddy?" Five-year-old Andrew's characteristic worried expression communicated even more concern than usual.

"He'll come to us." *Please, God, let that be true.*

"How do you know?" James asked. My eight-year-old's compelling hazel eyes were wide and questioning.

"He's leaving Kyiv today, and he'll follow us." I sounded calm and confident.

It was an act.

We didn't have to wait long for Jon. His van's cargo area was loaded, but he'd left Stephanie and the kids at their apartment. We added our two carry-on suitcases, musical instruments, backpacks, and a remote-controlled airplane that was Kiyoshi's special treasure.

While we were putting our stuff in the van, a middle-aged man, whom Jon knew, approached. They shook hands and talked. Like me, Jon had also been struggling with anxiety, and this man's calm confidence was a huge contrast to our experience of the past twenty-four hours.

When Jon told him our plan, the man was compassionate and understanding. I expected him to criticize our decision. No bombs had fallen on Ternopil. We should be strong and not abandon Ukraine in her hour of need. Instead, he emphasized there was no shame in leaving. Some people were built to live under stress and pressure, and others weren't. He didn't sound condescending, just matter-of-fact.

This permission to leave, coming from a Ukrainian, was profoundly comforting. The beginnings of guilt over fleeing were already taking root in my soul—and we hadn't even gotten into our escape vehicle. Months later, I would begin processing everything I set in motion that day, and his words would pave the way for self-forgiveness.

Once we loaded everything, we drove to Jon and Stephanie's apartment. When all twelve cousins were assembled next to the van, Jon laid out some ground rules.

"Kids, today it's really important that you listen and do whatever we say right away." He sounded intense.

"Yeah," I chimed in, trying to make my voice as comforting and gentle as possible, "and you need to understand that if we yell, it's not because we're angry. We just want to keep you safe, okay?"

The kids nodded seriously and climbed into the van. It had three rows of seats with belts for three people in each row, but that day, only the three people in the front had the luxury of seatbelts. The rest of us were packed in too tightly. Those in the front were Jon, who was driving, and the eldest child from each family: my Samuel and Jon and Stephanie's 12-year-old daughter. The second row had Stephanie, holding her 22-month-old and 4-year-old daughters, with her 6-year-old and 8-year-old daughters and 11-year-old son, Georgie, sitting side-by-side next to her. The final row had me, with Isaac and Andrew on my lap, and James, Peter, and Kiyoshi jammed in, hip-to-hip, beside me.

We made one stop before leaving town. We needed to say goodbye to Aaron and his Ukrainian wife Dara and their two young sons. They were choosing to stay. They walked to meet us on the main road to save us time. Everyone extricated themselves from the van, and we all exchanged hugs. All the adults had tears in their eyes. Was this goodbye for all time?

Aaron and Dara had been keeping our pet rats, and they promised to take good care of them. I hadn't considered evacuating with them. I was worried they wouldn't be allowed across the border, and I'd be forced to choose between turning back or releasing them into the wild.

Right before I climbed back in the van, Dara threw her arms around my neck and said fiercely in my ear, "We'll get your husband back to you!" Her confidence bolstered my courage. I wasn't in this alone.

Shortly before 8 am, all fifteen of us were loaded back into that nine-seat van. We were taking very little, and we had no idea if we would ever return. But we weren't grieving the things left behind. In that moment, we were just grateful to be leaving behind the fear and suspense that had engulfed us for the past day and night.

I was relieved to have taken the first step to getting my children to safety, but my relief was tempered by a pressing question: would George make it to us?

10

Through the Mountains

February 25, 2022: Day 2 of War
Western Ukraine

Despite the gravity of the situation, the overall atmosphere in the van was celebratory. Our family made a few road trips each year to visit these cousins, and my kids were thrilled that this time they would get to make a trip *with* their cousins. We parents were anxious, but our children seemed convinced it was a party.

"So, I called our friends who headed to Poland yesterday." Jon glanced back at Stephanie and me from the driver's seat. "They said they've been waiting in line at the Polish border for over twenty-four hours."

"Oh, my word!" I said, imagining how exhausted they must be after spending a day and a night in a car as it inched forward in line.

"Yeah. He told me a worker from the US Embassy told them it would've been better if they'd gone to Hungary, because the lines are a lot shorter there."

Stephanie spoke up. "Sounds like we should go to Hungary."

Jon glanced over his shoulder. "Is that okay with you guys?"

"Sounds good to me," I said.

"Great. I'll have the GPS take us south to the Carpathian Mountains instead of going by Lviv, since big cities could be targets. Um, Sharon?"

"Yeah?" I made eye contact with Jon in the rearview mirror.

"Can you be our communication person today?"

"Sure. What do you need?"

"Can you contact Anna and tell her we're coming to Hungary? See if we can stay with her?"

"Sure."

I went to work on my phone. First I texted Anna, our friend in Budapest, who had generously offered to house my family if war started. She had extended the same offer to Jon and Stephanie. I told her we were headed her way, but we had too many people in the van to continue legally after we crossed the Hungarian border.

I also texted friends in Ukraine to find out how they were. Now that I had made the decision to move forward with securing my children's safety, I felt liberated to do everything in my power to help others. I was so thankful for my smartphone and cellular data plan. Sitting in the far-back corner of that van, holding two children on my lap, I spent the hours of that ride tapping and swiping, monitoring all my chats, and speed typing with my thumbs.

Though the war was barely a day old, I discovered there was already a network of drivers evacuating people, and churches providing food and shelter. I connected people who were fleeing with those who could help them.

But amidst the good feelings that came from helping people, I was crushed with anxiety over the fate of our dog. If our friends all decided to leave Kyiv too, what would happen to him? I searched and searched for a pet hotel to house him until we could retrieve him. But so many Kyivans were fleeing, would the people who ran such businesses even stick around to care for the animals? Some people were offering to take in small caged pets to save them from being abandoned, but I couldn't find any place that would take a dog.

For three hours, we made good time. We passed gas stations with lines of cars and were grateful we had enough fuel to make it all the way to the border. The atmosphere in the van continued to be upbeat. The adults relaxed some, and the kids were acting like we were just taking a road trip with cousins—and they were loving it.

When we reached the Carpathian Mountains, we made a pit stop at a gas station with a restaurant and large convenience store. We wanted to buy enough food and water to sustain us for twenty-four hours, since we didn't know how long we would have to wait at the border. There were a few other cars when we pulled in, but no more than I had seen on previous trips. It was a pleasant surprise.

On a mission, I strode boldly through the doors of the convenience store—and then stopped abruptly when I noticed the COVID face mask on the man behind the cash register. I had forgotten to put mine on. I tensed, expecting someone to yell at me. I was about to run back to the van to search for a mask, but then I noticed that none of the other customers were wearing masks—and none of the masked employees seemed to care. After nearly two years of never appearing in public without a mask, it felt surreal to be barefaced in a store. But with bombs exploding all over the country and an invading army trying to take Ukrainian cities, COVID suddenly seemed insignificant.

I grabbed armfuls of the most sustaining snack foods I could find. A few of the kids were helping me, and I added some special treats they requested. As we carried the loot back to the van, I was shocked to see lines forming at the gas pumps. Clearly, we had been on the leading edge of the wave of evacuees crossing the mountains that morning. Now they were catching up with us.

We were about to leave when I remembered people had repeatedly told us to make sure we had toilet paper for the wait at the border. I ran back inside to buy packets of tissues, but there was already a huge line at the cash register from the new arrivals. Having just purchased over $50 of snacks, I decided I could help myself to some toilet paper with a clear conscience. In the women's restroom, I wound the loose end of a roll of toilet paper around itself until I had the equivalent of about half a roll. Hoping that would be enough, I hid it inside my coat and hurried back to the van.

We felt like our goal was almost within sight, but we were no longer making good time. Soon traffic slowed almost to a standstill. We were on a narrow, two-lane, mountain highway. The road was clear in one direction, but on our side, there was a long column of cars merely inching along. Eventually we reached a military checkpoint.

The soldiers were wearing full camouflage and had automatic weapons slung across their backs. My heart clenched. What were they looking for? They were courteous and efficient. They simply checked Jon's documents, then glanced at the luggage in the back of the van and waved us through. After that, traffic moved better for a little while, then slowed to a crawl as we approached another checkpoint.

We had to pass several of these to reach the border. There were long lines at each.

At one checkpoint, cars started cutting ahead by driving on the opposite side of the road. Jon ranted and gestured with his arms at these passing big shots in their fancy imported vehicles. They took no notice. Eventually he got so irritated that he positioned his large white van squarely in the middle of the road. No one could pass him on either side. Cars lined up behind him, blaring their horns, but he just sat there, immovable as a tank.

We were going through the middle of a little mountain village. Four weathered old men were standing by the road in front of their houses, watching. They kept looking at us, then looking at each other, and chuckling among themselves. I remember thinking it was probably the most entertainment they'd had in months.

Eventually, we made it through the mountains. The border was near, and we had to decide which crossing to use. Having visited Hungary many times, we knew we should not use the one recommended on the official website we consulted. Its wait times were routinely more than double or triple those of the smaller crossings. Instead, we called friends who lived right by the border, and they told us to go to a small crossing we'd never heard of before.

We arrived and joined the line just before 4 pm. The last section of the journey would normally have taken about two and a half hours. It had taken double that, but we were relieved it hadn't taken even longer. The line at the Ukrainian checkpoint was short and moving quickly, and soon Jon was talking to a border guard.

"How many people?" the guard asked in Ukrainian.

"Fifteen," Jon answered, handing him a tall stack of passports. Jon spoke Ukrainian better than many Ukrainians, having grown up in the country and having lived in a Ukrainian-speaking city for many years.

"Fifteen?" The border guard's voice sounded incredulous.

"Yes, fifteen. Twelve children and three adults."

The border guard walked around the front of the van, opened the sliding door, and surveyed Stephanie and me packed in the back with ten of the kids.

"Ah. Okay. Hmm . . ." He seemed to be having trouble deciding how to proceed.

"My kids and I can walk across," I volunteered in Ukrainian.

"Yes, that would be good." He looked relieved. "You see, it would be okay here, but the Hungarian side isn't going to like you going through with more than the legal number of people in the vehicle."

Even though it seemed the Ukrainian border guards wouldn't have given us any trouble, my six boys and I donned our coats and got out of the van. I didn't know if there was a Hungarian rule against changing one's mode of transportation between checkpoints, and I didn't want to find out by breaking it. If we had to pass the Hungarian checkpoint on foot, I wanted the stamps in our passports to show that we'd gone through the Ukrainian checkpoint on foot as well.

The boys didn't complain. We had crossed borders countless times, but never on foot. It felt like a fun adventure. There weren't many people walking across. We were processed and on our way long before Jon, Stephanie, and their kids got through.

Oddly, the Hungarian checkpoint was nowhere in sight, but it was clear which direction we were supposed to go. Instead of waiting for everyone else, we decided to take a stroll through no-man's-land, the territory between the border checkpoints that doesn't feel like part of either country. The sun was shining brightly on the trees and vegetation on either side of the narrow, winding, paved lane we were following. We were thankful for the opportunity to stretch our legs after eight hours of being sandwiched in the van. We walked down the middle of the road, only moving to the edge when a car needed to pass us.

After a while, Samuel became impatient. "I'm going to run ahead and see how far it is."

I opened my mouth to tell him to stay with me because I had the passports, but he was already off like a sprinter from the starting line, the end of his rattail bouncing with each footfall.

"Samuel! Samuel!! Samuel!!!" I called after him. He continued on as if he hadn't heard. Soon he was out of sight. I was upset by his rash behavior, but I couldn't leave the rest of the kids by themselves to chase after him. Besides that, I was pretty sure I couldn't catch him. I was in good shape for a forty-three-year-old mother of six, but he was a fifteen-year-old competitive runner, and taller than I was.

"What's wrong with him?" Kiyoshi's dark eyes blazed, and his tone expressed all the anger I felt. "Do you want me to bring him back?"

"No."

"C'mon, Mommy, let me go get him."

"You couldn't catch him. Either he'll get in trouble with a border guard and be sent back, or he'll get tired of messing around and come back on his own."

It seemed like Samuel was gone a long time, but in reality, it was probably only a few minutes before he came jogging back to us. I was relieved to see him, but still upset by his impulsiveness.

"Samuel, don't ever do that again! We're in no-man's-land. It's not a place to mess around! And you didn't even have your passport with you!"

"It's fine, Mommy," he said, completely unperturbed.

"No, it's *not* fine." I almost wished he'd been reprimanded by a border guard.

Before long, we reached the line of cars. It was much longer than the line at the Ukrainian checkpoint. It was barely moving. We decided to wait for Jon and Stephanie instead of continuing across on foot. While we had been traveling, Anna had reached out to our church network in Hungary. They found a van and a driver to meet us at the border so we could continue legally into the country. That van had not arrived yet, though, so we were in no rush to get across the border.

We stood off to the side of the road, watching the line getting longer. Jon and Stephanie's van finally showed up. The kids were excited to be reunited. I was comforted to see that evacuating with their cousins was protecting my children from experiencing the emotional trauma other kids in their position must be feeling.

The next few hours were like a tailgate party, van-style. We kept the sliding door open for much of the time, and the kids were constantly popping in and out. At one point, the older cousins were actually dancing on the side of the road next to the van. Now that we were officially out of Ukraine, the adults could relax, and it was hard not to smile at the kids' joy and enthusiasm. We all dined on the piles of snacks I'd bought and chatted as the van slowly inched toward Hungary.

11

George Breaks Curfew

6 am, February 25, 2022: Day 2 of War
Ukraine

After George said goodbye to Kiyoshi and me on the call early that morning, he prepared to leave our apartment with Olya to rendezvous with Yana and her son. Because of the curfew, he didn't know how they were going to get to the pickup point, and because of his spinal condition, he was afraid that if stairs were involved, he'd injure his back dealing with his suitcase. He frantically emptied his backpack, ditched his suitcase, and fled home with nothing but what he was wearing, his phone and laptop, his wallet and documents, and a few small personal items.

Most of the people in the apartment were still sleeping. It was a different scene from the tearful, agonizing parting of the day before, but it was still awful to leave everyone behind, not knowing if they would be safe. With a heavy heart and a guilty conscience, George said goodbye to our dog, wondering if we would see him again. George and Olya exited the building into the chilly air of an early morning in late February. They had no idea if they would ever return.

Before leaving, using the car-sharing app, George had looked for a car to rent to take them to the meet-up point with Yana, but the service was blocked in compliance with the curfew law. Next, he had called a taxi, but they weren't operating either. With no other choice, he and Olya headed to the closest subway station to wait for the first train, scheduled for 7 am.

The streets, usually filling with traffic at that hour, were mostly deserted. The air was still and quiet, a reprieve from the explosions

George and Olya had heard during the night. Despite the curfew, a surprising number of people were out, all headed to the subway as well. Worried eyes peered out of faces painted with exhaustion from a sleepless night. Some were engaged in urgent conversations on cell phones. George and Olya walked in silence, lost in thought. In his mind, George saw Kiyoshi's stricken expression when he heard that Jack would be left behind. George's stomach clenched as he imagined Jack abandoned on the street—lonely, confused, and frightened. Kyiv was huge—would we ever find him?

When they got to the station, a sobering sight met them. Instead of the usual bustle of morning rush-hour commuters, groups of tired people slumped on the floor. Many had spread blankets to sit on. Some even had pillows. Parents watched over sleeping children.

They were concentrated along the walls on the landings of the stairs that led down to the platform and near the pillars on the platform itself—anywhere a vertical surface could provide support for weary backs. They had bags containing whatever they thought most important to grab in those frantic moments before they rushed out of their homes to seek shelter. Tension and anxiety hung like stale cigarette smoke in the somber atmosphere. George surveyed the scene in shock and disbelief. It looked like about fifty people had spent the night there.

In the coming months, Kyivans would become accustomed to using their subway stations as places of work, school, and sleep as they did their best to carry on with normal life in the face of horrifically abnormal circumstances. As I sit here writing nearly three years later, Russia continues to target the capital of Ukraine with regular missile and drone attacks, and still the courageous people of Kyiv carry on. Many no longer bother to seek shelter when the air-raid sirens go off. What was once terrifying is now just a fact of daily life.

There was a subway train waiting on one side of the platform. The doors were standing open, and some people were already seated inside. It was going in the direction George and Olya needed. They quietly walked past our neighbors, who didn't have the good fortune of an apartment with a basement to sleep in, and they boarded the train.

George and Olya waited in silence for about twenty minutes. At 7 am, the subway speakers crackled to life with a bilingual announcement, first in Ukrainian, then English.

"Be careful; the doors are closing. The next station is Poshtova Ploshcha."

The familiar announcement was both comforting and jarring. The well-known words seemed out-of-place in a world that had changed so drastically. The train doors slid shut, and George and Olya were on their way.

They got off at the second stop to switch to a subway line that ran all the way to the place where they were to meet Yana. They would be late, but they were relieved to be on the final leg of the fastest route. Two stops before their destination, a voice on the sound system announced that the train would be going no farther. All passengers needed to exit.

George and Olya rushed up to street level. The atmosphere was radically different from the tense calm of their walk to the subway station. Panic prevailed. Frantic people rushed to leave the city. George and Olya were still two and a half miles (about four kilometers) from Yana. Traffic on the street was moving, but it was getting heavier, and they didn't know how much longer Yana would wait.

As they power-walked, George and Olya tried to flag down passing cars. This is a common practice in Ukraine. Usually you can find a willing driver (for a small fee), but today no one was stopping to pick up extra passengers.

George spotted a car pulling to the side of the road a short way ahead to pick up two people who were waiting. With a surge of hope, he took off sprinting. Maybe he could convince the driver to give them a lift. As soon as he reached the car, George opened the back door and leaned in.

"Can we get a ride?"

The driver shook his head. "I have to pick up more passengers."

"We just need to get to the end of the metro line."

"Oh, okay. Hurry, get in!"

"Thank you! Thank you so much!"

Olya jogged up, pulling her suitcase, and she and George quickly slid in with their bags. George leaned back and relaxed slightly. Maybe they would make it in time.

The spot where the driver let them off was about half a mile (800 meters) from Yana. They quickly walked the remaining distance. She waited, and they finally reached her at 7:40 am.

Traffic was crawling, but it was better than the day before. And this time, they were starting near the city's edge. As they inched along, George spotted a family by the side of the road. A young mother was half-sitting, half-leaning against a low wooden railing, her shoulders slumped forward and her head in her hands. The hood of her dark coat was thrown back, and her straight, brown hair hung down around her face, isolating her in her misery. Two young, school-aged children wearing backpacks stood beside her. They looked like they were maybe six and eight years old. Bags on the ground surrounded the small group, and a man, probably the father, stood a short distance away. It wasn't clear whether they were stranded or whether they were waiting for someone to pick them up.

George's eyes were drawn back to the woman, so obviously distraught. He imagined she was overwhelmed by being torn from her home and possibly having to say goodbye to her husband. With the institution of martial law, Ukrainian men between the ages of eighteen and sixty were not allowed to leave the country. If this mom and her kids planned to flee Ukraine, the father would not be able to accompany them. Maybe she was wondering where they would go and if they would be safe. Helplessness and grief overwhelmed George. Would anybody help them? Traffic slowly moved on until the family was lost to view.

George and his companions were traveling on a large divided highway, the main artery out of Kyiv in this direction. Bumper-to-bumper traffic clogged their side of the road. By contrast, the opposite side of the highway had been turned into a two-way road for armored vehicles and troop transport trucks that moved quickly in both directions. As Yana's car neared the city limits, the buildings gave way to trees. George was reassured to see Ukrainian soldiers and tanks positioned among the trees to the right. They were all pointing away from the road—to the north—waiting for the enemy. Every few minutes, George and his companions heard distant explosions. The atmosphere in the car was tense.

It took an hour to get fully out of Kyiv. After that, traffic slowly thinned. By the time they were forty miles (sixty-five kilometers) outside the capital, traffic was moving steadily. The sun was shining brightly, and the explosions had faded behind them. Except for there being more cars on the road than usual, the day had all the appearances of a typical midmorning on the cusp of spring.

George relaxed. As he did, the most traumatic moments of the morning came crowding back into his mind. Again, he remembered the haunting look on Kiyoshi's face when he heard that George would have to leave Jack behind, and it released a well of pent-up emotion. Then he remembered our friends who were sheltering at our apartment with their two young daughters. He thought of those little girls cowering in our basement, hearing explosions so close that they wondered if they were going to survive the next one, and he wept. It felt wrong that he was safely out in the sunshine while others were still trapped in the nightmare.

Their objective was to drive 260 miles (420 kilometers) west to Ternopil, which was on the way to Hungary. There, they would part ways. Yana planned to go to Slovakia, and Olya had decided to stay in Ternopil. George would travel on with a missionary family that was also en route to Hungary via Ternopil. They had fled Kharkiv, a city in the far east of Ukraine, just nineteen miles (thirty kilometers) from the Russian border, and had already been on the road for over twenty-four hours. They would stop in Ternopil to sleep and agreed to take George with them in the morning.

During the hours on the road that day, George was busy on his phone, connecting those who needed help with those who could give it—and desperately searching for a way to ensure that our dog would be cared for. But, like me, he couldn't find a good option for Jack. Then, when all hope seemed lost, the solution presented itself unexpectedly.

The Ethiopian family with the two young girls who were sheltering in our apartment contacted George. They had decided it was too dangerous to stay in Kyiv—they couldn't wait any longer for the convoy the U.N. had promised to organize for its employees. But they felt too conspicuous to evacuate on their own. Their skin color set them apart, they barely spoke Ukrainian or Russian, and their car had special UN license plates.

George connected them with Yurii, a Ukrainian friend who lived in Kaharlyk, a town just south of Kyiv. Yurii owned and operated a small trucking company. During the early days of the war, he pivoted from driving cargo to running an evacuation service, saving lives at the risk of his own. He agreed to drive into Kyiv first thing in the morning to collect this family from our apartment. George asked if he would also take our dog and care for him until we could get him. Yurii agreed.

Brimming with gratitude and relief, George exhaled and smiled for the first time that day. Some of the tension left his shoulders.

Over fourteen hours after starting their journey, George and Olya, with Yana and her son, finally reached Ternopil. Friends of ours took in Yana, her son, and the parrot. Though they were strangers, they received a warm welcome. In the coming months, over 30,000 displaced people would settle in Ternopil, which had a pre-war population of 225,000. The city also would serve as a way station for an even greater number of people fleeing further west. Yana, her son, George, and Olya were part of the first wave of these displaced people, many of whom would find welcome, places to sleep, and hot meals through local churches.

George and Olya met another friend, who drove them to Jon and Stephanie's apartment and gave them the key. It was 11 pm by the time they arrived and walked up the stairs to the fifth floor. This apartment had been our family's home for four years before we moved to Kyiv, and we had visited Jon and Stephanie here on a number of occasions. Entering it now felt both familiar and eerie.

It was dark and devoid of life, but it looked as if the people who lived there could return at any moment. There were still shoes and coats in the entryway walk-in closet. Children's toys were strewn about as if left in mid-play. The rumpled, unmade beds looked like they were simply waiting until bedtime brought back their usual occupants. In the kitchen, dirty dishes were piled in the sink, and the uneaten remains of a hurried breakfast littered the table.

George and Olya were exhausted, both physically and emotionally, but they couldn't rest yet. Seven of the friends who had been sheltering at our Kyiv apartment had also found ways out of the city. They would be arriving in Ternopil within hours, some by train, some by bus. George and Olya readied Jon and Stephanie's apartment for guests. They tidied the kitchen and searched for clean bedding. After that, Olya sent George to bed while she stayed up to make food for the other travelers, who would soon arrive, tired and hungry. Since she was staying in Ternopil, Olya could sleep in. George was leaving as soon as curfew ended at 7 am.

George stretched out on a bed they had made on the floor in the open kitchen area. He found comfort in the familiar surroundings, but his mind was spinning from the events of the last two days. He couldn't disconnect from his phone and the possibility that someone else might need his help. Eventually his exhaustion took over, and he succumbed to a profound oblivion. When our friends arrived and ate their late meal, just feet from where he was lying, he slept on, heedless of everything until his alarm woke him at 6:30 am.

12

THE KINDNESS OF STRANGERS

6 pm, February 25, 2022: Day 2 of War
No-Man's-Land, Dzvinkove Border Crossing

The sun went down on us as we waited to cross the Hungarian border. The sky slowly faded to black, and still the single-file line of cars stretched far ahead. By then we could see the Hungarian checkpoint. It looked so close, but we knew it could still take hours to reach it.

Though the checkpoint was in sight, I was reluctant to leave the cozy van to stand in the pedestrian line. Eventually, I could put it off no longer, as we knew our ride had arrived. I gathered my kids and a blanket or two to ward off the cold, and we walked to the end of the pedestrian line. Like the line of cars, it was much longer and moving much more slowly than its counterpart on the Ukrainian side of the border.

It was fully dark. The comfort of the sunny afternoon had given way to the darkness of a night with a biting wind. Three-year-old Isaac started coughing, an awful, wrenching sound. I winced each time it wracked his tiny frame.

I unzipped my coat and picked him up to cuddle in a blanket next to my body, but he struggled and protested until I put him down. I draped the blanket around his shoulders and did my best to hold it closed in front, but his coughing continued. Anticipating a long wait in the wind and desperate to protect him, I rallied his five older brothers to form a ring. We squeezed together until all the gaps were closed, shielding Isaac from the wind with our bodies. He accepted this compromise, and our human fortress slowly moved forward in line with the other refugees.

A few of the people near us made conversation. We shared where we had come from and how we had experienced the beginning of Russia's full-scale invasion. One man told me about a place to sleep. I thanked him and explained that someone was waiting for us with a van to take us further.

I was so thankful for our Hungarian connections. Our friends had not only organized transportation from the border, they had also arranged accommodations at a Christian retreat center, since Anna's apartment wasn't equipped to sleep fifteen extra people.

I wondered about my fellow evacuees. I couldn't imagine what I would do if I were in this line with no one to call and no place to go. At least not many of them had kids.

After a while, the people around me told me to cut to the front of the line because I had kids. Maybe they heard Isaac's coughing and were as concerned for him as I was.

It's common practice in Ukraine to let parents with small children go to the front of the line, but I almost never took advantage of it. When others suggested I should, I usually smiled and shook my head. But these people were insistent, and Isaac needed to get out of the cold. I thanked them and apologetically started to make my way forward. I didn't get far.

Another mother was in line a short way in front of me.

"I have kids too!" she snapped at me.

It was true. She had a boy and a girl, maybe eight and ten years old. They looked as if they were dressed to go on a skiing expedition. Although we had donned our coats before getting in line, my kids had been dressed for spending the day inside a van. But I had neither the confidence nor the forcefulness to argue that my sick three-year-old needed to get out of the cold sooner than her kids, so I meekly fell into line behind her. My boys and I reformed our protective circle around Isaac and prepared to wait as long as it took. Isaac's wracking cough continued.

Soon everyone nearby was muttering and grumbling at the mother in front of us. Several became more insistent, and before long, they shamed this woman into letting us go ahead. I felt a little sorry for her as we moved past, but I knew I needed to get Isaac into the waiting van as soon as possible.

So after about forty minutes in the pedestrian line, we found ourselves handing our passports to a Hungarian border guard. I don't remember if he was speaking English, Russian, or Ukrainian, but I remember gentleness, compassion, and concern as he told me there was transportation and a place where we could spend the night. I assured him we were okay, and soon he stamped our passports and handed them back.

It was just after 11 pm, Ukrainian time. The border crossing had taken seven hours. We had never waited at a border for so long, but refugees were spending over forty-eight hours at the Polish border. We were thankful for our relatively short crossing time.

Because I had delayed so long getting into the pedestrian line, Jon and Stephanie and their kids made it across before we did. Now they were parked beside a second van. Two Hungarian men whom I had never met welcomed us. They were from a church near the border. One had dinners neatly packed in gallon-size, zip-top bags. As he passed them out, he told us in broken English that his daughter had made them. Each contained a sandwich, a banana, a drink box, some snack foods, and a square of yellow paper with either a happy face or a heart drawn on it.

As I held my bag and looked at a simple happy face smiling at me, I nearly broke down sobbing.

We had made it. We were safe. And we were not alone.

The boys and I climbed into the waiting van, grateful to get out of the cold. The kids exclaimed over the various goodies in their meal bags as the two vans pulled out and headed into Hungary. At that point, I hadn't slept for forty-two hours. Although I struggle to stay awake on road trips, during all the hours on the road that day, I had never even felt drowsy. But now, having accomplished my mission of getting my children out of Ukraine, I could barely keep my eyes open. I didn't know the men I was with, but I trusted them instinctively.

The rest of that trip is a blur. I remember being half asleep with my forehead leaning against the back of the seat in front of me, feeling the gentle swaying motions of the van as it traversed the darkened Hungarian countryside. At some point, I was aware that the van was stopping, and then the sliding door beside me opened.

Disoriented, I blinked hard several times and looked around to get my bearings. We were at a rest stop. Jon's van was there too, along with a third van. One of the Hungarian men with us made me understand we were supposed to continue on in this new van.

I roused myself enough to transfer all my drowsy kids to the second vehicle and make sure they were all buckled in. I thanked the two men who had picked us up, and they said goodbye and left. Overwhelmed by the events of the last two days, I didn't think to ask their names or what city they were from—and then they were gone. I have forgotten what they looked like, but I will carry the memory of their extraordinary kindness with me for the rest of my life.

We didn't stop again after transferring to the second vehicle. It was dark and silent, and everyone but the driver was asleep or dozing. I was vaguely aware of the trip—long and monotonous, experienced through a fog of exhaustion. In lucid moments, I texted my family to update them on our progress. After several hours, the moment finally came when the van slowed almost to a stop and made a right turn, followed immediately by another right. I briefly heard the crunch of gravel under the tires, and then we were standing still.

With a start, I realized where we were. The Christian retreat center that had agreed to house us had served as the campus of a Bible college for many years, and my mother-in-law, Pam, had been on staff there for over a decade. Instead of taking us to the dormitories in the main building, as I had expected, our driver had taken us to a parking space that was significant to our family. It was the spot right outside Pam's old apartment, where we'd parked many times—back before our family outgrew the number of seats in our car. Jon and Stephanie's van pulled in beside us, and we emerged from the vehicles, all except for the youngest children, who were fast asleep.

It felt like the middle of the night, but we had arrived in the early hours of a new day.

Our driver said two apartments were ready for us. One was the unit Pam had called home. I was delighted by the prospect of staying in her old place, but I didn't want to take the privilege from Jon and Stephanie and their family.

"We'd love to have Mom's old apartment," I said hesitantly, "but I totally understand if you guys want it. We can stay in the other one."

"Oh, no, you can have it," Jon said, visibly relieved. "I don't think we could handle being there. Too many memories. It's not the same without her."

My kids and I climbed the stairs to the beloved upstairs unit that had been our favorite destination for many years. How many times had we arrived late at night after a long day of travel, made our way up these very stairs, and climbed into our waiting beds? The kids were delighted to be back in "Grandma's house." Of course, it would have been infinitely better if Grandma had been there to welcome us, but these walls held so many wonderful memories. Her presence seemed to linger on. It felt like a homecoming, something we all desperately needed.

We got our meager belongings transferred upstairs from the vans. I located all the toothbrushes and got everyone ready for bed. Then we figured out where each person would sleep in the cozy two-bedroom unit. It was hard for everyone to settle down after all the upheaval, but eventually all six boys were quiet in bed. Calm descended on the apartment as I set about getting myself ready for sleep.

I located my toiletries and arranged them in the bathroom, thinking about how wonderful a hot shower would feel, but I couldn't find my shower cap or bath mitt. Then it hit me. I had used both on the night before the beginning of Russia's full-scale invasion and had left them hanging in the bathroom to dry. In the frantic half hour of packing on the morning we fled, I'd forgotten to retrieve them.

The shower cap I could easily replace, but I felt like someone had knocked the wind out of me as I realized the Moroccan exfoliating mitt, precious because of who had given it to me, was gone. My arms fell to my sides, and I stood frozen in the middle of the bathroom, fighting tears.

It was the first of many similar realizations that would blindside me over the coming months. Random experiences would trigger memories of special things we had left behind. Over and over,

I would find myself yanked out of the present, forced for the hundredth time to relive the pain and trauma of fleeing our home with little warning.

Once I was finally ready for bed, I had an even harder time settling down to sleep than the kids had. It was daytime in California, where my family and close friends were awaiting news. I had to update them. It was around 6:30 am when I finally lay down on the queen-size bed in the room that had once belonged to Pam. The furniture had been rearranged since she moved out, and that made the room feel strange.

I lay with my back to the empty half of the bed where George should have been, a forlorn feeling lurking at the edges of my consciousness. I tried to banish it by focusing on the positive. It was 7:30 am in Ukraine, and George was on his way out of Ternopil to come to us. If all went according to plan, we would be reunited in about twenty-four hours.

13

The Power of Togetherness

6:30 am, February 26, 2022: Day 3 of War
Western Ukraine

George later told me his alarm went off at 6:30 am. The apartment was dark and quiet. He quickly gathered his few belongings, replaced them in his backpack, and looked for someone to lock the apartment door behind him. He poked his head into the living room and saw some of the ladies from our team asleep. Carefully shutting the door again, he headed toward the bedrooms.

In the second bedroom, George finally found the person he was looking for, a young, blond man sleeping beside his wife. George quietly roused him. He awoke easily and sleepily followed George. They hugged long and hard and said muted goodbyes just inside the apartment door.

His heart heavy over leaving all his friends, George walked down the concrete stairs from the fifth floor. It was just after 7 am, and George's ride, a large, white van, was waiting. The driver's door opened, and a man slowly got out. His shoulders were slumped, and the eyes peering from behind his glasses were weary. His family had spent the last two days driving. When Russia started bombing their city at dawn on February 24, they had loaded three kids, an adult daughter, and a few belongings into their van and fled west. After stopping in Ternopil for the night, they were on the road again.

"Thanks for taking me," George said, greeting the father with a hug. We'd known him for years. Like George, he was also from the American Midwest.

"Of course," the man said. "Thanks for offering to drive."

"How are you?"

"Ah . . . really tired."

Suddenly, the stillness of the morning was shattered by the wail of an air-raid siren. The two men quickly jumped in their seats, slammed the doors, and hit the road. Before long, they were in open countryside heading toward the mountains. As they drove, they talked about their experiences over the past two days. Everyone was still in shock.

Traffic was good. Every gas station had lines of cars, but they had a full tank. Once they got into the mountains, though, they encountered the same long waits at military checkpoints that we had experienced the day before.

During one of these waits, George had to pull off to the side of the road to allow one of the van's occupants to find a place to relieve herself among the mountainside bushes. It pained George to see about twenty cars roll past while they waited.

Once she rejoined them, George eased back into line. Since there were no cars on the opposite side of the road, he pulled out and drove ahead until he reached his former spot in line. The driver who had been behind him immediately let him back in.

That day, no one was cutting to the front. Instead, the shared hardship brought out the best in people, and they treated each other with kindness and consideration.

9:30 am, February 26, 2022
Vajta, Hungary

Meanwhile, I had awakened after only three hours of sleep. During the previous two days, the only rest I'd gotten had been some fitful dozing on the van ride from the border to the retreat center. Jon and Stephanie offered to take care of my kids so I could sleep more. Jon was going grocery shopping. I gave him a long list of things we needed to stock a new kitchen, and I prepared to go back to bed.

I couldn't rest without checking my messaging apps first. One of my friends in Kyiv was at her breaking point from all the explosions, but she didn't know how to leave. I asked George to put her in touch with our friend Yurii, who had evacuated the Ethiopian family and Jack from our apartment.

Within hours, Yurii was at my friend's apartment, like a special-order evacuation shuttle. He took her to his church in his hometown. She was able to spend the night in a private guest room and hitch a ride farther west with other evacuees the next day.

My friend later told me that when I contacted her, she just wanted someone to pick her up and get her out of Kyiv. It seemed like an impossible dream, and she didn't even bother to voice it. But God heard her unspoken prayer and sent Yurii. Throughout the multiple stages of her evacuation journey, she repeatedly experienced things that she later described to us as God taking care of her.

At one point, she was waiting at a crowded station to get a spot on an evacuation train. She saw a mother with a young child and felt a mental nudge to help them. She obeyed the prompting and passed the time helping the mother entertain her toddler.

When the next train arrived, the conductor prioritized people traveling with small children. He waved the mother and her child and my friend aboard. They took their seats before passengers without children were allowed on. The train couldn't accommodate everyone, and in the end, people were shoving wildly to get a standing-room-only spot.

Eventually, after days of travel, my friend made it safely to her parents' home in Spain.

After I got her connected with Yurii, I went back to bed. The apartment was quiet. My kids were next door with their aunt and cousins. My husband was safely on his way to us, driving through the part of Ukraine that was least likely to come under attack. And yet, I couldn't sleep. For three hours, I held my eyes closed and lay perfectly still, but I couldn't even doze. It was emotionally exhausting to be so sleep-deprived but unable to rest. Feeling guilty that Stephanie was taking care of twelve kids on her own, I finally got up, dressed, and left the apartment.

The sun was shining as I stepped onto the porch and made my way down the stairs to the entrance of the two-story unit where Jon and Stephanie's family was staying. I didn't bother to knock; I just let myself in. I heard the happy sounds of kids playing.

My eight-year-old James caught sight of me. “Hi, Mommy!” He ran over and gave me a quick hug around the waist, smiling up at me with his captivating hazel eyes.

“Hi!” I squeezed him back, comforted by his affection.

James ran back to play with his cousins. Reassured to see he was clearly enjoying himself, I searched for Jon and Stephanie. They were seated at the kitchen table.

“Thanks for watching the kids,” I said. “How have they been?”

“Oh, they’ve been great!” Stephanie paused. “How are you?”

How could I answer that question? Did I even know how I was?

“How are any of us?” I shrugged. “I’m glad George is safe and on his way.”

There was a pause.

“We have some news,” Jon said. “Mom’s coming.”

“What?” My hand flew to my mouth, and my eyes opened wide, blinking back tears formed from some combination of joy and shock. “She’s coming here?”

It was hard to believe. My mother-in-law was one of the most comforting people I knew. Pam’s coming wouldn’t make up for everything we had been through, but it would go a long way toward making things better.

“When?” I asked.

“Monday,” Jon said.

“What’s today?” I asked, disoriented.

“Saturday. And Paul and Melanie are coming with their kids. Tomorrow.”

The news just kept getting better. I shared a special bond with Melanie, one of George’s five sisters. We had lived together when I visited Kyiv before George and I were married, and she had been one of my bridesmaids. I saw her even less than I saw George’s mom. I couldn’t believe that the next day she would be arriving from the Middle East with her husband and five teenage kids. My older boys would be ecstatic.

Once it got dark, my kids and I went back to our apartment. I had trouble sleeping again. George was at the border, and I kept checking my phone for news of his progress and monitoring all my messaging apps for news of anything else.

George entered Hungary at 12:50 am Hungarian time. Even though there were now no obstacles standing between him and us, I couldn't relax. I finally managed to put myself to bed at 3 am, feeling how desperately my body needed rest. I slept lightly, knowing George would come in about three hours.

George called my cell phone when he arrived. I was up in an instant. I quietly made my way to the apartment door, careful not to disturb my sleeping kids. Through the blinds, I saw George's familiar silhouette in the soft, pre-dawn light. This was the moment I'd been hoping and praying for.

In an instant, I had the door open and stepped into his waiting embrace, wrapping my arms around his waist.

"Hi." I pressed my face into his chest.

He stroked my long hair. "It's good to see you."

"It's good to see you too." I had never meant it more.

We stood in the doorway with our arms around each other for a long moment, holding each other up in our exhaustion. George had been driving for almost 24 hours straight, and I had only slept a total of 6 hours since the beginning of the full-scale invasion 72 hours earlier.

I hadn't thought to request extra bedding from the retreat center staff, and we only had one twin-size comforter between the two of us. It was chilly in the apartment, and we cuddled together under the small blanket, drawing warmth and comfort from each other.

My mind wandered back over the fears that had assailed me during the past three days: having to face the uncertain future without George by my side . . . being forced to figure out a new life in a different country on my own . . . needing to find a job to support six growing boys . . . raising my children alone . . . watching my precious sons grow up without their dad.

Those awful visions now dissipated like smoke in the wind. We were together again. There was much wrong with the world, but this was definitely right.

14

An Uncertain Future

February 27, 2022: Day 4 of War
Vajta, Hungary

I expected to sleep well now that George was with us. I was wrong. Soon I heard his breathing settle into the even cadence of slumber, but still I lay there, wide awake.

Our family was back together. Now what? Could we stay in Pam's old apartment until it was safe to return to Ukraine? What about helping other refugees? How soon could we get started?

And when could we go home?

My back ached from lying in one position for so long, and I carefully rolled over, trying not to disturb George or dislodge the small blanket we shared. The room got brighter and brighter with the growing day. My thoughts continued to whirl, and I became more and more frustrated with my inability to sleep.

The kids would be awake soon, and my opportunity for rest would be gone. I had to sleep *now*. My body couldn't continue on a mere three hours per day.

Lecturing myself did nothing to help me relax.

Soft footsteps shuffled outside our room. I quickly rose and intercepted eight-year-old James.

"Is Daddy here?" He glanced past me at the bedroom.

"Yeah, he got here a couple hours ago."

"Where is he?"

"He's sleeping."

"Can I see him?"

"Yeah, just don't bother him. He's really tired."

James nodded and peeked into the room. George's head was poking out from under the blanket. James quietly withdrew and let me shut the door. He looked up at me with a huge smile on his face, his expressive hazel eyes dancing, and gave me a tight hug around the waist. Though I had been downplaying the danger George was in, James later told me he had been worried he would never see his dad again.

Soon all the kids were up. I fed them breakfast and tried to keep them quiet. Around lunchtime, George emerged from the bedroom. He looked groggy, and his dark hair was disheveled, but he got a big grin on his face as soon as he saw the kids.

"Daddy!" multiple voices exclaimed simultaneously. All the boys ran to him. Six pairs of arms tried to encircle him at once. George laughed as he struggled to maintain his balance in the midst of the excitement.

We headed to Jon and Stephanie's apartment. The family that came out of Ukraine with George was there too, and their two youngest children quickly found playmates among the twelve other children. The family's two older daughters worked side-by-side with the adults to prepare meals and wash the constant piles of dirty dishes. It felt like there were people everywhere, but though the logistics were challenging, the sense of community was invaluable. We needed each other.

Over the coming days, we would spend most of our waking hours together in that apartment. We worked shoulder-to-shoulder in the kitchen, we minded one another's children—and always—we talked. We often dabbed teary eyes with squares of toilet paper, but we didn't have time to give in to our pressing grief. We were all scrambling to figure out our next steps.

That first afternoon after George arrived, Jon and Stephanie drove to Budapest to meet Paul and Melanie and their five teenagers at the airport. We didn't tell any of our children the true purpose of the trip, because we knew they'd enjoy the surprise. Jon and Stephanie texted me when they were almost back. I called the kids to come outside just as the van was pulling up.

My eleven-year-old Peter ran out the front door, and when he saw his cousins, his mouth split open in a humongous, toothy grin. He ran back toward the apartment to shout the news to the rest of the kids inside.

Paul and Melanie's youngest boy made it to the front porch first and grabbed Jon and Stephanie's son Georgie in a bear hug. "Hiiiii!" Georgie screamed. As soon as he was released, he rushed past his cousin to greet everyone else. My thirteen-year-old son Kiyoshi got the next hug.

"When did you decide to come here?" Kiyoshi exclaimed, his hands raised in an expression of surprise. No one seemed to hear him. Everyone was shouting and laughing. Jon and Stephanie's toddler was walking around at knee level, wide-eyed at all the commotion.

Meanwhile, my autistic nephew came up to me, a big, open-mouthed smile on his face. Despite his natural aversion to touch, he was so pleased to see me that he let me give him a hug.

The rest of the kids finally made it out of the apartment to welcome everyone. Kiyoshi now had his hands on top of his head in consternation. "When did you decide to come here?" he repeated, to no one in particular. This time he got an answer.

"Yesterday," replied the only girl cousin in the group of new arrivals.

"I just walked here, you know," Paul and Melanie's oldest son, a tall, lanky blond, said.

"That must have been a long walk," Kiyoshi joked.

"It *was* a long walk," he agreed with a straight face.

It takes a while for twenty-three people to exchange hugs and greetings. Everyone was talking at once and going from one person to the next. It all blended together in a joyous cacophony.

In the middle of it all, I noticed my autistic nephew disappearing around the corner of the building. That was understandable—all our commotion had to be overwhelming to his specially wired brain. But I knew he too was overjoyed by the reunion, because he had stuck around to greet everyone in turn before heading off to put some distance between himself and all the noise.

We spent the rest of the day together, enjoying the comfort of time with loved ones. I was astonished that this large family had dropped everything and flown from their home in the Middle East to be with us.

Melanie explained. "When we evacuated from Iraq because of ISIS, we thought we were fine. People told us we should talk to someone, but Paul and I both said, 'We're fine. We don't need to talk to anyone.' But that next year was the hardest year we ever had. It even affected our marriage."

I nodded.

She continued, "We didn't realize it was because of what had happened to us until we finally started talking to a counselor. We don't want you guys to have to go through the same thing. That's why we're here. We want you to be able to talk about what you're going through."

Tears welled up, and I hugged Melanie. "Thank you."

The next day, February 28, Pam was flying in from Tbilisi, in the Republic of Georgia. George and I asked for the privilege of being the ones to meet her in Budapest. The drive was just under two hours. It was our first chance for private conversation since being reunited. We struggled to understand our new reality and make plans for the future.

The latter seemed impossible.

We agreed we'd return to Ukraine as soon as it was safe. But when would that be? One month? Six months? Where should we stay in the meantime? When we first arrived at the retreat center, I assumed we could set up house and stay as long as needed. That wishful thinking was a result of something I would later come to call *trauma brain*, a mental state that normalizes irrational or dangerous behavior because one's perception is skewed by traumatic events.

I was beginning to have doubts about my plan. Even if the people who managed the property repurposed it as a refugee shelter, we were not normal refugees. We held passports to a country that was not at war and could return there. Besides that, if we chose to stay in Europe, financial support from US churches gave us the option of finding a place to rent.

George and I never discussed whether we would stay in Europe. That was a given. We both knew we would remain as close to Ukraine as possible until this nightmare was over.

Pam's flight was on time. She and I shared a long, tearful embrace. Before driving back to the retreat center, we stopped at a supermarket. Besides food, I bought a queen-size comforter and duvet cover for George and me. Conscious that our money wouldn't last forever, I was careful to choose a cover that was on sale. My favorite color is purple, and it had a lovely floral print with multiple shades of purple and lavender. It was a gift from God to me, his traumatized daughter. Over the coming weeks, simply looking at it would make me pause, smile gently, and sigh contentedly. As we moved from one location to the next in search of a stable place to live, that purple print would become a sign of home.

On the drive back to the retreat center, we debriefed with Pam. Throughout our marriage, anytime we had faced a difficult decision, we had always consulted her. Now we were in the middle of our greatest challenge, and we didn't even need to pick up the phone to call her. Amazingly, she was already there to offer her support and wisdom.

Pam agreed that staying at the retreat center long-term wasn't viable. We had to be sensitive to the needs of refugees who had nowhere else to go. Though she didn't have any ideas about where we should relocate, she was supportive of our decision to stay in Europe. We arrived back at the retreat center with the barest glimmer lighting our dark path forward.

15

A Welcome Intermission

March 1, 2022: Day 6 of War
Vajta, Hungary

The next day, more visitors arrived: three pastors from the United States. After they finished unloading their suitcases, it looked like Christmas morning in Jon and Stephanie's living room. There was a new set of clothing and a brand-new toy for each of the fourteen children. For the adults, they had some new laptops and smartphones.

Their concern for us was a major motivation behind their trip, but it wasn't the only reason they'd canceled all their plans and flown almost half-way around the world on short notice. All of these men had been long-term missionaries in Hungary, and each of them had cared for refugees who came to Hungary during their years of service in the country. They knew Eastern Europe and wanted to get their American churches involved in this new refugee crisis. Theirs was a fact-finding trip as much as a mission of mercy.

Once the gift-giving was done, we discussed what else they could do. I sat next to George in the corner of the living room listening to the brainstorming session.

"So, how can we help?" Phil, the most energetic and vocal of the three pastors, opened the discussion.

"Man, I don't know. There are so many needs," Jon said.

"Let's just take your van and go into Ukraine," Phil said. "We can take a bunch of stuff and go to Ternopil and see what the needs are."

"Yeah, they could probably use medicines and medical supplies," said Mike, a soft-spoken, retired-Marine-turned-worship-pastor.

"We should take a bunch of power banks too. You never know when the electricity could be cut off," Paul said.

"Once we're there, we could buy a few more vans and evacuate people." Phil kept having ideas.

The direction the conversation was taking made me uneasy. This was morphing from a simple aid delivery into an evacuation project. They'd need people to drive these new vans.

So far, no one had said anything about George going, but I was nervous they would ask. He never said no to a request for help. It was one of the many things I loved about him, but right then, I almost wished he was a little less selfless.

We had just gotten him back. I hadn't recovered from the incredible strain of those three days of separation, of not knowing if we would see him again. I wasn't sure I would recover, and I was not prepared to let him head back into danger so soon.

But if others needed his help, how could I possibly deny them? I felt cowardly and selfish as I contemplated asking him not to go.

While I wrestled with these thoughts, more visitors arrived. Our Ethiopian friends were passing through our part of Hungary en route to Brussels, Belgium. We invited them to spend a night with us.

They loved the idea, and we decided, once again, not to tell our kids ahead of time.

They arrived just after 11 am. We called our kids outside as our friends were getting out of their car. There were the two parents, Aron and Lomi, their two elementary-school daughters, and an adult relative who lived with them like a nanny.

Eight-year-old James summed up all our feelings when he exclaimed, "Oh my goodness! I thought we weren't even going to see you guys ever again!" His eyes were wide with joy, and his eyebrows arched in surprise.

Everyone laughed, and we all hugged each other. Now our party of family and friends hanging out in Jon and Stephanie's apartment totaled forty people.

There was a big field beside the building, and soon someone organized an epic adults-versus-kids soccer game. The winter grass was dull and dormant, but the sun was shining brightly through the crisp air. The kids were a ragtag group of little guys who were just being allowed to participate for fun, slightly older kids who had never played much soccer, and a few teens who actually knew what they were doing.

The adult team had great athletes like George, his brother Jon, and brother-in-law Paul. Jon had actually been on the path to becoming a professional soccer player when he had been a teenager himself. Perhaps to even things up a bit, Aron, the father from Ethiopia, joined the kids' team.

I assumed the kids were going down, but in actuality, we adults never had a chance. It was hilarious, exhausting fun for all, and exactly what we needed.

Later, Lomi and I sat together and shared our experiences since the morning we had awakened to the sickening realization that Russia had launched a full-scale invasion of Ukraine.

"Sharon, it was terrifying, because our apartment is on the top floor," she told me. "We were so scared! You can't imagine how glad we were when George told us to come to your place!"

Lomi said that when George had to leave our apartment without our dog, her daughters wept, heartbroken both for Jack and Kiyoshi. Lomi's eyes got wide when she described listening to explosions nearby, wondering if the next bomb would hit our building. That terror was what pushed them to flee without the protection of the convoy the UN had promised to organize for its employees.

Though we'd known each other for less than a year, Lomi and I always connected on a deeply personal level, as if we both sensed in the other a kindred spirit. In that conversation, I was finally able to take steps to process my own trauma, reliving the most difficult moments of the first days of the war through storytelling. I sensed a touch of healing as we talked, the slightest relaxing of the strangling iron bands that had clamped around my heart.

Everything had changed, and the future was a looming question mark, but in that conversation, we experienced something familiar and stable. As I looked at Lomi's compassionate face and expressive eyes, I realized that while we couldn't be neighbors anymore, we would always remain friends.

Some local churches had dropped off donations of used clothing. Because we had been the first evacuees to arrive, they had brought the things to Jon and Stephanie's apartment. By this time, half of their living room floor was covered with plastic trash bags full of things that people had collected from their own homes.

Seated on the floor, all the moms sorted clothes by age and gender. We passed items back and forth as we found things that might be good for someone else's family. I picked out a few more changes of clothing for each of my kids.

Lomi found a coat she liked. "Oh, this is so nice! Can I have this?" Her eyes were sparkling. "I'll trade it for mine."

"Sure!" I wondered why she didn't want her Columbia jacket, which looked great to me. "Are you seriously getting rid of your coat?"

"Yeah, I spilled coffee on it when we were evacuating, and I haven't had a chance to wash it."

Her explanation didn't make sense. Couldn't she just wash it after getting settled in Brussels? But after wearing something through such traumatic experiences and living in it for several days of exhausting travel, I can now understand why she might have been sick of it, why she might even have felt strongly about never wanting to see it again.

"If you don't want your coat, I'll take it!" I laughed and stood up to try it on. The navy-blue jacket was a good fit for me and the perfect weight for early spring. All I had was my knee-length down coat, and I knew that would be too warm within a few weeks.

Despite the time we spent sorting donations, that day was a vacation from reality, an intermission in the middle of a tragic drama. We were able to set aside our fear, pain, and uncertainty for a few hours and enjoy conversation and laughter while our kids engaged in carefree play.

The next morning, Aron and Lomi and their family resumed their journey. We all hugged tightly before they drove away. They made it to Brussels two days later and began rebuilding their life.

Shortly after they left, we had another meeting in Jon and Stephanie's living room. Jon was preparing to take pastors Phil and

Mike and his brother-in-law Paul into Ukraine. No one had said anything about George joining the expedition, and George hadn't offered. I was relieved.

All the adults crowded into the room to pray for these men, who were deliberately heading into danger to help others. We sat on every available surface, including the floor. Some stood against the walls. Several of the mothers held small children on their laps.

As we prayed, I experienced a complicated mix of emotions. I was grateful George wasn't going. At the same time, I felt guilty he was staying. I could imagine the thoughts and feelings Stephanie must be having, and I was amazed she was willing to let her husband go. I didn't know if I could bring myself to do the same, and I was relieved no one was asking me to.

We prayed passionately in turn, until everyone had a chance. Then we all headed out to the gravel driveway. There were hugs all around, and the men climbed into Jon's van and left, our hearts and prayers following them.

They had barely gotten on their way when more newcomers arrived. It was George's twin sister, Renée, and her sixteen-year-old son, Josh, from Tbilisi, Georgia. Despite our joy at seeing them, we weren't able to sit around and catch up. George had an urgent mission.

16

War Isn't Up My Alley

March 2, 2022: Day 7 of War
Vajta, Hungary

I was relieved George was not going back into Ukraine, but he and I both desperately wanted to help. How? The answer was something we never could have imagined.

We had a friend in Ukraine who ran a small nonprofit that did disaster-relief projects around the world. With the start of the full-scale Russian invasion, he suddenly found himself in the middle of the world's largest hot spot. He told George he needed bulletproof vests, ballistic helmets, and combat boots. George promised he'd do his best, but he had no idea where to begin.

Before Jon and the other men left for Ukraine, one of the pastors had given George a lead on an acquaintance in Budapest who was a former British commando. Shortly after Jon and the other men departed, George headed into Budapest to meet this man at his place of work, a shooting range, and see if he could acquire military-grade protective gear.

When George arrived at the address, a clean-shaven Englishman with close-cropped, graying hair greeted him. The man held himself with poise and confidence. His polo shirt couldn't conceal his thick chest and broad shoulders. Massive, tattooed biceps protruded from the sleeves.

He welcomed George with a firm handshake and led him past several small rooms. In one of them, a man was tinkering with what looked to George's untrained eye like an assault rifle. They stopped in the room opposite. Guns were mounted on the wall, and a haze of blueish smoke hung in the air. There were a few armchairs and a low table with shot glasses and a bottle of whiskey. George felt like he was in a movie, about to negotiate with arms dealers.

A man speaking on a phone occupied one of the chairs. He was above middle age with gray hair. He glanced at George and the British commando as they entered.

"Please, have a seat," the Englishman said, producing a cigar box and offering one to George, who politely declined. His host chose one for himself and took a few moments to trim the end and light it.

"Can I get you some?" he asked George, motioning toward the whiskey.

"No, thanks. I'm fine."

"So, how can I help you?"

"Well . . ." George didn't know how to start. "This isn't really up my alley. I'm a pastor."

"That's fine." The man laughed good-naturedly. "It's not up many people's alleys."

"I need body armor and ballistic helmets. What would that cost?"

"Level-three or level-four?"

"Ah, I don't know. Let me call my friend."

George put him on the phone with our friend in Ukraine and sat back. After getting all the details he needed, the Englishman called a factory in Mexico for a quote. They said they'd get back to us later.

The whole time, the third man in the room had been constantly busy on his phone, texting and carrying on loud, agitated conversations. George couldn't help overhearing him say he needed a safe house near Kyiv.

George thought of the church in Kaharlyk that was housing the people our friend Yurii was evacuating. George asked a few questions and learned that a group of former military men was setting up an evacuation operation to get people out of Ukraine. Intrigued, George wondered if he could help.

That evening, George and I discussed the possibility and decided he should return to Budapest the next day. These hardened soldiers seemed clueless when it came to basic knowledge about Ukraine. By contrast, George had lived his entire adult life there, traveling up and down the country countless times. He knew the places, people, and languages. His network included almost twenty churches all over the country. And that wasn't all.

Half a year before, George had joined a nation-wide training cohort to become a Ukrainian police chaplain. The newly trained chaplains had not yet turned in their final papers when the invasion started. The planned graduation gala in Kyiv was postponed, and everyone had applied their training to the unthinkable situations in which they found themselves. Some jumped into evacuating people from dangerous areas. Others acquired and delivered aid. Chaos had descended on the country, but these brave men and women were already strategically positioned to bring help and hope where it was needed most. If George wanted to know the situation on the ground in any part of the country, all he had to do was ask in the chaplains' chat group, and he'd get an immediate answer.

The evacuation operation was happy to accept George's help. The sooner they could start working, the better. International military experts predicted Ukraine wouldn't hold out long. The city of Kherson had been overrun. Mariupol was under siege. Kyiv was predicted to fall within days. George headed back to Budapest, and so began an unconventional partnership that would dominate our lives for the coming weeks.

Meanwhile, we heard back from the Mexican factory. They informed us that the minimum order for the gear we needed was $26 million.[1] We were taken aback. Our friend in Ukraine said he couldn't raise that much.

George continued to search for body armor. Ultimately, he was able to connect our friend with a US-based group with millions of dollars of gear for Ukrainian defenders. They wanted a non-governmental channel to ensure their donations went to the Territorial Defense Forces and other poorly funded Ukrainian soldiers. Our friend was perfectly positioned to be that conduit.

---

1. *Three years after these events, George contests this amount. He remembers it being closer to $2–4 million. However, the amount I recorded in the daily journal I was keeping at the time was $26 million.*

When George arrived in Budapest to help on the first day, he discovered the evacuation operation had moved into a large army tent. There were several maps of Ukraine, with safe and dangerous zones marked in different colors, updated whenever new intel came in. A life-size cardboard standup of Winston Churchill stood in one corner, and a headless dummy wearing army fatigues in another. A well-worn couch, a few matching armchairs, a pool table, and several desks completed the decor. Despite the cold weather, the interior was warm, thanks to a heavy-duty space heater blasting hot air. Extension cords from the building next door powered computers and lights.

George spent that day observing, listening, and learning. It was an eye-opening experience. These seasoned men, all former military, talked casually about things George had never considered.

One man, a retired US Marine, was trying to get a vehicle to go into Ukraine and pick up clients. "There's no way I'm going in without a car!" he said passionately. "I made that mistake in Afghanistan. Had to fight my way out. Almost didn't get the lady out alive. I told myself I'd never go in without a car again!"

One of the men in the tent had been hired by an NGO to evacuate a group of children from an orphanage near a conflict zone. If they fell into the wrong hands, they could be sold into the sex trade. The man working on their case was constantly on the phone, trying to cut through the red tape preventing them from being moved. Every third word out of his mouth was an expletive, but he seemed to care deeply about the fate of those kids.

It took about two weeks, but eventually, the children evacuated safely, and our church contacts resettled them with their caretakers at a youth camp in Western Ukraine. It had been a favorite destination of our own children.

That first day, George learned people were paying enormous amounts for safe passage out of Ukraine. Relatives living abroad often sent the funds on behalf of their loved ones. For $15,000, they could order a five-seat car to extract up to four people. The so-called "Uber drivers" were former military men who had been part of similar operations in other parts of the world. Besides safe passage out of Ukraine, the fee covered protection, food, and lodging in safe houses.

George found it off-putting that these "independent contractors," as we started calling them, were profiting from war and suffering, but the men with whom he spoke seemed sincerely motivated by a desire to save lives. Why else would they risk their own? If they could get people out safely, we wanted to help.

17

Yurii

February 27, 2022–March 3, 2022
Kyiv Oblast, Ukraine

While all this was happening, our friend Yurii, the Ukrainian trucker, had continued to evacuate people. On the evening of February 27, George's twin sister, Renée, sent an urgent message to our family chat. Ira, a friend in Ukraine, had posted on Facebook, begging for someone to help her. She and her husband and two sons were in a house in Bucha with another family. Bucha is a suburb of Kyiv, now known for the infamous Bucha massacre that would take place under Russian occupation during March 2022.

George called Yurii to see if he could evacuate them, but Yurii didn't answer. All George's sources told him the fighting in Bucha was intense. It was impossible to get through. Ira and her family would do best simply to shelter in place, but that was a terrifying prospect. The house was located near the epicenter of the battle. With each explosion, the building jumped like a frightened animal. Ira and her family cowered in a corner, praying for the nightmare to be over.

A little before 2 am, George finally managed to get in touch with Yurii, but he simply confirmed what everyone else was saying. If the family could get out of Bucha, Yurii would pick them up in Kyiv. Otherwise, they just needed to lie low. Disappointed, George gave Ira's number to Yurii, anyway.

We prayed.

About an hour later, Ira texted George to thank him. Yurii was on his way.

We had no idea what had happened to change Yurii's mind. We were happy for our beleaguered friends but alarmed for Yurii. We had been worried about Ira and her family, but at least they had some shelter. Yurii was driving into imminent danger. We knew he wore a bulletproof vest on these missions, but that was no guarantee of safety.

George asked Ira to keep us updated and let us know as soon as she was safe.

We waited anxiously.

One hour.

Two hours.

They were still waiting for Yurii. Would he be stopped before he could make it to them? Would he be shot at? Or injured . . . or worse? We didn't even think of sleeping.

Finally, a little after 5:30 am, we got a text from Ira. She and her two sons and the other family were with Yurii on their way to his hometown, Kaharlyk, which was still safe.

However, we later learned that Ira's husband, Kolya, didn't escape with them. When Yurii arrived, Kolya was gone on a mission to retrieve their family's cats. With explosions and the sound of gunfire all around, Yurii realized they couldn't wait. He took everyone present and left immediately. Later they learned from neighbors that Russian tanks rolled down their street five minutes later. That night Yurii saved nine people from the trauma of Bucha's bloody occupation.

We finally went to bed, exhausted and elated. Later that day, we discussed the daring evacuation over cups of coffee in Jon and Stephanie's apartment.

"Wow," Jon said, "when you talk to Yurii in peacetime, he's a little intense, you know? It's like, whoa, man, settle down! But at a time like this?" He paused and shook his head. "Now I know why God made him that way."

The rest of us couldn't have agreed more.

Ira later told us how her husband eventually managed to escape Bucha. Russian soldiers stopped Kolya at a checkpoint as he tried to walk out of town with their cats. They told him if he wanted to leave, he'd have to get permission from their superiors and directed him to a nearby kindergarten they had repurposed to process people.

Kolya headed in the direction they indicated, but as soon as they were out of sight, he ducked onto a side street. Why should he follow their instructions? This was his home, not theirs, and he wasn't about to let any interloping Russians tell him what to do.

He encountered a group of people also trying to evacuate on foot. Some of them told Kolya that Russian soldiers had taken their cell phones and laptops. The soldiers at the checkpoint hadn't even searched Kolya; that was supposed to happen at the kindergarten.

To increase his odds of escape, Kolya separated himself from the group. He made it to a bridge out of town, where he met volunteers who were evacuating refugees. They took Kolya to his parents' home in Kyiv. He left the cats there, then enlisted in the Ukrainian Armed Forces.

Later Kolya learned that the Russians had shot the men who had gone to the kindergarten.

Ira's trip to Kaharlyk took hours longer than usual because there were so many Ukrainian military checkpoints. But eventually they made it, and Ira texted George a heartfelt thank-you for the role he had played in their safe evacuation. She also sent a photo of one of her sons petting our dog, Jack. She said Jack had been therapeutic for them, and Yurii's family was taking good care of him.

Several days later, on March 3, George received an urgent text from Yurii. Things around Kyiv were getting more and more dangerous. The Russian army was trying to encircle the city, and some special forces had even managed to infiltrate the capital. But Yurii had continued doing evacuations. His text said his van had just been shot up. He was lying low, hoping to be able to make it back to safety.

It was a surreal, helpless feeling to know a friend was in a position so precarious that he might not survive. We called an emergency prayer meeting in Jon and Stephanie's apartment.

God, protect him! my heart cried, but that seemed so inadequate in the situation.

"God, blind the eyes of the Russian soldiers. May they not even be able to see Yurii or his van," someone else prayed aloud.

Yes! That's it! Yes, God, do that! Please do that! I agreed silently.

We waited in suspense for hours. Finally, Yurii texted George that he had made it back to safety on foot. One of the bullets had pierced his van's engine, making the vehicle undrivable. Unfazed, after making it home, Yurii had found another vehicle and evacuated more people that same day.

We were all in awe of the heroism and bravery of this selfless truck driver. Ukraine needed more people like him.

18

More Relocations

March 3, 2022: Day 8 of War
Vajta, Hungary

After Pam's arrival, family discussions focused on long-term plans. Those of us who had evacuated struggled to wrap our minds around our new reality. In our traumatized state, evaluating options and making decisions felt overwhelming. We leaned heavily on the input and wisdom of the others, especially Pam. It was a relief not to have to work through these dilemmas in isolation.

We all believed the war couldn't last long. The US and the EU would put a stop to this outrage, and we could probably return to Ukraine in half a year. It didn't make sense to relocate to the United States for such a short time, but everyone was realizing what George and I had already discussed. We couldn't stay at the retreat center. We had other options. More and more refugees were arriving each day. We needed to move on to free up space for those who had nowhere else to go.

Our tribe completely filled two apartments, and it looked likely that soon we would have more people. George had a third brother. David was a missionary in Russia. He and his wife Deborah lived with their four kids in Siberia. Initially, they didn't think the war would affect them, but things quickly escalated.

The international community reacted to Putin's invasion with official statements of condemnation and economic sanctions. At the same time, the Russian government passed laws to support the so-called "special military operation" in Ukraine. They made it illegal to discredit the use of the armed forces of the Russian Federation or to spread "false information" about them. "False information" included referring to the "special military operation" as a *war* or *invasion* or saying that it was killing Ukrainian children. The penalty for breaking these new laws ranged from fines to up to fifteen years' imprisonment.

Anti-Ukraine and anti-foreigner sentiment grew in the country. David and Deborah knew was evicted from their apartment. Their landlord claimed that renting to foreigners was now illegal.

The Russian government started arresting people on charges of terrorism or spreading false propaganda. A Ukrainian friend living in David and Deborah's city was arrested and forced to delete his Facebook account. Before releasing him, the police threatened him and warned that he was under surveillance. His young daughter came home from her government-funded kindergarten spouting anti-Western propaganda: Russia was being forced to defend itself from Ukraine, and the EU and the US were at fault. The family received terrifying phone calls from people who said they knew where they lived and where their kids went to school.

These developments made David and Deborah uneasy. Not only were they vulnerable as Americans, but David had strong ties to Ukraine, having lived there for seven years. Many of his friends and family still lived there. Beyond concern for their own safety, David and Deborah were worried their presence might create problems for the church they had started. The situation in the country was deteriorating, and they realized that if they wanted to leave Russia, they had to act fast.

The international community was discussing cutting Russian banks out of SWIFT, the international network used by financial institutions to exchange information securely. If this happened, David and Deborah would have no way to access their primary bank account, which was in the United States.

In the meantime, many of the world's airports had banned flights from Russia. In order to leave the country, the family decided to fly to Saint Petersburg in the far west of Russia and hire a car to drive them to the Finnish border. But then they learned the taxi companies that used to provide that service had discontinued it during COVID. Finally, a friend outside Russia found them six spots on a flight from Saint Petersburg to Dubai. He had to purchase the tickets using cryptocurrency because the airline was no longer accepting credit card payments for flights originating in Russia.

From Dubai, the family could easily travel anywhere in the world, and they decided they would join us in Hungary.

They paid cash for air tickets to Saint Petersburg from their remote location and hurriedly packed a few suitcases. The situation was gut-wrenching. How do you condense your whole life into a few bags in the space of two days? How do you say goodbye to all your friends when you have only forty-eight hours, you're fleeing an oppressive regime, and your cover story is that you're just going on vacation? In their haste, they ended up forgetting special items, and they left with only a few close friends knowing the true reason for their trip.

Despite the obstacles, everything went according to plan, and their family of six made it the 1,200 miles (1,900 kilometers) to Saint Petersburg in plenty of time for their March 3 flight. But they couldn't relax. They still had to clear passport control to board the plane. Was David already flagged in the Russian system as a Ukrainian sympathizer? Would they be detained for questioning? Arrested? They shared all these concerns in a secure text message and asked us to pray. We privately passed their request to all the praying people we knew.

Then we waited. We were doing a lot of that in those days—unable to make contact with people, anxiously checking for updates, praying and hoping.

We finally received a text that they had boarded their flight without trouble. We celebrated, but personally, I was still worried. I imagined Russian police storming aboard the plane while it was parked at the gate and dragging David off. I didn't relax until I knew they were finally airborne.

Once they were safely gone, David and Deborah found out from a neighbor that the police had come looking for them. Their neighbor had said they were on vacation.

Once the family was on its way to Hungary, the rest of us decided to leave the retreat center as soon as possible. A pastor in Debrecen, a Hungarian city located 80 miles (130 kilometers) from the Ukrainian border, had offered us an apartment, and we accepted.

I packed quickly. With groceries plus donations and gifts we'd received, we had twice as much stuff as when we arrived. Once again, I regretted having bought so much food, but at least this time I could take it with us.

We weren't the only evacuees who had decided not to stay. The family with whom George had left Ukraine was flying to the United States the next morning, and another American family who had arrived at the retreat center shortly after us had already returned to the US. Both were leaving their vans in George's care. It was bizarre to go from not owning a vehicle to suddenly having two at our disposal. But it wouldn't be for long.

The next day, March 4, the head of the professional evacuation service called George. He needed to borrow a fifteen-passenger van to evacuate people from Kyiv and asked if George could find one through his church contacts. In exchange, the evacuation operation would make a generous contribution to the church, and they would return the van within a few days.

George couldn't find any church vehicles, so he checked with the owners of the two vans in our care. Could he volunteer their vehicles for the mission? Both families immediately gave their approval. There was some question about the road-worthiness of one of the vans, but the evacuators said it didn't matter. They would have a mechanic standing by to look at it as soon as we could deliver it to them in Budapest, then their drivers would take the vehicles into Ukraine.

These plans developed while we were waiting for one of the vans to return from a run to the airport. In the meantime, we packed all our things into the other van. The rest of George's extended family moved out of the retreat center and went to Budapest to meet David, Deborah, and their kids, who were flying in that morning. We would rendezvous at a Budapest hotel where we'd all booked rooms for the night.

Once the other van returned, George and the kids and I checked out of the retreat center to move to Budapest. I hadn't driven for years and was nervous about being behind the wheel again. One of the vans was a huge nine-seater that I wasn't sure I could manage. George gallantly took it, leaving me with a seven-seat minivan. We buckled the kids into the minivan and headed out, George leading the way. The minivan handled well, and I was soon at ease. It didn't seem to have any issues, and I wondered why the family who left it with us said it needed work.

We made it to Budapest in about ninety minutes. Traffic was super heavy, and the evacuators needed the vehicles as soon as possible. Every minute mattered. George pulled into the bus lane and zipped along to the right of all the stopped cars. I hated to break the law, but I had no choice, because I didn't know where we were going. I called him.

"We're in the bus lane!" I said as soon as George picked up.

"It's okay. We're from Ukraine."

"And that's relevant how?" I retorted sarcastically.

"Our country is at war! We can drive in the bus lane!" He hung up.

His logic didn't make any sense to me, but I gritted my teeth and followed him. I breathed silent apologies to every car we passed, hoping they would see our Ukrainian license plates and have compassion rather than judging us. I was also praying we wouldn't get stopped by the police.

Without warning, the van shut off. I was coasting. I felt frantic, but I knew I had to stay calm. I had all the kids with me. My left foot instinctively felt for the clutch so I could turn the key to restart the engine while still rolling. There was no clutch. It was an automatic. I didn't know how to restart an automatic while coasting, and there was nowhere to pull over.

"Kids, pray! The van quit, and I don't know what to do!" I spoke loudly so my words would carry to the back.

"Okay, Mommy!" several voices answered.

The van continued to coast while I considered the problem, then suddenly, I knew what to do. While still rolling, I put the van in park and turned the key in the ignition. It worked.

"Thank you, God!" I said aloud. "Thank you, kids!"

I heaved a sigh of relief, but it didn't last long. About a block later, the van shut off again. I quickly put it in park and restarted it while coasting. But it kept dying, and each time it did, the distance it would travel before dying got shorter. I was losing momentum.

I finally realized it would be impossible to reach our destination without becoming a hazard. At that moment, the van died again. I spotted a parking spot a few car lengths ahead. I got the van restarted and pulled up next to the curb just as it shut off.

I called George and explained. He parked and walked back to us. Thankfully, the hotel where our whole clan was staying for the night was just around the corner. We unloaded the van, and the kids helped us transport all our stuff on foot.

After we checked in, George took the vans to the independent contractors. He enlisted the aid of Caleb, yet another American pastor and former missionary to Hungary who had dropped everything to fly to Europe in response to the war in Ukraine. After the engine cooled down, the minivan I'd been driving cooperated better, and the two men were able to deliver both vans. George later told me the man in charge of the evacuation operation was so relieved to have vehicles that he almost cried when they showed up.

While George was delivering the vans, I was figuring out how we were going to sleep eight people in the two-bedroom hotel apartment unit we had reserved for the night. George and I would share the double bed in the front bedroom. That left two twin beds and a narrow couch for the six boys. Thankfully, the family that had returned to the United States that morning had given us a thin camping mattress. One kid could use that, and I made another makeshift bed on the floor for the two smallest children by folding our queen-size comforter into a thick pad.

After we put the boys to bed, George drew a bath for me. I slid into the tub until I was submerged to my chin and allowed the hot water to pull the tension from my body. Afterwards, George and I made love for the first time since we had been reunited. For days, life-and-death needs had constantly bombarded us, and our intimate life had been the first casualty. Every day we were busy until late into the night, monitoring all our chat apps and social media, scanning for people whom we could help.

Our friends in Ukraine didn't have the luxury of sleeping in safety. The war never took a break, so it felt wrong for us to pause for sleep. I'm surprised we didn't work out a shift system, so one of us could always be manning a phone while the other slept. But we hadn't figured that out, just like we hadn't figured out how to fit in couple time. When we finally put ourselves to bed for a few hours early each morning, I had always been too exhausted for anything but sleep. George had been patient and understanding. His selfless gentleness made our union on that night even more beautiful than usual.

As we snuggled afterward, I was thankful for many things. I had been sad to leave the familiar retreat center, but at least we had a comfortable place to spend the night. And the next day we were moving closer to our beloved Ukraine. If we couldn't move back home right away, being close to the border was the next best thing. And we had the equivalent of a small village of loved ones making the move with us. What could be better?

19

Relocating Yet Again

March 5, 2022: Day 10 of War
Budapest, Hungary

The next day was our second moving day in a row. Leaving the hotel apartments was easy, since we had only been there one night. We hadn't developed any sort of attachment. We hadn't even settled in.

Since we had given our vans to the independent contractors, we no longer had enough vehicles to transport our whole tribe to Debrecen. Somehow, George's sister Melanie procured a tour bus, free of charge. It belonged to a professional soccer team, and its driver attended a church in Budapest. He agreed to take our group to Debrecen if we would cover the fuel.

The only difficulty was meeting up with him. There wasn't a parking lot within walking distance. The only place large enough to accommodate a tour bus was a bus stop about a block away, and the bus wouldn't be able to park there for long. The driver gave us a time to be in place. We'd need to get everyone and all our things onboard in the space of five minutes.

When Melanie told us the plan the night before, I was completely overwhelmed. The prospect of carrying our collective mountain of stuff to the pickup point a block away—with all the little kids in tow—made me want to cry. But it was a miracle that Melanie had found us a bus, so I simply thanked her and tried to figure out how to approach the challenge.

It turned out I didn't need to do anything. In the morning, several of my nieces and nephews knocked on our door and asked for our bags. George's brother David, who had arrived the previous day from Siberia with his family, had organized them into a squad of porters. They collected all the luggage from everyone's rooms. Then, while one stood guard over the stuff outside the hotel, the rest of them walked back and forth, transporting it all to the bus stop, where another cousin stood guard until the job was done. Except for Uncle David, who was busy supervising his crew, the adults simply watched over the little kids, who were happily playing with each other in front of the hotel.

George's brother Jon had recently returned from Ukraine, and he and George were deep in conversation. I didn't think much about it until George approached me.

"What do you think of me staying here to talk with the pastors who just got back from Ukraine? They've got a lot of ideas from what they saw there, and they think I could help. You and the kids could still go to Debrecen with everyone else."

"Sure." I was used to George's out-of-the-box thinking and last-minute plan changes. We probably seemed slightly insane to most people, but it worked for us.

"You'll be okay?" he asked.

"Yeah, we'll be fine," I said. "Look how happy the kids are with their cousins! And I'll have Mom and the rest of the ladies." I was looking forward to some girl time.

"Okay, thanks. I think it's really important. The independent contractors have intel that Russia's brought in Chechen soldiers. They're supposed to be really brutal. They're worried things are about to get a lot worse in Ukraine. And they said the safe house in Kaharlyk has been compromised, because Russia's trying to surround Kyiv. We don't know how long we have to get people out."

"That doesn't sound good." This was bad. Awful things could happen, maybe even to people we knew.

"Yeah, the pastors want to try to get everyone from the Ternopil church out."

"Everyone?"

"Everyone who wants to leave."

My stomach clenched as I thought of beautiful Olya in the path of raping and pillaging Chechen soldiers. Hopefully, she would evacuate. Even though Ternopil was far from the Russian troops around Kyiv, enemy soldiers could easily sweep down from Belarus. “Wow. You stay here and do whatever you need to do. We’ll be fine.”

“You’re amazing.”

“I know.” I batted my eyelashes at him and laughed as he gave me a squeeze and kissed my forehead.

The older cousins had almost completed moving the luggage to the bus stop. It was time to move out. The adults gathered the little kids and started the migration. Without having to manage any bags, we reached the stop much sooner than I expected.

When we arrived, the older kids met us beside a huge collection of suitcases, wheeled carry-ons, backpacks, shopping bags, musical instruments, and random articles. Melanie had taken a few people ahead in her rental van, but our group still had twenty kids and five adults. We took up the entire bus stop. We looked like a tour group, so it was fitting we were waiting for a tour bus.

We stood by the curb, some of us watching oncoming traffic, some of us minding little kids, all of us impatient to start the next leg of our journey. There was a sidewalk stand beside us selling chimney cakes, a Hungarian specialty. The tantalizing aroma of freshly baked pastry and cinnamon filled the air. Several of the kids asked if we could get some of the tubular confections.

Expecting the bus to arrive any minute, the adults decided against it because the cakes were made to order, and the wait time was at least five minutes. The kids were disappointed, but the adults stood firm. Every five minutes, the kids would bring up the subject again.

“See, we would’ve had time! Can’t we get some now?”

Finally, the bus arrived. The driver jumped out and quickly opened the cargo compartment. David and the teenage porter squad loaded our things. George and I shared a tender embrace and a kiss on the lips, then he hugged each of our kids goodbye. Once everyone was aboard, the size of the bus dwarfed even our large group.

The older cousins congregated toward the back. From the sound of their rowdy laughter, they were having a great time. I took seats for myself and my two youngest kids at the front of the bus. Andrew and Isaac were thrilled to be so near the driver and able to see out the enormous front windows.

The trip took three hours. Our destination was what I could only call a mini-hotel. Surprisingly, despite the influx of Ukrainian refugees, it was nearly empty. It was ideal. It felt like we were all staying in one large house, but we had separate rooms and bathrooms. We occupied every available room in the two-story building.

Soon after we arrived, all the husbands drove into Ukraine, except for George, who was still in Budapest. Feeling the threat to our friends and family still in Ternopil, these men went to help them evacuate. Suddenly, we ladies were on our own.

George's mom and sisters made it their mission to mitigate the difficulties for the three mothers who had been displaced. They kept the pantry and fridge stocked and often ordered takeout for everyone. What would have seemed impossible on my own was bearable because of their care.

The mini-hotel was the fourth place where the kids and I had stayed since leaving our home in Kyiv two weeks earlier. The first two had cost next to nothing, but the last two were another matter. The mini-hotel would cost our family about $140 per night. It was a good price, considering the seven of us required two rooms, but I knew it would add up fast. How long could we keep paying?

I had voiced this concern when we arrived, but the other adults already had credit cards out, ready to check-in. I realized that unless we were willing to sign long-term lease agreements, we weren't likely to find a better deal, so I pulled out my card too. We needed a place to sleep, and I was too overwhelmed to deal with more than the most urgent needs. I would just have to trust God that, when the bill came, there would be money to pay it off.

Though I was uneasy about the price, the timing of our stay was perfect. My son James's ninth birthday was in less than two weeks, and I was excited for him to have a party with so many relatives. Having his cousins around would relieve the bitterness of not being able to celebrate with any of his friends in Ukraine.

The days we spent at the mini-hotel were therapeutic. There was a common kitchen and dining area on the first floor. We ate together, and the adults shared morning coffee and evening herbal tea after the little kids were in bed. The older cousins played card games and board games that my nephew Josh brought with him from Tbilisi. The hotel property was fenced, and the younger cousins enjoyed the freedom to run around outside. In the evenings, the older kids watched movies and introduced my son Samuel to the Marvel universe.

We were a close-knit group, with shared memories, inside jokes, and common goals. We sometimes went years without seeing each other, but we always looked forward to the next reunion. For me, being together diminished the pain of being displaced.

If home is where your heart is, I had found a temporary home in that mini-hotel in Debrecen, Hungary.

20

The Whole Gamut

March 6, 2022: Day 11 of War
Debrecen, Hungary

For days before arriving at the mini-hotel, I had been at the mercy of my emotions. Tears leaked from my eyes at every reminder of the war. The day after our arrival was different. I couldn't feel anything. I operated on autopilot, detached, uninterested.

I wondered if it was part of the normal response to trauma. I wasn't sure which I preferred—this almost-dead half-existence, or the sharp pain I had felt for so much of the previous ten days.

George called at lunchtime with important news about the evacuations from Ternopil.

"Aaron and Dara are coming to Hungary with their kids. And Olya's coming, too, with her little brother."

"Oh." I should have felt joy at the prospect of seeing my brother-in-law and his wife and our former apartment-mate Olya. *What's wrong with me?*

"Aaron and Dara will stay in Debrecen with you guys. We found a place for Olya and her brother here in Budapest. I'm thinking of coming to Debrecen to meet her and go back to Budapest with her. Might make the transition easier for her."

"That's a good idea." To myself, I thought, *Olya is going to be so traumatized when she gets here, like we were when we first got out of Ukraine. She'll probably want to stay near me and the kids. How is she going to feel about having to go to Budapest?*

"And I'll get to see you and the boys." George broke into my thoughts.

"Oh, that'll be nice." It was a white lie. I knew I should feel pleased by the news, but I didn't feel anything.

When George arrived that evening, Andrew and Isaac, our two youngest kids, jumped up and ran to him.

"Daddy!" they exclaimed, throwing themselves at him.

George laughed and smiled as he kneeled to hug them. "Hi, boys!"

I gave him a mechanical hug and a peck on the lips, going through the motions, because I still couldn't sense my feelings. While George greeted his mom and sisters, I went looking for the rest of our boys. When I told them George had arrived, they reluctantly pulled themselves away from their various activities to give their dad a quick hug and a smile before running back to their cousins. I noted the contrast between how excitedly our two youngest sons reacted to seeing George again and how casual the older boys were about it. Andrew and Isaac had seemed happy enough since moving to the mini-hotel, but I realized it wasn't natural for them to be separated from their dad for so long.

"I have something for you." George smiled at me.

"Really?" I managed to feel some interest.

He produced a small, crumpled, purple plastic bag from his backpack. I immediately recognized it. It had been "hidden" for months in his sock drawer in Kyiv. I had discovered it one day when putting away his laundry. Realizing it must be a gift for me, I had replaced it without looking inside.

"Sorry it's not wrapped." He handed it to me.

I reached in and pulled out a beautiful necklace. Faceted purple beads were suspended at regular intervals on three chains of varying lengths that all hung from a single clasp.

"Thank you. It's beautiful."

This man had evacuated from Ukraine with almost nothing but the clothes on his back, but he had still found the presence of mind to pack this token of his love and preserve it through everything that had happened. On a normal day, I would have felt a warm rush of joy and pleasure over his devotion, but that day I merely noted the facts dispassionately.

We took seats in the dining area to talk.

"How are things going with the independent contractors?" I asked, trying desperately to make conversation to mask my lack of interest in anything.

"I don't know." George sighed. "They don't always tell me everything, so I feel like I'm not really part of their team. I've been able to give them good intel, but I feel like I don't always have the full picture. I don't know if I'm really being effective there." He sighed again. "They actually offered to hire me."

"Really?"

"Yeah. Then I'd be an official part of the team and know more, but I don't like the idea of taking money to help people. What do you think?" He fixed his gentle blue eyes on me, waiting for my input.

I was silent for a moment, contemplating. "Honestly, I don't know. That's a hard one. If hiring you means they could get more people out safely, then, sure, I guess it would be a good thing. And you could always use the money to help even more people."

"Yeah, I guess you're right. I'll have to think about it some more."

After feeling emotionally numb all day, as I anticipated Olya's impending arrival, I had strong emotions. However, instead of joy, I felt horrible guilt. She had lived with our family for over two years, and I felt a responsibility to house her, but we didn't have room for both her and her teenage brother.

She arrived too soon. I wasn't ready to face her, but I followed George out to greet her. The group she was traveling with was just stopping for a few minutes to allow Olya and me to see each other before continuing to Budapest.

The door on the side of the van slid open to reveal a tangle of bags and people's limbs, with a pregnant woman, a toddler, and two cats thrown into the mix. One of the cats was a sphinx, a blue-eyed furless creature with the disposition of a demon. He was under Olya's care. He belonged to a married couple who had been part of our team in Kyiv. The wife had chosen to stay in Ukraine with her husband. As displaced people, they didn't know if they could find housing that would allow pets, so they had tearfully entrusted their beloved animal to Olya.

Olya extricated herself from the van. Her wide blue eyes were brimming with tears, and she clasped me in a desperate hug. "I didn't know if I was going to see you again."

I had also wondered the same thing, but I didn't say so. I was so knotted with guilt over not being able to offer her a place to stay that I couldn't think of anything to say. But if Olya was upset about having to go to Budapest, she didn't show it.

"How is Isaac?" she asked after she released me.

"He's sleeping."

"Can I see him?"

I led her inside and took her upstairs. It was quiet; all the little kids were in bed. The older kids were watching a movie in one of the rooms downstairs. We walked to the last room on the left. Isaac and Andrew were asleep on a twin bed just inside the door. The light from the hallway streamed over them. Three-year-old Isaac was the picture of peace and innocence, his thick lashes curling gently against his delicate cheeks. Olya sat on the edge of the bed, leaned over, and kissed him tenderly, her long, blonde hair brushing his face.

Olya had known Isaac almost from birth. His disposition of sunshine and sweetness had always imparted calm and a sense of well-being to the person holding him. Olya was one of many guests to our home who would practically get in line for some "Isaac therapy." Later, when she joined our household a few months before Isaac's second birthday, she had worked hard to become one of his favorite people.

I could only imagine the thoughts and feelings going through her now. Her home was far behind. The future was dark and uncertain. She had reached her adopted family, but we weren't inviting her to stay. How could we let her go?

We didn't linger in the room. Olya's ride was waiting, and they still had two and a half hours to reach Budapest. As we said goodbye and hugged, I detached myself from the situation to survive the guilt. Olya got back into the van, and they drove away into the darkness with George following close behind.

The next morning, March 7, I woke up shortly before sunrise. My capacity to feel emotion was back, and I was overwhelmed with anxiety. My first thought as I lay in bed was of our dog, Jack. Now that the safe house in Kaharlyk had been compromised, I feared for his safety.

I didn't want to be thinking about this right now. I shouldn't even be awake. I quietly rolled onto my side and curled into the fetal position. When we first evacuated, I had been unable to sleep for more than three hours at a time. That level of insomnia had passed, but I still had not slept for more than a five-hour stretch. I desperately wanted to go back to sleep now, but it was impossible.

I knew the family keeping Jack had him outside in a doghouse. Images of cruel Russian soldiers roaming the streets and using him for target practice kept replaying in my mind. If they were gunning down civilians, what hope did a dog have of escaping their malice? My heart thudded in my chest, my throat constricted, and my breath came in quick pants.

I tried to relax and breathe through the strangling anxiety, and an idea took shape. If the independent contractors were still using the church in Kaharlyk as a safe house, they might be planning an evacuation from there. Could they get Jack?

I grabbed my phone and texted George. Within two hours, it was settled.

The independent contractors were organizing a convoy of tour buses to bring out all their clients. Some were at the safe house in Kaharlyk, and the man who would be in charge of the convoy said he would take responsibility for Jack. A retired US Marine, he seemed more than qualified to get our dog.

George contacted me later that day to say he was accepting the job offer from the independent contractors. He had discussed it with other pastors, and they agreed it made sense, since the contractors had the experience and money to make a large-scale evacuation happen. George could help them get more people to safety by filling in the gaps in their knowledge base and skill set.

In addition to a salary, they offered to put George up in a hotel. Ever since we parted, he had been sleeping on the floor of a crowded apartment with others who had come to Budapest as a result of the violence in Ukraine.

The mission was urgent and all-consuming. George quickly got pulled into a rhythm of working as many hours as needed and being on call twenty-four hours a day. He brought on five more people to help—some in Hungary, some in Ukraine—and split his salary among those who needed it. Once the large-scale evacuation was underway, the contractors gave George and his team an entire tour bus to fill with people, free of charge, and we were able to use the vacant seats in the rest of the buses for non-paying passengers.

That evening, Melanie joined me as I was tidying up the kitchen at the mini-hotel. She and George's brother Aaron had gone grocery shopping for everyone that day. She went over to the refrigerator and reached up to retrieve something from the top. Turning around, she offered me a small bouquet of tulips wrapped in clear cellophane. The blossoms were purple, my favorite color.

"Thank you!" I said, taking them.

"Aaron picked them out for you."

I was touched but a little puzzled. It seemed so random. But nothing about our life since the onset of the war had been predictable. At least this unexpected event was a welcome one.

I loved receiving tulips in the spring. In fact, George gave me a bouquet of tulips every March 8, in celebration of International Women's Day.

I suddenly realized why Aaron had gotten flowers for me. Tomorrow was International Women's Day, and George and I would not be together.

My posture wilted. I stared at the floor.

When I learned about this old Soviet holiday after moving to Ukraine, I was amazed that there was a day to celebrate all women. In the US we had Mother's Day and Valentine's Day, but there was nothing for single, childless women. I thought it was wonderful to designate a day to honor all the women in your life. There was a move in Ukraine to boycott the holiday because of the way Soviet culture had used it to justify subjugating women for the other 364 days of the year, but despite the controversy, I still loved the celebration.

Every year, George got flowers for all the important women around him. I remembered my first Women's Day, just over two months after we married. George went out early in the morning to buy tulips for me, his mom, his sisters, and his two young nieces. He made the day for those two little girls, and I was impressed by how thoughtful and caring my husband was.

We always celebrated with a special outing for just the two of us. Even after we had kids, George made it happen, though it was the hardest day of the year to find child care. Typically, all our regular babysitters would be unavailable. One year, he asked a single male friend to watch our kids. He had the day off because of the holiday, and since he was single, he wasn't taking a significant other out.

This year, there would be no celebrations. George and I were in different cities, and anyway, who felt like celebrating? I looked at the delicate blossoms, the only festivities this Women's Day was likely to offer, and my heart filled with gratitude for my brother-in-law's thoughtful gesture.

The surge of positive emotions stirred up the ever-present pain right below the surface. I blinked back tears as I searched the cupboards for a large glass to hold my tulips.

21

Women's Day Getaway

March 8, 2022: Day 13 of War
Debrecen, Hungary

The next morning, George called. "Happy Women's Day! Would you like to come to Budapest to visit me?"

"What?"

"I worked it out with Renée to watch the kids so you can come! There are trains to Budapest from Debrecen all the time."

"Wow. . . um . . . yeah, that would be great." I tried to sound excited to mask my anxiety. How was I going to find my way to the train station? I hadn't left the grounds of the mini-hotel since arriving. And how was I supposed to buy a ticket in a country where I didn't speak the language?

In the end, the Hungarian pastor who invited us to Debrecen booked my ticket online and drove me to the station.

The train ride was a treat. My compartment was half empty, and I spent the three hours reading and writing, two of my favorite activities. When I arrived in Budapest, George was there to meet me, and we hugged and kissed right on the platform.

We dropped off my things at his hotel before heading out for dinner. There were many restaurants within walking distance, and we chose one we had discovered on a visit to Budapest in happier days.

Our waitress spoke English. "Where are you from?" she asked.

George and I looked at each other. How could we explain? Saying we were Americans wouldn't do our situation justice. It felt like our very identities had been altered by the experience of being displaced. I wanted to communicate some idea of all we had been through, what we had lost, and how much we were hurting. But saying we were from Ukraine might be confusing, since we were obviously native English speakers.

"We're from Ukraine," George finally said. "We're Americans, but we were living in Kyiv when the war started, and we evacuated here to Hungary."

"Oh," she said, drawing the word out. "I'm sorry for what's happening." She paused, then added, "I'm Polish-Russian, and Putin's a madman!"

George and I love date nights, but eating out is stressful. George has celiac disease, and I am intolerant to a long list of ingredients. It's always a gamble if we will find anything to eat that won't make us feel unwell. This night, the waitress patiently helped us select our meals, and we both enjoyed our food.

We spent the evening catching up on our separate lives since the kids and I had relocated to Debrecen. George took several calls and answered a number of text messages, all related to the evacuations. Under normal circumstances, I would have been upset by the constant interruptions, but these weren't normal circumstances.

He put the phone down after finishing another text and turned back to me.

"The guys at the command center think things are going to get really bad. They all say Kyiv is going to fall within seventy-two hours."

"No!"

"I hope they're wrong, but they seem to know what they're talking about. They have some sort of intel. We've got a short window to get everyone out. There are so many needs, but we decided the priority is to get people out and aid in. We came up with a motto: People—west; aid—east."

"Who's 'we'?"

"Phil and the other pastors working with me."

Our conversation continued in this vein. It was hard to talk about anything but the war and the effort to save people from it. These world events had swallowed up our lives.

After the meal was over, we enjoyed a pleasant stroll back to the hotel, hand in hand, and then we agreed to call it a night. Neither of us had been sleeping well, and we were both exhausted. But we were in good spirits. Despite a war, being displaced, and living hours apart, we had managed to celebrate Women's Day together. We said good night and snuggled up to each other, grateful to be together.

The next day, March 9, George didn't have to be at work at the command tent until 10 am, and we enjoyed a leisurely morning together in bed. As he left, we agreed to meet up for a late lunch. When I got to the command tent, George was deep in the middle of something. I smiled at him and tried to minimize the interruption my arrival had caused.

While I waited for George to finish, I looked around at the eclectic decor and wondered where they had found the life-size cardboard standup of Winston Churchill and if anyone actually used the pool table. It was covered with maps.

When he had a free moment, George introduced me to the retired US Marine who would be responsible for evacuating our dog. He had a neatly trimmed black beard and mustache and black hair. He gave me a firm handshake, looking me straight in the eye.

"Thank you so much for agreeing to get Jack for us," I said. "The kids will be so happy."

"Yes, ma'am!" He stood at attention, chest out, shoulders back, fists clenched by his sides. "I will bring your dog home!"

He was treating this favor like a serious mission. I was reassured Jack would be in capable hands.

I listened as the group discussed the logistics for the evacuation convoy. They had hired eight tour buses from Kosovo, and they were on the final countdown for sending them into Ukraine. They were selecting rendezvous points in each city along the route. A Ukrainian lady, one of the extra people George had recruited, was communicating these locations to each of the waiting clients.

At the moment, they were trying to choose a safe rendezvous spot on the southern edge of Kyiv, near the highway out of the city. It needed to have a parking lot large enough for a tour bus. George knew the perfect spot. It was a shopping center just inside the city limits, located right on the main highway out of Kyiv. They marked it down as the rendezvous point for Kyiv and moved on to the next order of business.

As I watched and listened, I was impressed by the way George confidently and effortlessly provided answers to the needs the contractors had. They had a skill set and level of experience that put them in a separate category from most people, but they listened with attention and respect anytime George spoke.

Over the next few hours, I continued to observe. A few times I hesitantly offered input of my own. I was surprised when everyone listened closely and seriously considered my ideas. Soft-spoken and unassertive, I wasn't used to this. People often ignored me in group contexts, simply because they couldn't hear me. Rather than force my way into the spotlight, I would give up and keep my thoughts to myself.

George maintained that people needed to hear what I had to say. Over the years, he developed an almost psychic sense about when I had something to share, and he'd call a halt to the conversation to give me the floor. He didn't need to do that on this day. If I simply cleared my throat, this group of men, which included battle-hardened, intimidating warriors, immediately stopped what they were doing to pay attention.

Around 3:30 pm, someone asked if I wanted a ride back to the hotel.

"Well, George and I were supposed to get lunch together, but . . . maybe he's not going to have lunch today?" I wasn't sure what to say.

My words had an immediate effect. George's boss informed him they didn't need him right then, and he should take me out to eat. Caleb, one of the pastors on George's team, said he and George just needed to shoot a quick video. I got to watch as they produced the second in a series updating churches in the United States.

They asked people to pray for the convoy of buses that was going to try to cross the border into Ukraine later that night. They also explained that there was lots of aid available in Western Ukraine, but there were people starving in Eastern Ukraine, hiding in freezing basements without water, food, or electricity. There was an urgent need to transport the aid farther east. George already had a network of brave men ready to go—they just needed wheels.

He made an appeal for funds to buy vehicles to establish an aid pipeline.

The previous video had presented the need for a van so a church in Eastern Ukraine could evacuate people. In less than twenty-four hours, we had raised the necessary funds. The church bought a van that they used to get people out of the city of Mariupol, where tens of thousands of civilians would eventually die in the Russian bombardment, siege, and occupation.

As soon as George finished the video, everyone chased us away and promised not to contact George unless it was absolutely necessary. Someone loaned us a car, and we drove to a nearby Mexican place that had gluten-free options. The food was amazing, and we agreed we'd found a favorite restaurant.

The independent contractors did end up needing George. He spent half the meal on his phone, but I didn't mind. It was a great opportunity to see his work and, in a small way, participate.

22

Can We At Least Have James's Birthday Party Tonight?

March 10, 2022: Day 15 of War
Debrecen, Hungary

As I rode the train back to Debrecen after my visit to George in Budapest, George's mom initiated a three-way call with him and me. Awkwardly, Pam told us that our children and I needed to move out of the mini-hotel the next day and relocate to Budapest to rejoin George. Her motivation was two-fold: to provide for my two youngest children, who missed their dad, and to care for one of her other displaced daughters-in-law, who seemed to need more quiet and privacy than the mini-hotel could offer with all of us living there.

Some of the extended family had already moved out. Everyone else was trying to plan their next steps. I was the exception, content to live one day at a time, thankful for each morning and evening we got to spend together. While I knew it couldn't last indefinitely, I had no desire to end the arrangement. I assumed my kids and I would stay until the last of the extended family left the mini-hotel, and then we would move to George, if he hadn't rejoined us yet. I should have announced my plans. It could have spared much hurt and misunderstanding.

George's mom and sisters, who had come to Hungary to help the displaced families, had been handling all the organizational details for our large group. It was a huge job, and I had been happy to let them take over. Reeling with shock and pain, I didn't feel like recruiting bus drivers or reserving hotels. It was wonderful not to have to think about any details. I just showed up with my kids when and where I was told, and almost magically, we had transportation, places to stay, and food. I will always be thankful for this loving care that cushioned us from many of the difficulties of the refugee experience.

I suppose we all got so used to the system that it seemed natural to extend this careful planning to include scheduling when everyone would leave the mini-hotel. Since one family needed more space, while my family needed to be reunited with George, the logical solution was for my kids and me to move to Budapest as soon as possible. My Japanese reticence may even have invited that conclusion. On the surface, I looked unbreakable and steady, someone who could handle another sudden relocation. In truth, I was more fragile than I allowed anyone to see.

When Pam called, I had left my train compartment to take the call in the open area at the end of the train car, so I was standing when I heard the news that we needed to leave the extended family the next day. I immediately felt lightheaded. Overwhelmed with grief, I had to crouch to regain my balance. I felt like my children and I were being exiled from the family haven. It seemed unfair and too abrupt. It was true that my two youngest kids missed George, but I didn't agree that the situation was as serious as Pam thought. To me, the greater harm lay in tearing the four older boys away from their cousins. They would be devastated. But I didn't voice any of this. It felt selfish to insist on my preference when it was in my power to help others in the extended family. But I felt left out. Did no one see the needs of *my* family?

I said little during the phone conversation, not trusting myself to be able to speak without breaking down crying. Shortly before we hung up, I managed to string a few words together in a perfectly even voice. "Can we at least have James's birthday party tonight?"

Pam happily agreed, and I spent the rest of the train ride trying to pull myself together enough to organize a party four days ahead of schedule. Since I'd been in Budapest for two days, I hadn't started shopping yet. Now I would only have a few hours to create a party for thirty-three people from scratch, and I had no idea where to find everything I needed.

As soon as my train arrived in Debrecen, I was on a mission. As I power-walked through the main lobby of the train station, a tantalizing aroma grabbed my attention. Fresh pastry and cinnamon. Somewhere nearby, someone was baking chimney cakes. I had found the birthday cake.

I followed my nose to a little bakery stand inside the train station. In barely comprehensible Hungarian, I asked for twelve chimney cakes. The lady who took my order seemed astonished at the volume, but she nodded that they could do it. She tapped her wristwatch and showed me ten fingers twice. It made me feel like a child, but I appreciated her effort to find a way to communicate with me. I understood it would take twenty minutes to fill my order. I found a seat nearby to read while I waited.

I kept rereading the same paragraph without any idea of what it said. In frustration, I finally gave up. My thoughts were tumbling inside my head, a mix of practical concerns about the party and worry about how my kids would take the news about moving out.

The one thing I couldn't think about was the rejection I felt. When I tried to come to terms with being asked to leave the family refuge, my thoughts disintegrated. My pain, like the whirling blades of a branch shredder, splintered everything that came near, even my attempts to understand why this was happening.

As a child, I experienced repeated rejection. My mother died of cancer when I was only five, and for years afterwards, most of my school classmates shunned me. When I was in fourth grade, I remember once standing in line to go into class after recess, and I heard a girl behind me say, "Her mom died." I don't think she meant for me to overhear, because when I glanced over my shoulder, she was cupping her hand around her mouth as if to keep the sound from traveling. She was pointing at me. I faced forward again without saying anything. I could feel the stares of the other kids. I knew I was marked, an outcast.

Things improved after my dad remarried when I was eleven, but by then I had developed a social unease that I carried into adulthood, a deep conviction that nobody wanted me around. If they didn't reject me outright, I told myself it was because they were just being polite. If they got together without me, it confirmed my suspicion that I was not welcome. I suffered in silence, but I ached to belong somewhere.

When I married George, I found a deep sense of belonging with his large family. Finally, I had a group of peers who I knew accepted me unconditionally. For years I'd basked in the security of their love, but now it felt like they were shoving me out into the cold and slamming the door in my face. The logical part of my mind said they weren't actually rejecting me, but it couldn't communicate with the emotional part. I was profoundly hurt.

Finally, I saw the chimney-cake lady signaling to me. I jumped up and rushed to the window to take the cakes.

As I was walking out of the station, a man fell in beside me and started making conversation in English. He made me mildly uneasy, but I answered his questions, because I didn't want to be rude. As soon as he heard I was from Ukraine, he wanted to know where I was staying and if he could help me. Those final two questions made my unease flare into full-blown alarm, and I stopped speaking to him. For decades, sex traffickers had targeted Ukrainian women who were seeking a better life in the West. I knew that in the midst of the refugee crisis, they had to be out in force, plying the borders of Ukraine looking for vulnerable females traveling by themselves.

I ignored the man and ordered a taxi with the Bolt app, which is like the Uber of Europe. While I waited, the man finally gave up and left. I felt like I'd had a narrow escape. If I'd just arrived from Ukraine, alone and without money or anyone to call, would I have been taken in? I shuddered.

The taxi driver already had my destination from the app, so I didn't need to try to speak Hungarian. My emotions, frazzled from the encounter with the man at the train station, settled as we rode in silence. Then the driver stopped, said something incomprehensible, and motioned out the window as if to ask if this was the right place.

I didn't recognize anything. I shook my head and said, "*Nem*," one of the few Hungarian words I had managed to master. My heart started to race. How was I going to get back to the hotel if I couldn't communicate? I would have known what to say in Ukrainian, but I was so helpless here. I scrambled mentally for a solution. I was just about to get out of the car when the driver seemed to figure out where he needed to go. Immensely relieved, I sat back while he drove the remaining distance.

I entered the mini-hotel feeling like the family outcast. As a result, I was nervous about interacting with everyone, but as soon as I walked in, the other ladies rallied around me to help with the party. They put themselves fully at my disposal to ensure it was a success. I concluded that the tension was all in my own mind.

While we were planning, my eldest son, Samuel, joined the conversation. As soon as he heard we were going to throw James a birthday party, he said, "Can we celebrate my birthday too?"

"Samuel!" I said, assuming his request was a nonsensical prank to get attention. His fifteenth birthday had been almost two months earlier.

"But I never got to celebrate," he protested. "Remember? I was going to have a party with my friends, but then you sent me to Ternopil, and then the war happened."

I felt like I'd had the wind knocked out of me. The war had stolen from my son his much-anticipated party with friends. I hadn't even remembered. I started to cry. "Of course we can celebrate your birthday too!" I said.

The party began at 9 pm, to give George time to drive from Budapest after work. It was a simple affair, but sharing it with so many loved ones made the time extra special. Each family gave both of the birthday boys a gift. Everyone talked and laughed late into the night.

I decided not to tell my kids about leaving the next day. It would have ruined the evening. As a result, the family had fun. I may have been the one exception, because I was heartsick over having to move out, but I did love seeing my children's joy. I had been right to call for this party, despite the challenges of organizing it so quickly.

The kids stayed up well past their bedtimes. I appreciated having George's help getting them settled for the night. Since the call with Pam on the train that morning, we hadn't had time to talk privately about the coming move, but George wasn't acting upset. I decided not to bring it up. My emotions were so raw that I wasn't sure I could discuss the situation without whining or badmouthing someone. It was easier just to keep my feelings to myself. George finally headed back to Budapest around 1 am. When I finally collapsed in bed, I was exhausted, heartsick, and dreading the next day.

23

My Epiphany

March 11, 2022: Day 16 of War
Debrecen, Hungary

I woke at 6:30 am. Like every morning since the full-scale war started, the first thing I did was check the news from Ukraine. It wasn't good. Russian missiles had hit Lutsk and Lviv overnight, two cities in Western Ukraine that should have been safe from the violence happening elsewhere in the country.

As I lay in bed contemplating how long Russia's reach had become, I suddenly heard an air-raid siren, followed by distant explosions. I couldn't believe my ears. It felt like a repeat of my incredulity on the first day of the war when I heard the first siren in Ternopil—except this time, it seemed even less likely that Russia would be attacking.

Putin wouldn't dare launch missiles at Hungary, would he? It wasn't possible I was hearing what I thought I was hearing. I quietly slipped out of bed, careful not to rouse Andrew and Isaac, who were sharing the room with me, and stepped into the bathroom. Silently shutting the door, I cracked open the window.

The sound was unmistakable: a loud wail that rose and fell, punctuated by percussive roars. I stood riveted to the spot, unwilling—or unable—to accept the evidence of my own ears. I kept trying to convince myself it was all in my head, yet I couldn't deny I was hearing actual sounds.

Was I misinterpreting normal noises that had mundane explanations? Or was I hearing things that weren't there? I had no idea, and I continued to stand by the bathroom window, taking no action, hoping the sounds would just go away.

Eventually they stopped, and I went back to bed. I was exhausted, but for the next two hours I lay awake, on the verge of a panic attack. My throat was constricted, my chest tight, and my heart racing. I couldn't draw a full breath, but I forced myself to breathe as calmly as possible and fought to maintain control.

When I saw the rest of the family later that morning, no one said anything about hearing unusual sounds. I concluded my traumatized mind had played a cruel trick on me. Maybe a security alarm had been going off at the same time that noises from a construction site had been mimicking explosions. Or—maybe the sounds I had seemed to hear so clearly had all been in my mind. Was trauma causing me to lose my grip on reality?

We had a special visitor late that morning. My childhood church in California had sent John, one of the associate pastors, to offer us moral support and personally deliver special gifts to help our displaced families through the difficult time.

Everyone had asked for different things. I had requested some of our favorite board games and a large rolling suitcase to help us with the next move I had known was coming sooner or later. In addition, one of George's sisters had sent an essential oil diffuser to go with the prized oils I had carried out of Ukraine. My sister had sent some clothes for me. One item—a plum-colored dress with three-quarter sleeves—became my new favorite outfit. Functional yet elegant, it was made of a delightfully soft, stretchy fabric, like a reassuring hug. I didn't have many clothes. Throughout the rest of that spring, I practically lived in that dress.

Pastor John reassured us that the church would take care of all our expenses. I was overwhelmed with gratitude. I had been worried about paying for our portion of the mini-hotel, and before we even checked out, the bill was covered.

After Pastor John left, I knew I had to work quickly. The train trip to Budapest was three hours long, which meant we had less than three hours to leave the hotel if we wanted to make it to Budapest before bedtime. I still had to pack, buy train tickets, and find a place for us to sleep.

Our possessions seemed to have doubled during our week in Debrecen. In addition to the gifts from my church and sister, there were all the birthday presents from the night before. As I surveyed everything spread out on the beds in my room, the ever-present tightness in my chest increased, and my throat constricted. I tried to take a deep, calming breath, but my strangled lungs only allowed a shallow panting rhythm.

I slid to the floor and sat cross-legged, slumped forward, my elbows on my knees and my hands supporting my face. I had no idea how to accomplish everything. I didn't even know where to start.

As I sat there paralyzed, Pam came into the room.

"How are you doing, honey?" she asked.

I looked up at her. "I'm totally overwhelmed," I said, matter-of-factly. "I don't know how I'm going to get us ready to go in time, and I still have to find a place for us to stay." Then I sighed.

"Would it help if I got someone to find a place for you?" She sat down on the edge of a bed.

"Yeah, I guess so." I sighed again. I stood up and moved to sit next to her, glad for her company. "You know, I heard air-raid sirens this morning. And explosions. It sounded so real."

"What?"

"Right after I woke up, early this morning. I heard them. Of course, it wasn't real. But I could have sworn I heard it. Maybe it was all in my mind. I don't know."

"Oh, Sharon," Pam said, concern and sympathy etched on her face. "I'm so sorry." She wrapped her arms around me. I leaned into her, deeply comforted. It was a relief to tell someone about that experience.

She told me how much she appreciated my willingness to move out, because she felt it was really important for my sister-in-law. I nodded, willing my face to be a mask of tranquility. If it was that important, I was prepared to do whatever it took to make the move happen within the next few hours.

But I still hadn't told my kids.

I went downstairs to find them and enlist their help in packing their things.

"Hey, boys," I said, after I gathered them in the dining area. "We're going to move to Budapest today."

"What?" several voices cried in unison.

"Why do we have to leave today?" Kiyoshi was shouting.

"Well . . ." I spoke slowly, choosing my words carefully. I was unwilling to say something I didn't believe to be true, but I also did not want to blame anyone for the situation. "Daddy's in Budapest. Don't you kids miss him?"

"No!" the four older boys answered right away. They talked on top of each other in a rush to explain.

"We'd rather be with our cousins!"

"Yeah, we hardly ever get to see them!"

"Why do we have to leave?"

Andrew and Isaac, the two youngest boys, were silent.

"Well . . . " I opened my mouth and shut it again. They weren't making this easy. I tried again. "Your uncle's been in Ukraine, and his family hasn't seen him for a little while. They need some time alone."

"Then why don't they just move out?" Kiyoshi said.

I sighed. "I'm sorry. I don't want to go either, but we have to. Please go pack your stuff."

At that, my fifteen-year-old son Samuel's face twisted into a grotesque contortion, and huge tears overflowed his gray eyes, dripped down his cheeks, and splashed on the floor. I was shocked.

"Why, Mommy?" His voice was high-pitched and desperate. "We've been watching the Avengers movies, and we were going to watch the last one together tonight!"

I felt his acute pain and disappointment, made worse by the sudden change of plans and the unfairness of the forced separation from his cousins. His tears were about much more than a missed movie. The movie was just the final link in a chain of losses stretching back to leaving Kyiv without a chance to say goodbye to his friends.

At that moment, I had an epiphany. I had been wrong to agree to move so soon. No matter how inconvenient it might be for the rest of the family, my responsibility in this situation was to safeguard the emotional health of my own children. This painful situation served to awaken the hibernating mama bear within me, and God knew my children were going to need her during the coming months.

I made eye contact with Samuel. "Okay, we'll stay one more night so you can watch your movie. Will that be good?" I looked at the rest of the boys. They all nodded.

I found Pam. "I'm not going to do this to my kids," I told her, with uncharacteristic abruptness. "We're not leaving today. We'll go tomorrow." I should have shared how much I personally wanted to stay, how deeply it hurt me to leave before the rest of the extended family, but advocating for my children was a major victory. Learning to stand up for myself would have to wait for another day.

The war didn't just drop physical bombs on the territory of Ukraine; the reverberations decimated families and ways of life for people all over the country. Even after we crossed the border, this dynamic continued to affect us. Figuring out how to navigate the unthinkable was like stumbling through clouds of dust from the collapse of a city. We couldn't see clearly, all landmarks were obscured, and when we called out to loved ones to find them in the chaos, the voices that answered were weak and indistinct. We all did the best we could amid horrific stress and uncertainty, but sometimes we made decisions we later regretted. Pam has since told me that if she could do it over again, she would do some things differently. So would I. But though the experience was painful, it was necessary to form me into a mother ready to fight for her children.

After my announcement, everyone quickly adjusted to my new timeframe and helped me in every way they could. Without the pressure of having to catch a train in a few hours, I found fresh purpose and determination. I worked quickly and soon finished packing.

The boys made the most of their time, knowing it was their last day. In the evening, Samuel and the rest of the older cousins watched the final Avengers movie. The extra time made it possible for George to help with the move. That night after work, he borrowed a car and made the five-hour round-trip to Debrecen to take most of our things to Budapest. The next day, the kids and I would only need to manage our backpacks and musical instruments.

I went to bed late again but felt more at peace than on the previous night. Even though it would be painful to leave the extended family, maybe Pam was right. Like me, she was just trying to protect the emotional health of all her children, including children-in-law and grandchildren. For her, part of that meant reuniting the boys and me with George—and I had to admit it sounded wonderful to have our immediate family back together. In less than twenty-four hours, that would be our new reality.

24

The Airbnb

March 12, 2022: Day 17 of War
Debrecen & Budapest, Hungary

The next morning, the kids and I said goodbye to everyone, and Melanie drove us to the train station. Because we had stayed an extra night, the boys offered no complaints about the move.

I hugged Melanie goodbye, tears forming in my eyes. Despite the additional day, it still pained me to leave the rest of the family. "Thank you for everything," I said. "I don't know what we would have done without you."

"Oh, of course!" Melanie dismissed my thanks with a wave of her hand. She looked at me intently. "Are you okay?"

No, I wasn't. I felt like a pariah. But even if I had wanted to explain, there was no time. We needed to board our train.

"I'll be fine," I said. It wasn't a lie. It was a proclamation. In a few days or weeks, I would be able to put this whole episode behind me and move on. I would be fine. I forced the corners of my lips into a tight smile.

Our train was already waiting on the tracks. It was scheduled to leave soon, so rather than rushing down the platform to our car, I decided to board the nearest car. We would make our way through the train to our reserved seats after we were safely aboard.

I helped the little kids get on, and the older ones followed. We were in the enclosed space at one end of the car. A sliding glass door separated us from the seating area. I tried to open it. It wouldn't budge.

I realized we'd better get off the train and sprint to our car, but just then, the exit door shut automatically. The train wasn't moving yet, but I couldn't get the exit to open. I made eye contact with Melanie through the window in the exit door and shrugged my shoulders at the inconvenience. She looked panicked and dashed out of sight.

"What's wrong with the door, Mommy?" James asked. The long lashes framing his hazel eyes were spread wide in alarm as he looked up at me.

"I don't know. It won't open."

"What are we going to do?" Kiyoshi asked calmly.

"Well, we can't really do anything right now." I looked through the sliding glass door at the seats beyond and shrugged. "At least we're on the train."

"You mean we're just gonna have to stand here for *three hours*?" Peter huffed dramatically and crossed his arms.

"I hope not," I said. "When the conductor comes through to check tickets, he'll have to open the door. We just have to wait."

I positioned Andrew and Isaac close to me so I could help my two smallest children balance once the train started to move.

Samuel's eyebrows shot up: my eldest son had an idea. "C'mon, guys, let's play *I Spy*! I spy with my little eye . . . something blue!"

His brothers joined in the game.

As the train lurched into motion, my phone chimed. It was a text message from Melanie: **The conductor says he will work it out. You're so brave, Sharon.**

I puzzled over the last sentence. *What does she mean, I'm brave? I'm just taking a train with my kids. It's not a big deal.*

The seven of us stood crowded together in the small space, making the best of the situation, until eventually the conductor came. I showed him our tickets, and he made sure we were able to reach our seats several cars down.

When we arrived in Budapest, our former apartment mate Olya was supposed to meet us at the train station with an old friend of ours, a Hungarian man named Imre. He had been making daily trips to the border in his van to pick up Ukrainians and take them to Budapest, where churches were helping them find places to stay. Since Imre spoke no Ukrainian or Russian, Olya had been going along to translate.

They happened to be in Budapest when we arrived and agreed to pick us up and take us to the Airbnb that George's brother Aaron and his wife had found for us. They'd shown me photos of a cozy apartment with enough beds to sleep eight, and I'd approved it to be reserved through the end of the month. When the kids and I got off the train, we didn't see Olya or Imre anywhere. There were multiple train tracks and a constant flow of people in both directions. I gathered the children close and stood paralyzed, watching the foot traffic, trying to decide which direction to go. Without knowing how to speak Hungarian, I felt like I couldn't even ask for directions.

I finally got out my phone and called Olya. She apologized for being late and explained there hadn't been anywhere to park near the station. Eventually we found her, and she led us about a block down the street to where Imre's seven-seat van was parked under an overpass. Including Imre and Olya, there were nine of us, plus more bags than people. The limited cargo space was already crowded with other items. Somehow, we managed to cram the kids and me and all our backpacks and musical instruments into the five back seats. I gave Imre the address, and we took off.

Parking in downtown Budapest is tricky, and when we reached our destination, Imre was dismayed to find there was absolutely no place to stop, let alone park. I could tell he wanted to make sure we met up with the landlord and help us get our things into the apartment, but he had to let us off about a block away.

I had been communicating with the landlord and was confident we could find him. The kids and I extricated ourselves and our things from the van, and I thanked Imre and Olya.

"Are you really sure you're going to be okay?" Imre asked for about the third time, his heavy, dark eyebrows furrowed in concern. Olya repeated the same question in Ukrainian, her wide blue eyes uneasy. She was clearly unwilling to leave us in this situation.

"We'll be fine," I reassured them both, forcing my lips into a smile. "He said he's waiting by that grocery store." I pointed.

"Okay, if you're sure . . ." Irme sounded doubtful.

"I am. Thank you so much for getting us." I smiled again as I closed the van door.

Olya kept looking back over her shoulder at us as they pulled out into traffic. I felt my heart sink as they drove away. Despite my brave words, I didn't want to do this by myself, but I didn't have a choice.

The kids and I all walked at the speed of three-year-old Isaac, the slowest member of the family. I called the landlord to let him know we were almost there. He stayed on the line. As we got closer, I spotted a man in front of the grocery store talking on a cell phone. I waved at him, and he came to meet us.

He was friendly and spoke decent English. He led us to an entrance right beside the grocery store and opened it. We entered a high-ceilinged corridor that led to a flight of stone stairs. They were polished to a sheen with use and slightly worn down in the middle of each step from the passage of decades of feet.

The landlord headed straight for these stairs, explaining that the elevator was broken. The steps climbed along the four sides of a large stairwell that extended all the way to the top floor of the building. Standing in the middle of this open space on the ground level, I tilted my head back and looked straight up. The stairs ascended to a dizzying height. I hoped we didn't have to go too high.

The flights were long, in keeping with the high ceiling we had seen in the entryway. I held little Isaac's hand, and we slowly climbed to the second floor. I hoped we'd stop, but our guide continued going. Thankfully, he stopped on the third floor and led us down an open balcony to the last apartment.

As soon as I stepped inside, I wanted to turn around and leave. The place felt dismal, nothing like the cozy pictures online. There was a large room, a tiny room, a shower room, and two toilets in adjacent closets. I was happy to have two toilets, but that was the only positive I could see. The large room had a sink, a fridge, a stove, a table and chairs, a queen bed, two twin beds, and a floor lamp that was leaning at an odd angle. I later found out that it didn't work. The tiny room had two small cots along one wall and a loft with a double mattress on the floor.

There was nothing inviting or relaxing in the whole apartment. Not a single couch or armchair. All the furniture was old and mismatched, as if it had been acquired at a flea market, and I soon discovered that the sheets and towels were worn and mismatched as well. Oddly, there was a second refrigerator in the entryway, but no washing machine anywhere.

As the landlord showed us around, seemingly proud of his apartment, I smiled and nodded. He offered to let us use the washing machine in his apartment. I thanked him and saw him out.

"This place is awful," Kiyoshi said, as soon as I closed the door.

"At least it has two toilets," I said.

"Yeah, but it's so depressing."

I couldn't think of an appropriate response that wouldn't be an outright lie. The apartment definitely had me depressed. It was sapping my desire to do anything. It felt like we'd landed in a ghetto. What did that make us? Second-class citizens? Rather than responding, I sighed and forced myself to do the next thing. I moved our stuff into the rooms. I'd feel better once George joined us. I just had to hold on until he got off work.

I heard my cellphone chime with a new message alert. It was a cryptic text from George: **It looks like I'm going to Krakow with Caleb and Paul to meet up with the key guys there. Caleb and I think I should go as the contact guy. You okay with that?**

My heart sank. My spirit wilted. And I had so many questions. When would this trip to Poland happen? How long would George be gone? What "key guys" would he be meeting?

I texted George back, but by the time I finally got answers to my questions, he had already committed to going. Things were happening so fast during those early days of the war. Everyone was scrambling to respond to the ever-changing needs of the moment, and George ended up being at the forefront of multiple projects.

He was leaving for Krakow in a few hours, as soon as he got done with work and brought our bags to us. He would be gone until sometime the next day. Samaritan's Purse, an international aid organization, had called the meeting and invited people on the forefront of helping in the midst of the crisis.

If I told George that the kids and I needed him, he would back out of the trip. But I knew we didn't need him enough to justify keeping him from this meeting. I could manage without him for a day or two, and the kids would be okay, as long as I was okay. George had a rare gift for drawing people together, and he could form valuable connections at this meeting that would make a huge difference in our ability to help and save lives. But it was hard to imagine worse timing.

In a single day, I had been deprived of the support and company of the extended family. If that hadn't been bad enough, now I was marooned with six kids in the worst apartment I'd ever seen in a big, unfamiliar city where I didn't speak the language. Why did George have to leave us at a time like this?

But having a pity party wasn't going to solve anything. I squared my shoulders and resolved to make the best of the situation. Creating a comfortable space in this apartment was beyond me, but at least I could provide a delicious meal.

"I'm going downstairs to the grocery store. Don't fight while I'm gone, and keep the door locked, okay?"

"Okay," several of the boys said in unison.

I returned within thirty minutes with enough food for the next few meals and a special treasure—gourmet frozen-pasta meals that only required the addition of a bit of water and a few minutes of cooking.

As soon as I opened the apartment door, James had news for me.

"One of the chairs broke!"

"What? How did that happen?"

"I was sitting on it, and Samuel pushed me, and it just broke."

"It just broke? Why did Samuel push you? Are you okay?"

"Yeah, I'm fine."

"Show me the chair."

"Kiyoshi put it back together. It's in the little room, so no one will use it."

It was a simple wooden chair with an upholstered seat. I examined it carefully. None of the wood was splintered. The pieces must have just come apart. I was relieved we hadn't caused irreparable damage.

Soon I had a late lunch ready, and we were sitting down to a hot meal. The remaining chairs were a little wobbly, but no one seemed to mind.

Before we began, we all bowed our heads, and I offered a simple prayer.

"Dear Father, thank you for this yummy meal. Thank you for taking care of us and providing for all our needs. Thank you that we have a place to sleep tonight. Please bless Daddy and give him a safe trip. In Jesus' name, amen."

"Amen," the kids echoed.

The food must have been delicious, because the kids ate quickly, asking for more until it was all gone. I ate a bowl of oatmeal, my backup plan whenever I couldn't find anything else.

"Let's get everything cleaned up, and then we can watch a movie!" I said.

"Yay!" came a chorus of voices.

"What are we going to watch?" Peter asked, bouncing in excitement.

"I don't know—I'll have to look."

The four older kids all helped with the kitchen chores. There was no dishwasher, so I said I'd do the dishes. I was surprised to see that the sponge had obviously already been used, and the bottle of dish soap was mostly empty and coated with grime. But the worst part was the drying rack, if one could call it that. It was simply a plastic tray covered with an absorbent pad that was less than clean.

I paused for a moment, wrinkling my nose and clenching my fists. Who knew what kind of germs were hanging out in that absorbent pad? But then I shrugged, sighed, and picked up the sponge. My shoulders slumped as I worked.

With COVID still an issue of global concern, these conditions were unacceptable, but I washed the dishes with the supplies provided and placed them to dry on the tray with its dirty pad. If this had happened three weeks earlier, I would simply have run downstairs to buy a new sponge and some paper towels. This obvious solution never occurred to me until I was writing this memoir. I had been bombarded with too many situations I couldn't control; now my brain was stuck in trauma mode. Each new disaster was simply something to survive, not fix.

After we cleaned up, I got out my laptop and sat on the edge of the queen bed to choose a movie. Three of the kids joined me, watching over my shoulders as I opened our video streaming service. Suddenly, the corner of the bed collapsed with a crash.

I felt horrible. We'd barely been in the place for two hours, and we'd already broken as many pieces of furniture! What would the landlord say? I shouldn't have let the three boys sit on the bed with me. I got everyone off and surveyed the damage. It was a wooden frame, and the long piece that ran from the head to the foot had simply come out of the slot in the footboard. I lifted up the long board, mattress and all, and fitted it back into the slot. Then, still supporting the wood with both hands, I used the side of my foot like a mallet to pound the footboard back into place.

I stepped back to admire my work, pleased I had been able to put it back together on my own. But how was I going to tell the landlord? He'd need to have it repaired, so it wouldn't collapse on his next tenants. I put a few of the wobbly chairs along that side of the bed to block it off and told all the kids not to sit there.

I retrieved my laptop and decided to try one of the other beds. There was an iron one that looked promising. The thin mattress provided little cushioning, but the frame was sturdy. The six kids and I perched on the edge while I chose a movie. I set up my laptop on a chair facing us, and we all did our best to get comfortable.

I pressed play, holding my breath to see if it was going to work. The internet connection was superb, and we were able to watch the entire movie without any streaming problems. Maybe the landlord was too cheap to buy a new sponge and a dish rack, but at least he provided good internet service, I noted to myself.

After we finished the movie, George called. He had finished work and was bringing us all the bags and suitcases he had transported from Debrecen to Budapest the night before. I took the two oldest boys with me to meet up with him. The only place George could find to stop was about a five-minute walk away. We found him parked illegally, blocking a narrow lane. Samuel, Kiyoshi, and I quickly retrieved our bags, said a hasty goodbye, and watched George drive away. I may have looked strong, my back straight as I stood on the sidewalk beside my two sons, but inside, I was crumpling under the weight of coping with so many challenges without my life partner by my side.

We trekked slowly back to the apartment building with all our things. Eventually we made it and stood before the broad stone steps. I entrusted the smaller bags to the boys and took the huge suitcase myself. I'm a slight woman, just over 5 feet 5 inches and under 120 pounds. This suitcase was well over half my weight. I had deliberately packed it with our heaviest things, since it had wheels. I hadn't anticipated having to heave it up multiple flights of stairs.

I wanted to sit on the bottom step and cry, but sooner or later, I'd still have to face the inevitable. Besides, years of having to be the one in the family to do all the heavy lifting—because of George's back condition—had taught me I could move anything I set my mind to.

You can do this, I told myself. *You figured out how to get Peter up the stairs with a broken femur when he was nine years old, and you'll figure this out too!*

I paused for a moment, staring at the ascending stairs, then I took a deep breath and began. I placed myself two steps above the suitcase. Using a rowing motion with my arms and a bit of help from my thigh muscles, I lifted the suitcase until it slid into place on the next step. Then I moved up another step and repeated the procedure. Lift, *thump* . . . step up . . . lift, *thump* . . . step up . . . lift, *thump*. I did this, one stair at a time, all the way to the third floor. By the time I got there, I was so grateful we weren't located on the fourth, fifth, or sixth floor.

I wish I could say the rest of the evening was uneventful, but it wouldn't be true. At some point, I heard one of the boys call out in alarm. "Mommy, the toilet's leaking!"

I rushed to investigate. Expecting to find a clogged bowl, I was already mentally assessing the best place in the apartment to look for a plunger. Instead, I found that the pipe connecting the antique toilet tank to the bowl had sprung a leak and was spewing water all over the floor. I quickly called the landlord. He said he'd be right over.

While we waited, the six boys and I stood just outside the toilet closet, watching the rapidly growing pool of water. The landlord appeared within minutes. He quickly located the shut-off valve. We used half of the available towels to mop up the small lake that had formed. The landlord apologized and said he'd have a plumber come the next day to fix the toilet and the shower.

"Okay, thank you." I smiled and nodded. *The shower? What in the world is wrong with the shower?* I wondered. We hadn't tried to use it yet. I guess we wouldn't have needed those towels anyway.

After the landlord left, it still wasn't bedtime. To combat the lonely, forlorn feeling of being stuck in this awkward apartment without George, I made a video to share in our family chat group. I gave a virtual tour of the apartment, humorously showing how you had to use two hands to turn on the tap in one of the toilets. The faucet wasn't anchored to the sink, so when you tried to turn the knob, the entire fixture simply twisted around. The solution was simple—just hold the faucet steady with one hand while turning the knob with the other.

The kitchen faucet had the same problem, but at least the design of the knobs allowed you to turn them without having to use your free hand to stabilize the faucet, I noted for the video. I told them about the toilet and shower. I showed the bed and explained how it had collapsed and how I had fixed it, and mentioned that one of the chairs had collapsed under James. I showed another chair that was so wobbly it actually rocked like a rocking chair, even with all four legs on the floor. Then I panned up to show the beautifully ornate crown molding on the antique ceiling. The apartment wasn't all bad, and it did have great internet, I narrated.

Feeling less isolated, I uploaded the video to the chat group. The time dragged in that dismal apartment, but finally, all the kids were resting quietly, and I could go to bed too. The only bed left was the one that had broken. I approached the opposite side from where it had collapsed and carefully turned back the covers. Gingerly putting my weight on it, I held my breath to see if it would come crashing down. It held. I pulled the covers over me and tried to get comfortable in the darkness.

The mattress was hard, and sleep was elusive. I was afraid to move, lest the bed collapse again. I was lying on my side, holding very still. My legs and back ached from being in the same position for so long. I tried to stretch without jostling the bed. Slowly, I shifted my weight. I reached out to God with my mind, inviting him into the middle of my misery. He was already there; I'd just been too busy coping to notice. Now I felt his comforting presence. *Good night, Lord.*

Eventually, I fell asleep.

25

A LITTLE TASTE OF HEAVEN

March 13, 2022: Day 18 of War
Budapest, Hungary

In the morning I had a text message from Pam: **I'm so sorry about the Airbnb!! I just heard it is horrible!!**

I wrote back: **Yeah . . . James and Samuel both seem to be allergic to something here. I think maybe the pillows. Everything seems really old and sort of decaying . . . I hate the fact that we are committed to renting this dump until the 30th.**

She responded: **I hate it so much for you. Feeling wretched about it all. You are such a trooper, Sharon!! I'll absorb the cost . . . Need to get you settled in a decent place. So sorry.**

Her sympathy reassured me that my feelings of being singled out and excluded from the family circle were misguided. If I had any doubts left, the text I received from Melanie shortly after 10 am removed them. She'd found a hotel in Budapest with vacancies, and she'd made reservations for us *and her family*. The seven of them were coming to us.

She sent a link. I tapped it and found myself looking at pictures of cozy rooms and sparkling bathrooms. I kept staring at the matching bedspreads. Compared to the haphazard decor in the Airbnb, that small detail seemed the epitome of luxury and good taste.

I had been planning to tough it out in the apartment as long as necessary, but literally overnight, our fortunes had changed. Melanie also told me that George's brother Aaron was working on getting our booking canceled and the money refunded. She said the video really helped with that.

I had never dreamed my video would create such a storm. I had only wanted to relieve my sense of isolation, but now we had hotel reservations, and part of the family circle was joining us in Budapest.

The kids were still eating breakfast when I told them about the hotel and showed them the website.

"What? A hotel?" James's expressive hazel eyes were wide as he stared at the pictures. "Is it five stars?"

"No!" I laughed. "But it does look really nice, doesn't it? And guess what? Uncle Paul and Aunty Melanie and their kids are going to stay there too."

There was an immediate frenzy of simultaneous exclamations.

"No way!"

"What?"

"When are they getting there?"

"Let's go!"

I smiled at their enthusiasm. We all needed this. "The sooner we're ready to go, the sooner we can leave."

The end was in sight, but this apartment wasn't done adding drama to our lives. Before he could finish his breakfast, my eldest son, Samuel, crashed to the floor as another of the apartment's wobbly chairs collapsed.

Thankfully, he was unhurt. He jumped up and stared at the chair. "Whaaaat?" He pointed at it and laughed loudly.

Kiyoshi reassembled the chair and put it in the other room beside the first one that had fallen apart. This was getting out of hand. Until that point, I had felt guilty about the broken furniture, like it was our fault. Not anymore. I realized chairs and beds should not break when used for their intended purposes. If a bed collapsed under the weight of three children and one slight woman, there was something wrong with the bed, not with us.

Everyone was upbeat and cooperative as we cleaned and packed. After we were ready to go, the landlord arrived with the plumber. I hadn't told him we were leaving.

He was all smiles, apologizing cheerfully and assuring me everything would be taken care of. I couldn't bring myself to smile and nod as I had the day before. Then he noticed our bags lined up in the entryway. He frowned and looked at me sharply.

"Where are you going?"

"My sister-in-law found us a hotel."

"Why? You have problem here?"

"Well, yes." I took him to the bathroom and showed him the faucet that took two hands to turn on.

"This is not problem. We fix now."

"You should fix the one in the kitchen too," I said, heading there. Then I showed him the unsanitary sponge and dirty drying pad. "Before the next person comes, you should replace these. It wouldn't cost much."

"Pshhh," he made a dismissive noise at me. "This is not problem. Stay."

"No, come look at this." I led him to the bed. "This broke last night."

He looked at me as if I was making it up. How could he doubt my word? Couldn't he see how rickety his furniture was?

"Watch," I said, removing the chairs I had lined up to keep the kids from sitting on the bed. Holding my breath, not wanting to get injured, I carefully lowered myself onto the corner of the mattress above where I had put the frame back together the night before. Nothing happened.

Now the landlord was glaring at me.

"Well, it collapsed last night. This part came out, and I had to put it back together again. And two of the chairs broke when kids sat on them."

Now his face was something between a sneer and a scowl.

"I have little kids. This apartment isn't safe. We have to leave." For some reason, I felt like I had to justify why we were moving out.

"I have another apartment. Come see."

"No, we're leaving." I walked back to the entryway.

"Come see," he insisted, following me and putting his hand on my shoulder. "It's not far."

The moment his hand made contact, I felt an angry strength fill me. "Don't touch me!" I stepped out of his reach. My eldest son, Samuel, later told me he was surprised to see me stand up for myself.

I called to the boys, "Kids, let's go!"

Everyone rushed to the entryway and pulled on shoes and coats. The seven of us were out the door with all our things in under two minutes. The landlord slammed the door behind us.

Eventually, I got all of us and our stuff down the stairs and out of the building. We nearly obstructed the wide sidewalk. We had three rolling suitcases, seven backpacks, a number of random bags, a violin, a flute, two ukuleles, and a bright-red, toy electric guitar.

Our Hungarian friend Imre was still in town, and Melanie had asked him to pick us up. He found a place to stop in our vicinity, but it wasn't a legal parking spot, so he couldn't leave the van to come help us. We were on our own.

I kept my eyes on the kids, making sure everyone stayed together and kept their distance from the traffic whizzing by just inches from the curb.

"Peter, hold the littles' hands!" I directed. "Samuel, Kiyoshi, James—help me with the bags, please."

They all took over their assigned tasks. I was proud of them. We worked well together in complex situations.

I took the huge suitcase and placed an oversized reusable shopping bag on top. The bag was crammed full of our queen-size comforter and the camping mattress. The mattress barely fit. As we walked, one end kept popping out and flopping around, and the bag didn't want to stay balanced on the suitcase. Every few steps, I had to stop to wrestle with the mattress or reposition the bag.

We're never going to make it at this rate, I thought in despair. I calmed my breathing and focused on putting one foot in front of the other. If I simply did that enough times, we would get there. And once we got to Imre, everything would be okay. I knew he would make sure we were taken care of.

The sidewalk was wide enough to accommodate two lanes of automobile traffic, and our cavalcade took up over half of it. We were a ridiculous spectacle. I could sense the stares of passersby, and I tried not to make eye contact. I was sure we looked every bit the part of refugees, limping along with all our worldly possessions.

I will never see these people again. It doesn't matter what they think of us, I consoled myself. *Just leave us alone*, I silently begged them.

And then a man approached us and addressed me in Hungarian. I wanted to disappear, but there was nowhere to hide. I assumed he must be telling me we were doing something wrong. I wanted to apologize, but I couldn't speak Hungarian.

I had no idea what he was trying to communicate. Was he saying that we were taking up too much space on the sidewalk? Or that we were breaking some local law? But that couldn't be it, because he didn't seem upset. I felt obligated to engage with him and make amends, if for nothing else than the fact that I didn't speak Hungarian.

I apologized automatically in Ukrainian, "*Vybachte. Ya ne rozumiyu,*" even though English would have been a more logical choice if I wanted to be understood in Budapest.

He switched to Russian. "Do you need help?"

My eyes filled with tears of relief and gratitude. "Yes, thank you!" I said, still in Ukrainian. Though I could understand Russian, I could hardly speak it.

He took the huge suitcase and uncooperative mattress from me and one of the smaller bags from the kids. Miraculously, the large shopping bag and mattress behaved perfectly for him.

As we walked, we exchanged bits of our stories. He continued to speak Russian; I, Ukrainian. He was from the extreme western part of Ukraine, between the Carpathian Mountains and Hungary, but he had been living in Hungary for years. He was friendly and compassionate.

We moved much faster with his help, and before long, we found Imre. I thanked the stranger who had seen and responded to our need, and then he was gone. I felt like God had sent us an angel.

It took only fifteen minutes to drive to the hotel, but it felt like a world away. It was a four-star, business hotel. There was a parking lot with plenty of free spaces. As we walked up to the entrance, we passed beautifully landscaped flower beds and peaceful fish ponds.

Our bags didn't seem incongruous here the way they had in the middle of foot traffic on a downtown sidewalk. Despite our awkward menagerie of luggage, I held my head high as we entered. We had a right to be here. We were paying guests.

The lobby was spacious and welcoming. There were couches, armchairs, and a water dispenser with paper cups. The man at the reception desk spoke perfect English and was helpful and accommodating. After what we'd been through, it felt like a little taste of heaven. We checked in under Melanie's name, received our key cards, and headed to our rooms. Melanie had reserved three double rooms for our family.

I handed Samuel and Kiyoshi each a keycard. "These are for your rooms."

"Whaaat? We have our own rooms?" Samuel asked, his jaw dropping, his gray eyes wide and staring at the keycard in his hand.

"Yeah, you do! Isn't that cool?"

While the four oldest boys settled in, I took the two youngest ones to my room. It was small but comfortable, with two twin beds and an armchair. I pushed the two beds together so George and I wouldn't have to sleep separately. The camping mattress saved the day again: I used it to make a bed on the floor for Andrew and Isaac.

Even if we had wanted to book another room to accommodate everyone, it wouldn't have been possible. With the influx of refugees, it had been hard for Melanie to find any vacancies in the city. She had taken the last rooms this hotel had. They were only available for three nights.

Thankfully, one of George's church connections in Budapest had told him about a rental apartment that would be vacant soon. Hopefully, it would be ready for us by the time we had to check out. But that was a problem for tomorrow. Or the day after. Today, right here, right now, we had a place to call our own.

26

Catching Up

March 13, 2022: Day 18 of War
Budapest, Hungary

Paul and Melanie and their kids made it to Budapest that evening. It was Sunday, and we met up at a church that was hosting an evening of Ukrainian worship music. Jon had come from Debrecen to lead it.

Shouts of joy and welcome reverberated as the kids ran to greet each other in the parking lot. Though we had only left Debrecen the previous day, it felt like we'd been apart much longer. I threw my arms around Melanie and squeezed tightly. When we hugged goodbye on the train station platform, I had no idea when I'd see her again. With my typical Japanese reticence, I hadn't voiced my feelings then, and I didn't now. I basked privately in the joy of the moment.

When we entered the church, the lights were dim, and they were already singing. Jon was a classically trained musician and talented songwriter. Several of his profound and poetic songs had gained such wide popularity that Christians of all persuasions sang them in churches across Ukraine.

As I looked around, I was amazed at how many faces I recognized. After spending nearly two decades in Ukraine, I knew people from all over the country. Many were there that night. We hugged and whispered warm greetings as we held each other. I had tears in my eyes. What had each of these dear ones gone through to get here? Where were they staying? Would they settle in Budapest? Maybe there was hope we'd have friends nearby.

I found seats for myself and the kids, then I closed my eyes and surrendered to the music. I breathed a contented sigh and felt tension drain from my body as a beloved melody and familiar words about God's love and goodness washed over me. I added my voice to the chorus of those around me. It felt like coming home.

Midway through the evening, Jon sang a song I had never heard. Had he just written it in response to the war? I listened intently and opened my eyes to read the lyrics projected onto a screen.

I quickly picked up the melody and was soon singing along. Then we got to the bridge, an impassioned plea to God:

Take away all our pain,
Wipe away all our tears.

The words catalyzed a flood of emotion. I couldn't sing another note. Overwhelmed by the trauma of the last eighteen days, I wept. As cleansing tears poured down my cheeks and sobs shook my body, I lifted my face to the ceiling and whispered the words in time to the music.

Once all the kids were in bed that night, I decided to catch up on the journal I was keeping, a habit I'd established a few days after leaving Ukraine. So much was happening so quickly that it was disorienting. Often by evening it was hard to remember the events of the morning, and keeping things straight in our minds from week to week would have been impossible. I realized someday we were going to want a written record of that time, because we were too traumatized to think clearly right now, let alone trust our memories.

Every night before bed, I typed a few sentences to document the most important events of the day. Whenever I had time, I went back and fleshed out the details. With the upheaval of relocating twice in two days, I had gotten behind. Despite how tired I was, I didn't want to let another day pass without recording events while they were still fresh.

George was on his way back from Krakow, and I didn't feel settled enough to go to bed without him. I was still up writing when he arrived at 2 am. I jumped up to greet him, wrapping my arms around his waist, inhaling his scent and melting into his reassuring embrace. We exchanged a few whispered greetings, but catching up would have to wait until later. George had urgent work. He shut himself in the bathroom so he wouldn't disturb me.

I went to bed, relaxing in the knowledge that our family was officially back together. I was in that disorienting place somewhere between waking and sleeping when I suddenly heard George's voice speaking in urgent tones from the bathroom. I jolted awake, my pulse throbbing in my throat. I lay still, straining my ears to make out what he was saying. Something about evacuations. He sounded worried. I contemplated going to him to offer my help, but realized there probably wasn't anything I could do except pray.

I tried to slow my racing heart with deep, steady breaths, but I could only inhale halfway before the persistent tightness in my chest stopped me. I lay in the darkness, my breathing quick and shallow, asking God to give George strength and wisdom for whatever challenge he was facing. Eventually, sleep reclaimed me.

I woke up at 7:15 am. It was March 14, my son James's ninth birthday and the nineteenth day of the war. My first thought was, *Why can't I ever sleep more than five hours anymore?* I stayed in bed, holding my eyes closed, willing myself to go back to sleep, but soon Andrew and Isaac woke up. George rose immediately.

"I'll take them to breakfast," he said. "Why don't you stay here and get some rest?"

"Are you sure?" I was already halfway out of bed.

"Yeah, you deserve it," he said fondly, kissing me on the forehead.

"Thanks." I pulled the covers over my ears in an effort to block out the kids' noises. After his trip and late night, George had to be as exhausted as I was. I was grateful he had somehow mustered the energy to care for the kids and had the selflessness to let me rest.

I lay in bed with my eyes shut, but I couldn't stop reliving the events of the previous day—especially the way the landlord had treated me like a liar when we were leaving the apartment. I wasn't used to people not taking me at my word. I felt violated.

And then there was the way he pressured me to go look at his other apartment. The memory of the weight of his hand on my shoulder made my skin crawl. Though my normal response to difficult situations was guilt or sadness, this struck a different chord.

Anger.

But I wasn't just angry at the landlord. I was angry that I'd ended up in Budapest on my own in the first place. If I hadn't left Debrecen in such a rush, none of this would have happened.

My anger needed a target, but I realized it wasn't fair to hold anyone else responsible when I hadn't shared my true feelings. If I was honest, I had no one to blame but myself.

Why did I always let myself get pushed around? Why couldn't I ever stand up for myself? I'd managed to advocate for the kids by delaying our departure one day, but why hadn't I also voiced my deep misgivings and hurt over the rushed move? Why did I always mutely acquiesce to what other people wanted? I worried so much about their feelings—why did I ignore my own?

At 10 am I finally gave up on sleep. I quickly dressed and found my way to the hotel restaurant. George, our kids, Paul, Melanie, and their kids were all there. Melanie spotted me and came over right away.

"Good morning! Isn't this place nice?" She gave me a hug.

"It's amazing! Thank you so much for finding it."

"Of course! We couldn't let you stay in that awful apartment! We just couldn't believe it when we saw your video! Aaron contacted Airbnb and Booking.com, and we're getting that listing removed from both sites."

"It wasn't *that* bad. I don't want to make any problems for the landlord. He was really nice. Well, at least until I told him we were leaving."

"Sharon, it was *bad*. And if we don't report him, he'll just take advantage of other people."

"I guess so."

She went on as if she hadn't heard me. "And who's that going to be right now? Ukrainian moms and kids, who have nowhere else to go. He'll take advantage of them. You don't want that."

"No, you're right. I don't want that to happen." I paused. "He touched me."

"He *what*?" Melanie practically roared.

"On the shoulder, when he was trying to convince me to go look at another apartment he had. And I was thinking, *I'm not interested in any apartment that you have anything to do with, because it'll just be another dump like this one.* But I didn't say that. I just said, 'No,' and then he put his hand on my shoulder. It wasn't sexual. More, kind of friendly, like he was trying to encourage me to listen to him. But it made me uncomfortable."

"Sharon, that was wrong! He had no right to do that! Of course you felt uncomfortable. Oh! I'm so sorry you had to go through that!" She had tears in her eyes. I started crying too. She wrapped her arms around me. "I'm so sorry, Sharon."

I let her hold me and gave into the emotions that suddenly overwhelmed me. The storm of sobs was violent but completely silent and quickly over. With all the activity from our collective eleven kids, no one noticed my crying besides Melanie. I thanked her and dried my eyes on a napkin.

Since I'd been so late coming to breakfast, I'd missed the chance to talk with George. He had to leave for a major planning meeting with a group of pastors and missionaries. The evacuation convoy he'd helped organize was in the process of picking up people from multiple safe houses in Ukraine. In just a few days, they would arrive in Budapest. With that project almost wrapped up, George was pivoting away from evacuations to focus on helping refugees. He gave me a quick kiss on the lips before he headed out.

After breakfast, Melanie offered to watch the kids so I could rest. I was grateful for the opportunity to nap, but it turned out to be a frustrating experience. My overwrought nerves refused to relax. At 5 pm I finally gave up.

While I had been trying to nap, George had been in a long meeting with four pastors, two of his brothers, and Paul. They were creating a network of drivers and vehicles to deliver aid all over Ukraine and developing a strategy to resettle Ukrainian refugees across Europe.

That meeting gave birth to the idea of creating communities for displaced Ukrainians. This vision captured George's and my imaginations and became the dream that animated much of what we would do over the next few years.

Once the meeting was over, George and I worked together to feed the kids dinner and get them ready for bed. We still hadn't gotten to talk, but it was great to have a partner again. George and I finally got to bed around midnight.

I didn't feel ready to sleep. George was busy texting, but I tried to start a conversation.

George looked up briefly and nodded. "Uh-huh. Yeah." He went back to his unfinished text message.

"Can you please put your phone down?" My voice betrayed a hint of irritation. I immediately felt guilty. After all, I had been the one to interrupt him in the middle of writing a message. It was probably critical. Everything he did those days had a life-or-death quality to it. But on the other hand, he and I needed to reconnect.

I took as deep a breath as I could manage around the constant tightness in my chest and let it out slowly. "I'm sorry."

"No, you're right. I'm sorry." He set his phone aside.

He gave me his full attention. I told him everything. I shared my feelings over being asked to leave the family haven—how it had made me feel rejected, excluded, less than. He finally heard first-hand about our experiences with the apartment and its landlord. I expressed my anger with myself for the way everything had turned out.

It was life-giving to pour out my heart to a sympathetic listener. George assured that me none of what had happened had been my fault and said he was sorry he hadn't been around to intervene. It was 12:45 am when we said goodnight, snuggled close, and went to sleep.

27

I'm Not Okay—No One Is

March 15, 2022: Day 19 of War
Budapest, Hungary

I woke at 5:45 am. After two hours of holding my eyes closed, I gave up. Maybe I was never going to sleep more than five hours again.

George had a breakfast meeting. Andrew and Isaac were still asleep when he left the room. Normally early risers, today our five-year-old and three-year-old were finally catching up on the rest that had been stolen from them during the chaotic weeks since the start of the war. I'll admit, I was envious.

Around 10 am, there was a soft knock on our door. It was Melanie.

"We're checking out now," she said. "We're flying back home tomorrow. Paul and I decided to go say goodbye to the rest of the family today."

"Wow. So this is it, then." I felt stunned. Who knew the next time they'd be able to visit from the Middle East?

"Yeah," she paused. "I can't get any more time off work. I hate leaving." Her eyes were glistening with tears. "I'm so sorry!"

"Don't be! I can't believe you came. I don't know what we would have done without you."

"I'd like to just quit my job and stay here and help. What you guys are doing is so important. I don't want to go back there. Will you pray for me?"

Melanie was normally strong and confident. I'd never heard her sound uncertain and forlorn.

I took her hands in mine, bowed my head, and talked out loud to God. The words flowed easily as I spoke the thoughts that came to my mind—encouragement and strength and the power of God. When I finished, Melanie wiped her eyes and hugged me. She was calmer, at peace.

"Thank you," she said. "That was a message from the Lord for me."

Later that morning, George and I shared a late breakfast outside at a table beside a fish pond. While our children ran among the flower beds and back and forth across the bridge over the pond, we enjoyed the fresh air and sunshine and the rare chance to talk. George told me about the meetings he had been in over the last few days, starting with the one in Krakow and ending with the meeting from that morning.

As a result of the Krakow meeting, our church network in Ukraine had become an official partner with Samaritan's Purse. Once they got their huge operation running in Ukraine, we would only need to call and tell them where we needed aid, and they would deliver it, free of charge. However, they weren't ready to start deliveries yet, and people were running out of time.

To bridge the gap, George was working to get vehicles into the hands of Ukrainian men who had started a grassroots movement to deliver aid and evacuate people across the country. These heroes were taking anything that would run, filling it to capacity with food, drinking water, and baby diapers, driving into dangerous areas, unloading the supplies, and offering rides to as many people as they could carry out. Then they would gas up and do it all over again. With the war in Ukraine making international headlines, it wasn't hard to raise money for this project.

What *was* hard was getting used to my husband being involved in such big doings. After three decades of missionary service, the Markey name was well known in our church circles, but even so, George and I had a low profile. We didn't like to organize large events, and we rarely spoke at them. We'd never aspired to build a megachurch—in fact, when the full-scale invasion started, we had been in the process of starting a network of house churches in Kyiv.

But overnight, we had been catapulted to the center of an international effort to help Ukraine. Along with other pastors, George was directing the use of hundreds of thousands of dollars of donations, and because of his connections, military-grade protective gear worth millions was on its way to Ukraine. We still didn't have a stable place to live, and yet George was a crucial part of multiple huge projects.

After breakfast, George left for another important meeting, his second of the day.

I was in our hotel room with Andrew and Isaac when my dad texted me shortly before noon: **Have you moved into Budapest yet?**

I told him about the events of the past few days, where we were staying now, where all the other displaced members of the Markey family were, and what their immediate plans were.

None of us had any idea what our long-term plans were.

I updated my dad on our housing status. The previous tenants had just left the apartment George had found, and the landlord was scrambling to get it ready for us in record time, since we had to check out of the hotel the next day.

We texted for about an hour until I sent him this message: **I can't wait to get settled and start talking to the Christian therapist who really helped Melanie and Paul after they had to flee Iraq. I'm not well. Ever since the war started, I find it almost impossible to sleep for more than five hours per night. I am physically exhausted, and when I am awake, I am almost constantly trying to keep a panicky feeling in my chest under control. A few mornings ago, I thought for sure that I heard air-raid sirens and distant explosions, even though the rational part of my brain knew that was extremely unlikely.**

Instead of texting back, he called, but the call wouldn't connect. I glanced at the little boys. I didn't want my three-year-old and five-year-old to overhear the disturbing things I might discuss with my dad. Isaac and Andrew were coloring pictures and seemed content.

"I'm going into the hall to talk on the phone," I told them.

Andrew looked up at me, his eyebrows tilted up in the middle in his characteristic worried expression. "You're leaving?"

"If you need me, I'll be right outside the room, okay?" He seemed satisfied, and I called my dad back as I stepped out and quietly shut the door behind me.

This time, the call connected. Feeling at home, I walked up and down the empty hallway in my socks while I talked.

Though I had been giving my family daily updates via text message, this was the first time I'd talked with my dad since evacuating. Dispassionately, I told him about the main events of the past nineteen days. Then I referenced something—I can't remember what—and suddenly I could hardly speak past the enormous, painful lump in my throat. I paused, trying to regain control. I stopped pacing near a huge potted plant and slid down the wall until I was sitting on the floor beside the plant.

"I'm sorry," I finally managed. "Sometimes I feel normal, and sometimes I just start crying."

"It's okay," my dad reassured me gently. "You've been through a lot."

I didn't know what to say. My emotions told me I'd been through an upheaval that would take years to process. But my mind was quick to point out that the kids and I had experienced none of the violence of war, so I didn't have the right to feel so torn up. Back then, I didn't know psychologists equate forced displacement with the death of a close relative, in terms of its psychological impact.

I stared at the dark carpet, tracing the large paisley pattern with the big toe of one socked foot as I blinked away tears.

Soon after we hung up, George arrived with a borrowed car. Some men from my childhood church were in Budapest, and we were meeting up with them for lunch at a park nearby. George made two trips to transport all six of our kids and me to the park.

When we got there, I was surprised to see a group of Ukrainian friends in addition to the guys from California. I went around smiling and hugging people. It was disorienting to be picnicking in a park, greeting friends as if life was normal and happy, when all of us had just been through the unthinkable.

Pastor John, who had visited us in Debrecen to deliver gifts, was standing with another man from my church. They looked my way as I walked up. "Hi, Sharon!" the other man said. "How are you doing?"

I wanted to give more than the automatic "I'm fine" as an answer. I wanted to talk about what had happened to us and help them understand what we and so many Ukrainians had endured. But I had no idea where to begin.

"Well, it's been tough." I paused, searching for words. Then it all came out in a rush.

"The kids and I were in Ternopil when the invasion happened. We didn't hear any explosions, just air-raid sirens. We spent half of the first day in a basement. George was still in Kyiv. He heard explosions. He tried to come to us, but he couldn't get out of the city. Everybody was trying to leave. The roads were jammed."

I rushed on. "The kids and I spent that night in a basement because there was an air-raid siren right after I put them to bed. I couldn't sleep all night. Martial law had been declared, and there was a curfew, but George was planning to violate it to try to get out of Kyiv early in the morning. I was so worried for him."

I paused to take a breath and slowed down. Speaking matter-of-factly, as if I was recounting something academic, I continued, "I honestly didn't know if I was ever going to see him again. It was the longest night of my life."

"But you're okay, right?" the other man said.

I opened my mouth to agree with him. I was okay, right? Then I stopped. I needed to be honest with myself and with these men. "No, I'm not. No *one* is." My voice was soft, but I spoke with fierce earnestness.

There was an awkward pause.

"Can I pray for you?" Pastor John asked gently.

"I'd love that."

Right there, in the middle of the park, he took out a small vial of oil and dabbed a little on my forehead. It had a rich, warm, woodsy scent. Then, in simple sentences, he asked God to comfort me, give me strength, and provide for our family. I felt seen and supported.

That night after the kids were in bed, George left the hotel to meet up with the retired US Marine who had taken on the assignment of getting our dog out of Ukraine. The convoy had finally made it to Hungary.

George got Jack, picked up the keys to our new apartment, and spent the night there. The next day, we would all move in. The kids knew about the move, but we hadn't told them about Jack. I hadn't wanted to get their hopes up, in case something went wrong. They were going to be so surprised.

28

EVERYTHING THAT MATTERS

March 16, 2023: Day 21 of War
Budapest, Hungary

The next morning, we checked out of the hotel. The kids and I packed up and moved all our things out to the parking lot to wait for George. I seated myself on a low wall beside a flower bed near our stuff. These bags contained all we owned. There was no guarantee that our apartment in Kyiv would survive. I knew we had to accept the possibility that we would never see the rest of our belongings again.

It was a sobering thought, but at that moment, it didn't make me sad. I had too much to be thankful for. Our family was together again, and we were moving into permanent housing.

The kids ran up and down the walkways between the flowerbeds while we waited. Eventually, George showed up in a borrowed car. He was not alone. To my surprise, our new landlord had come along to help us move. He was driving a pickup truck with a camouflage paint job and an extended cab. My eyes opened wide when I saw it. In almost twenty years of living in Eastern Europe, I had never seen a pickup truck.

Our new landlord was an American and a retired military man. He had a reassuring, sturdy presence, a friendly smile, and a firm handshake. With his help, we quickly loaded all our stuff into the bed of his truck, then the three oldest boys and I climbed into the cab. George took the three youngest kids.

Like Kyiv, Budapest is situated on a river that divides the city in half. Many bridges link the two sides. Our new apartment was on the opposite side of the Danube River from the hotel. As we crossed one of the bridges, I gazed at the elegant buildings lining both banks. This cityscape was breathtaking. We had passed through Budapest a number of times over the past fifteen years, and I never got tired of admiring this view.

After crossing the river, we drove into an older part of town. Narrow one-way streets crisscrossed each other in a confusing tangle, but our landlord knew exactly where he was going and expertly maneuvered his pickup through the tight spaces. Eventually he found a parking spot on a street that felt more like an alley, and we unloaded. George parked nearby. Everyone except three-year-old Isaac took a bag or two, and we followed the two men down the narrow sidewalk and around a corner.

There, sandwiched between two old buildings, was a gleaming new structure. George walked up to the glass door, produced a magnetic fob, and touched it to the keypad panel. An electronic tone sounded, and George opened the door and held it. The kids and I trooped inside. We were in a corridor leading to a peaceful courtyard full of well-tended plants.

George led us to another hallway with a pair of sleek, modern elevators with touch-sensitive-glass control panels and floor-to-ceiling mirrors.

"Whoa! Look at the elevator!" James's striking hazel eyes were wide, and his mouth was hanging open.

I felt as awestruck as my nine-year-old. Most of the elevators we used in Ukraine were relics of the Soviet Union. They were frequently dingy and poorly lit. The buttons were plastic and usually defaced. Often the floor numbers were no longer legible, so they would be scrawled in permanent marker on the panel beside the buttons. Sometimes a few buttons would be missing entirely. Stepping into this sparkling elevator with its touch-sensitive panel felt like stepping up in the world.

Since we couldn't all fit in one elevator, George handed me the keys and gave me directions. I took Samuel and James and a bunch of bags and tapped the six on the glass touchpad. When we got out, we walked through a door onto a balcony overlooking the courtyard. I glanced over the railing. It was a dizzying height. To my American mind, we were actually on the seventh floor, because in Hungary, floor numbering starts with zero on the ground floor.

The metal railing was made of horizontal stainless steel bars. It looked like a shiny ladder inviting a small child to climb. Images of my two youngest ones falling to their deaths on the pavement far below flashed unbidden in my mind. I felt nauseated and lightheaded. Our apartment opened directly onto this balcony. I would have to be super vigilant and always keep the door locked so the little ones couldn't get out unsupervised.

Ours was the second apartment. As soon as I opened the door, I heard Jack's nails clicking on the laminate floor as he came to greet us. He didn't bark or show other signs of excitement. He walked slowly with his ears and tail down. He definitely recognized me but seemed worried. Samuel and James came in right behind me.

"Jack!" Samuel squealed, leaning down to pet the dog.

"Jack's here?" James raised his eyebrows in excitement and glanced at me for confirmation before he stepped around Samuel to see for himself.

George arrived with Isaac, Andrew, and Peter. All the kids rushed to pet Jack, exclaiming happily. Jack stood very still and quiet, barely wagging his tail. Kiyoshi, the child with the closest bond to Jack, was downstairs with our landlord waiting for another elevator.

George glanced out the door. "Here they come! Here they come!"

We vacated the entryway so Kiyoshi would have a clear view of Jack as soon as he stepped inside.

When Kiyoshi saw all of us watching him, he stood in the doorway and flashed us a silly grin. It took him five long seconds before he realized the sad-looking animal standing beside him was his beloved pet.

Then the moment of recognition came.

He drew in his breath sharply. "Jack!" He dropped to his knees beside the dog and rubbed his ears. "Jack!" Kiyoshi rested his forehead on the dog's head, his dark hair mingling with the dog's tawny fur.

Jack came alive. He wagged his tail with conviction and whined repeatedly.

He had been waiting for his boy.

I blinked to clear the tears of joy from my eyes and finally inspected our surroundings. The fully furnished apartment was compact and cozy. With all of us in it, some would have called it cramped. It had two bedrooms, one bathroom, and an open kitchen and living room. The ceilings in the bedrooms slanted down to within two feet of the floor along one side of each room. Abundant natural light streamed in through skylights placed in the sloping ceilings.

Each bedroom was equipped with two twin beds pushed together in the middle of the floor, creating a king-size bed. At first glance, it didn't seem possible to accommodate a family of eight. The sloping ceilings eliminated the possibility of bunk beds, and there didn't appear to be enough floor space to fit more beds. But we had experience living in close quarters.

Once, the eight of us and Jack had lived for almost a month in an office space that we shared with two other people. After that, we spent two and a half years in a two-bedroom, one-bathroom apartment. By now I was an expert at finding creative ways to maximize limited space. Impressed by my ingenuity, my dad once joked I had a future in interior design for submarines.

I liked challenges, and figuring out how to make this small space work for our large family would be fun. I was already getting ideas. At the same time, part of my mind warned me that living like this might have an adverse effect on us in the long run. Maybe we should look for a larger apartment.

Our landlord's voice brought me back to the present. "This place is worth five hundred euros a month. You can pay me or not pay me. Stay as long or as little as you like."

"Wow, thank you!" George said. "We can pay you," he added quickly.

Our landlord nodded. "Sorry they didn't have time to get cleaners in here before you moved in. I think they painted."

"That's fine," I said. "We're just so grateful to have a place to stay."

"Go shopping for whatever you need. Drapes, dishes, furniture. We'll take it out of your rent."

"Wow, thank you!" I said.

"Thank you," George chimed in. "Do you think we could get a dishwasher?"

"Yeah, this place needs a dishwasher," our landlord agreed. "You pick something out and let us know what it costs."

Our new landlord was being incredibly generous on so many levels. The one I appreciated most was his assurance that we could stay as long or as little as we liked. Normal practice in Hungary was for tenants to sign a one-year contract and pay a significant deposit that they would forfeit if they moved out early.

This requirement of committing to a year was a roadblock to those who had been displaced by the war. We had no plans to stay long term. We were going back to Ukraine soon. We were sure the war couldn't last long. The international community wouldn't allow Putin to get away with his outrageous behavior. It violated all accepted norms of modern international relations. You can't just steal the land of a neighboring country.

Of course, Putin had done exactly that in 2008 in the Republic of Georgia and again in 2014 when he annexed Ukraine's Crimea, and no one had stopped him then. But the current situation was clearly on another level. This was a full-scale invasion that was killing thousands of civilians, including women and children. The US and the EU would get involved this time and put an end to this madness, and we'd all go back home and pick up life where we'd left off.

As soon as our landlord left, Kiyoshi and I decided to walk the dog. Jack loved going on walks.

"C'mon, Jack! Let's go outside," I called to him.

He slunk over to me, his head down, his ears back, and his tail between his legs. It was strange. I rubbed his ears then put his leash on and opened the apartment door. To my consternation, instead of following me out, Jack put his belly on the floor, splayed his legs, and braced himself against the threshold.

"That's weird," George said. "He did the same thing last night when I tried to bring him inside the building."

"And now he's doing it to not *leave* the building?" I asked no one in particular.

Kiyoshi and I finally got Jack out the door. He hugged the wall as we walked down the balcony to the elevator. Once the elevator doors opened, he fought again to keep from getting in.

"Jack, what's wrong?" Kiyoshi asked. "Don't you want to go outside?"

Once we got Jack out of the building, he started to act more normal. Kiyoshi and I explored the neighborhood together, walking the length of a quiet, tree-lined, residential street a block away. When we got back to our building, Jack didn't resist entering or getting on the elevator. Maybe he had just needed some time to acclimate. I could definitely understand. We all needed some time to get used to all the changes.

We spent the rest of the day deep-cleaning the kitchen. We scoured the counters and floor. We scrubbed layers of caked-on grease off the stove's exhaust hood. We soaked the exhaust screen in the bathtub in hot water and dish soap until the water looked like coffee.

George drove to the Mexican restaurant where he'd taken me when I visited Budapest for Women's Day and picked up dinner for everyone. After the hours of hard work, it tasted even more amazing than I remembered. The atmosphere in the small apartment felt cozy and celebratory.

We had to improvise with the sleeping arrangements. I spread our comforter with the lovely, purple cover over the bed in the smaller bedroom, claiming it for George and myself. Samuel, Peter, and the two smallest boys chose the king-size bed in the other bedroom, cuddling together in the middle of it like a litter of puppies. The couch in the living room converted into a double bed, and Kiyoshi and James slept there. There weren't any sheets or blankets for the couch, but we had sleeping bags, a gift Melanie had pressed me to accept before they left. I hadn't anticipated needing them so soon. Four pillows came with the apartment, and we had acquired two more since evacuating. It was enough, since the two youngest boys weren't picky about whether or not they had pillows.

As George and I settled into bed under our purple comforter, I experienced a profound sense of contentment. Maybe we would never see most of our things again, but right here in this tiny apartment, we had everything that mattered. We had each other. We had food and clothing. And we had a place to sleep for as many nights as we wanted. What more could we ask for?

29

Settling In

Thursday, March 17, 2022: Day 22 of War
Budapest, Hungary

I awoke to sunlight streaming through the skylights. The effect was cheerful and homey. I lay in bed gazing around the room. I took a deep breath, held it for a moment, and let it out.

I repeated the exercise, just to be sure.

I could breathe deeply again. The strangling tightness in my chest that had been part of every waking moment for weeks was completely gone. What could it mean? I continued to take deep, even breaths, enjoying the new freedom.

George left in the morning to meet with two pastors who were helping him organize his new humanitarian efforts. My mission for the day was less urgent but no less important for our family. I was going to turn this little apartment into a comfortable space for us.

The first order of business was to finish cleaning. I had the kids dust, sweep and mop, and disinfect the bathroom with vinegar. Meanwhile, I washed all the windows and skylights inside and out till they sparkled in the copious sunlight.

After a few hours of work, we decided to take Jack and explore the large park nearby. We'd heard great things about it. One American friend had even compared it to New York City's Central Park. Having always wanted to see Central Park, I was excited about living so close to its Budapest equivalent.

We found the park easily and began exploring. We came to a running path with a reddish, springy surface. We hurried across, careful not to impede any of the runners.

"Look, Samuel," I said, "you could come here to go running every day!"

"Ummm, yeah." His voice sounded flat, and instead of perking up, his tall, lanky frame folded in on itself.

"Don't you want to start running again? Uncle Paul and Aunty Melanie got you those nice shoes."

Ever since leaving Ukraine, our fifteen-year-old budding distance runner had practically abandoned the sport that had been his passion before the war. It hadn't helped that he'd accidentally left his running shoes in Ternopil when we evacuated. But when we were living in Debrecen, Paul and Melanie had bought him a top-of-the-line pair of Nike running shoes. Samuel had happily gone running with Melanie once or twice when we were in Debrecen, but he hadn't run at all since. I was concerned about his lack of interest in something that had given him so much joy and satisfaction.

After the running track, the path took us past a number of playing courts, including an enclosed miniature soccer field with an electronic scoreboard and covered bleachers. We kept staring at all the possibilities, amazed by the variety of sports represented.

When we reached the end of the sports complex, we noticed a little skate park and a small rock-climbing wall off to our right. We might have gone that way, except for what we saw directly in front of us. Peeking through the trees was a humongous, red-and-white balloon. Curious, we headed to investigate.

We soon came to the edge of a huge playground. The balloon was on top of some sort of structure in the middle. The whole area was fenced, with child-proof latches on the gates. A sign indicated that dogs were not allowed. Kiyoshi volunteered to stay with Jack. The rest of us entered the playground.

We found ourselves on a multicolored, springy surface. There were large holes here and there enclosing small trampolines, the perfect size for one person to jump. There were also some odd swellings of the ground, which we discovered were tunnels for kids to crawl through, complete with domed skylights. We frolicked on the trampolines before venturing farther into the play area.

The next section was for slightly older kids and included a zip line. We passed a series of dry, concrete waterways that I realized must be filled in the summer to provide water fun for the kids. There was a remarkable variety of playground equipment. Some things were familiar—like slides, swings, and see-saws—others were puzzling, until I saw how kids were using them. Every few steps we stopped to stare at something new and interesting.

Finally we made it to the section designed for the most adventurous play, and there was the structure with the red-and-white balloon. It looked like a hot-air balloon, but it was actually a forty-foot-tall jungle gym, and the majority of the climbing occurred inside the balloon.

There were too many play structures to list, but we soon discovered our two favorites. One was a tall, corkscrew slide with a digital stopwatch that displayed the time it had taken you to go down, accurate to the millisecond. The older boys became obsessed with getting the fastest time and achieving personal bests.

Beside it was my favorite; I dubbed it the whee-saw. A yoke shaped like an inverted V balanced atop a tall pole. Each end of the yoke supported a saddle with handlebars. Two riders would take turns pushing off the ground. The yoke would tilt and send them soaring high in the air while also spinning around the central axis. It looked like a crazy ride. I wanted to try, but the line was too long.

We spent about an hour enjoying the playground. Eventually, hunger and the need to check on Kiyoshi forced us to leave. We found him and Jack, and we all returned to the apartment for lunch. Afterwards, the four oldest boys asked if they could go back to the playground by themselves. They stayed out until after dark. George got back before them with dinner for everyone from a takeout place he'd discovered nearby.

The older boys finally returned shortly after 7 pm. They burst into the apartment, talking all at once.

"I did the slide so many times!"

"It was so fun!"

"We have to stay here!"

"Yeah, this apartment is fine. It's totally worth living here to be by this park!"

"Wow!" George managed to fit the word into a short pause between exclamations. "Sounds like you really liked it!"

So, it was decided. We wouldn't be moving to a bigger apartment—unless we happened to hear of something near the park. I had already known I could make this small space work for us. I was looking forward to the challenge, and having the kids on board would make it easier. And it wasn't like we were deciding to live in these cramped quarters forever. It was just a temporary arrangement until we could go back to Ukraine.

You can put up with just about anything when you know it's only temporary.

Having decided to stay in the apartment, I devoted the next day, Friday, March 18, to adapting it to our needs. I separated the two twin beds in the kids' room, put them along opposite walls, and pushed the foot of each bed under the sloping part of the ceiling. The room felt 100% larger, and I had utilized twenty square feet of space that was otherwise useless due to the low clearance. Next, I moved the two twin beds George and I had been using into the kids' room.

Working in the 10 x 18-foot space felt like playing Tetris, but eventually I figured out a configuration that allowed me to fit all four beds, two bedside tables, two wardrobes, and an organizer unit to hold toys, while still leaving a bit of space free for a play area. I shook my head in amazement as I surveyed the result. No one who had seen the room in its former configuration would have imagined it could accommodate all this—and it actually felt more spacious than before. Later, we would even figure out how to fit in a full-size Yamaha keyboard for the piano players in the family.

The kids helped out for a few hours, doing whatever I asked. Once they finished, the four older ones went back to the park. A little after noon, Anya, a member of our team from Kyiv who had also evacuated to Hungary, showed up to babysit. George and I walked her to the park with Andrew and Isaac.

We found the other boys on the slide with the stopwatch. They came running when they saw us. Nine-year-old James wrapped his arms around my waist and took a moment to lean into me, then he smiled up into my face with his beautiful hazel eyes before repeating the ritual with George.

"Wow, this place is amazing!" George said. "Are you guys having fun?"

"Yeah!" the boys all exclaimed.

I noticed that the whee-saw was free.

"George, you've got to see this! It's the most amazing thing. It's sort of like a seesaw, except you go really high and spin around. We were watching people do it yesterday!" I grabbed his hand and pulled him toward the playground toy. "C'mon, let's do it while there's no line!"

He followed easily, and we both climbed into our saddles and grabbed the handlebars. George launched himself with a powerful push off the ground that sent him high in the air in a huge arching motion. As he descended, I was propelled almost equally high in an arch that corresponded to the U-shape of his descent. I clung to the handlebars as the ground receded to a distance of at least six feet.

George kicked off the ground again, and I felt a ticklish feeling in the pit of my stomach as I descended abruptly. My face split into a wide, open-mouthed smile. I tried to kick off the ground, but we were moving so fast with such a wild, spinning motion that my feet hardly made contact with the sand before I was being hurled up and to the side again. I gave up—I just held on and enjoyed the ride while George did all the work. Hearty laughter bubbled up from somewhere deep inside me, and soon I was belly laughing uncontrollably.

It felt oddly similar to sobbing.

For so much of the last three weeks, I had managed my emotions with iron restraint. Ensuring the kids' safety and care was all-consuming. I couldn't allow myself the luxury of sitting with my pain. The tears I shed were quickly dried, the feelings diverted somewhere they wouldn't hinder my ability to function. But as I began to laugh, those diverted emotions found a crack in my reserve and rushed out, a mighty torrent. The laughter brought profound relief.

I was familiar with the cleansing power of tears. I'd never known laughter could be as potent.

George and I gave Anya a key to our apartment and left the kids with her. Our landlord had loaned us a car so we could go shopping. We went to two discount stores to get small household items, then we went to IKEA. Among many other things, we bought sheets, pillowcases, a kitchen counter unit with storage underneath it, two desks, and a double bed. I was careful to choose the smallest possible bed that would accommodate two people because our bedroom was small, and I wanted to fit in a writing desk. Our new bed was only four and a half feet wide, but George and I agreed it would be fine. No matter how big the bed, we always ended up sleeping close together in the middle. When we were done shopping, we bought dinner for Anya and the kids from the IKEA food court.

When we got back to the apartment, we were amazed and relieved to see an open parking spot by the curb just outside the building entrance. God was smiling on us. We asked the four older boys to come downstairs to help.

"You were gone for six hours!" Samuel chided us, as if our roles were reversed, and he was the parent. The fact that I had to tilt my head back to look up at my oldest son reinforced the illusion.

"It was that long?" I asked, genuinely surprised. "Sorry. We needed to get a lot of stuff."

The six of us went back and forth, transporting things in stages: curb to entrance, entrance to elevator, elevator to apartment. Once we finally got everything into the apartment, the limited floor space was a tangle of shopping bags and boxes of furniture that needed to be assembled. I couldn't wait to get started, but I knew I'd have to wait until tomorrow.

While the kids ate their late dinner, they told us about their day.

"Guess what?" Kiyoshi said. "We made some friends!"

"You did? Wow!" I said.

"Yeah, it's these two boys," Peter interrupted. "They're from Ukraine, but their mom is American, or something. I dunno."

"No, she's Ukrainian," Kiyoshi corrected him.

"Well, maybe, but she lived in America. So, yeah." Peter tossed his head, flinging his unruly hair out of his eyes.

"And we're going to meet them at the park again tomorrow!" Kiyoshi's eyebrows were raised, his dark eyes wide and dancing. He was making big gestures with his arms.

"That's amazing! I'm so happy for you!" I said. "What are their names?"

"Dima and Andriy," Kiyoshi said.

While George oversaw getting the kids ready for bed that night, I made up the four twin beds with the new sheets we had just bought. Once again, the camping mattress came to the rescue, as I used it to make a fifth bed on the floor. The five older kids all chose a spot and snuggled in. Even with the camping mattress, we were still one bed short, so I had three-year-old Isaac get in bed with eleven-year-old Peter. Peter loved little kids and had a winsome way with them.

Fifteen-year-old Samuel noticed and sat up. "Isaac, you want to sleep with me, right?" he said.

"No." Isaac was still sitting up and gave an emphatic shake of his head.

"C'mon," Samuel patted the bed beside him, "sleep with me!"

In answer, Isaac simply threw himself down on the bed beside Peter.

From then on, each night Isaac chose where he would sleep. The sweet-tempered baby of the family was a favorite with everyone. Some evenings, heated quarrels would break out among the older boys as they tried to influence Isaac's decision in their own favor. Though it put me on edge when they fought, I was heartened to see their love for their littlest brother.

This game of *Where Will Isaac Sleep?* became a new evening routine. The war in Ukraine had shattered so many of our family rhythms, and I knew I needed to reestablish them as quickly as possible. I never imagined not having enough beds would give us a new custom that would imbue our temporary quarters with a sense of home.

That night, with our new bed not yet set up, George and I slept on the couch. We could feel the wooden frame poking through the cushions. We shifted around, trying to find the least uncomfortable spots. It felt like we were camping out, but even so, we were grateful to have a place to call our own. As I drifted to sleep, I was excited for the next day, when I could continue the process of building a little nest for our family.

30

Building Our Nest

Saturday, March 19, 2023: Day 24 of War
Budapest, Hungary

Every day when I awoke in our new apartment, I experienced the same sense of well-being that had so surprised me the first morning. On this morning, I took a deep breath, held it for a few seconds and slowly let it out. It was still hard to believe I could breathe deeply again.

George had to leave to look at an office space for rent. Over the past three weeks, a handful of Ukrainian refugees had come to the forefront of the work he was doing. We realized the next phase would be to organize them into a team to serve other refugees. We'd need an office, and a church in Budapest was offering to rent one for us.

My goal for the day was simple: make the apartment comfortable and convenient for our family. The next order of business was to assemble the most important pieces of furniture. I asked Samuel and Kiyoshi, my two eldest, to assemble one item each. I decided to work on the bed George and I had gotten.

I went into our room and surveyed the scene. There was a large wardrobe against a far wall. Before I had moved the beds out, it had been blockaded behind them. The awkward position meant we would have to vault across the bed to reach the wardrobe. Alternatively, we could bend at a forty-five degree angle to crab walk around the foot of the bed under the low ceiling. This arrangement was not going to work.

Despite its size, the empty wardrobe was easy to slide across the slick laminate flooring. I put it in the only other place it would fit, behind the door. I pushed it as far away from the door as possible, but the sloping ceiling stopped it well before it cleared the area the door needed to open freely. Now the door would only open about eighteen inches. It wasn't ideal, but we could live with it. George and I were both skinny. *It's a good thing I'm not pregnant*, I thought wryly.

Next, I set to work assembling the bed. I looked through the wordless instruction booklet and chuckled at the cartoon figures illustrating having a second person help you and calling customer support. I was confident I could put this bed together on my own. And as soon as George went back to get the mattress that we hadn't been able to fit in the car with all the furniture, we'd have our own bed again.

I pulled the pieces out of the box. It was a soft, unfinished wood. Pine, if my guess was correct. I screwed them together as the instructions showed. It wasn't complicated, and soon I had a bed frame in the middle of the room.

That's when I noticed the problem. There was nothing to support a mattress. It was just a rectangular frame on legs with a short headboard. There was one beam running down the middle, but most of it was empty space. Something was missing.

I scanned the directions again, and I saw it: a little note that this item needed to be purchased along with another item. How had we missed that? George would have more shopping to do. In the meantime, I'd better unblock the bedroom door. It would be impossible to maneuver the other item through the partially barricaded entrance. I shifted the wardrobe until I could open the door completely.

Now the wardrobe was standing in the middle of the scanty floor space. There was barely room to move, and the thing was blocking two of the three skylights. I frowned. I'd transformed our sunny bedroom into a dark, awkward confine. Discouraged, I left the bedroom to check on the older boys' progress.

Samuel had finished assembling a shoe rack.

"Good job, Samuel!"

"What do you mean? It was easy," Samuel said.

"Okay, well, thank you. Could you put it in the entryway and put everyone's shoes on it, please?"

Now we wouldn't constantly be tripping over multiple pairs of footwear every time we tried to enter or leave the apartment.

Kiyoshi was still working on his project, a kitchen counter unit with shelving below. I'd given him a complicated project because he was our family's LEGO prodigy, but he had reached an impasse. I helped him figure out the problem and get back on track again.

I returned to our bedroom to keep working. As soon as I entered the room, the imposing presence of the massive wardrobe pushed back at me. I cringed. I wanted to flee. Our bedroom was supposed to be a sanctuary, but this cramped, shadowy space was the least restful place in the apartment. I was doing an awful job of creating a nest for our family.

George came back around lunchtime with guests: our Hungarian friend Imre and four Ukrainian ladies. Olya, Anya, and Tanya were all teammates from before the war, and Ira was the friend whom Yurii had evacuated from Bucha just minutes before Russian forces overran the neighborhood where she was hiding in a basement with her two sons.

These ladies would become the first members of the team we were forming to help Ukrainian refugees in Hungary. It was wonderful to welcome these friends into our new space. Even though the apartment floors were still clogged with the things we'd bought the day before and I was woefully unequipped to entertain, I was genuinely pleased to host them. We'd known each of these ladies for years, and they brought a feeling of home with them.

We hardly had any food in the apartment, since we'd spent all our time shopping for furniture the previous day. Kiyoshi was still busy with the counter unit, so I asked Samuel and Peter to buy lunch for everyone at a nearby shawarma stand. On hectic days in Kyiv, these wraps filled with tender sliced meat, veggies, and savory sauces had been an option I had sometimes used to cover a meal for the kids. I never had any trouble finding a volunteer to buy the food, because it was one of the boys' favorite treats. I was surprised when both Samuel and Peter objected.

"Uh, how are we supposed to order?" Samuel asked.

"Yeah, they don't speak English," Peter said.

"They might," I said hopefully. "And even if they don't, you can just point."

"Naw. I don't wanna," Peter said.

"Samuel?" I looked at my fifteen-year-old son.

"No."

"C'mon, just try it. We've got to learn to function here. There are ways to make yourself understood." I thought back to my early days in Ukraine before I had learned to speak the language. In order to communicate, sometimes I resorted to pointing, pantomiming, and indicating numbers on my fingers.

"Uh-uh." Samuel shook his head, looking down.

I was taken aback and a little puzzled. This was the boy who had tried to convince me to let him walk himself to and from school in first grade. He was always confident and independent, but right now he looked uncertain and scared.

If we'd had this conversation just a month before, I wouldn't have accepted no for an answer. But I realized the kids had been through enough. If they didn't want to figure out how to order food in a foreign language, I wasn't going to force them.

Despite my brave words, I could relate. I had invested nearly two decades in learning Ukrainian. It was by far the hardest language I'd ever studied, but I persevered and finally reached a comfortable level of fluency. Then, in a single day, all my years of work were annihilated. Now I had to start over from scratch—and everyone said Hungarian was even harder than Ukrainian. I wanted to cry and give up before I'd even begun.

But at least I knew how to manage in a place where I couldn't speak the language. My four older kids couldn't even remember a time before they knew how to speak Ukrainian. For them, linguistic helplessness was a new and frightening experience. Maybe I'd have to take a break to buy lunch myself. Even if I was practically clueless in Hungarian, I was adept at communication.

Imre, fluent in English and Hungarian, came to the rescue. "I could go with them and help them order."

"That would be great!" I said. "What do you think, boys?"

"Okay," Samuel said.

"Yeah, I guess," said Peter.

"Thanks so much," I said to Imre.

"No *probléma*!" he said cheerfully, using a humorous mix of English and Hungarian.

While they were gone, I got to listen in on George's conversation with the Ukrainian ladies. He spent most of his time in meetings now, and this was a rare opportunity for me to participate in one.

"Well, yeah, the apartment is a little small," he was saying in Ukrainian, "but Sharon's doing an amazing job. Thanks to her, it's already starting to feel like a home."

I wanted to argue that it was still a mess and had a long way to go, but this unexpected praise warmed and filled me. I would replay his words in my mind later when I felt discouraged by how slow my progress was.

The meeting was a brainstorming session about the best ways to help other refugees. When it was over, George made another trip to IKEA. Sadly, the part we needed for our bed was out of stock. There was an alternative, but it cost twice as much. We wanted to find the best deal we could, since we were spending our landlord's money, so we ended up camping out on the uneven couch for three more nights. When the item was still out of stock on the fourth day, we gave in and bought the more expensive option. We realized our generous landlord would have told us to spend the extra fifty bucks in order to get a good night's sleep.

By Thursday, March 24, the bareness of our fridge and pantry was becoming a real problem. We could eat takeout for only so long. There was a grocery store practically across the street from our apartment, but when it came to many of the foods that were staples for us, either I couldn't find them, or the quality was inferior to what we were used to.

In Ukraine, I had done almost all our grocery shopping online. I had favorites lists, and when we needed to restock, I just logged into my account, clicked a few buttons, and submitted my order. If I did this before noon, I'd have my groceries before dinner. No matter how massive the order, the delivery fee was always negligible. I'd heard Hungarian stores also had grocery delivery service, but I hadn't looked into it yet. So on this morning, George and I decided to make a big grocery run using our landlord's car.

It's always challenging learning where everything is in a new grocery store. When you're shopping in a new country, you also have to decipher labels in a foreign language and figure out how the food is organized in that country.

When I first moved to Ukraine, it took me a while to get used to the fact that the unsweetened cocoa powder I used for baking was not shelved near the flour and sugar. Instead, it was on the row with the coffee. It boggled my mind every time I needed to buy it, until someone finally pointed out that it was for making hot cocoa, which was a hot beverage like coffee.

We still hadn't learned these sorts of details in Hungary, and we spent a long time trying to find everything. It was especially hard to locate the dried beans, lentils, and chickpeas, because we never imagined they would be shelved by the fresh produce. I got out of breath as I power-walked with my heavily laden cart up one aisle and down the next, but I forced myself to keep going, rushing to find each item on my list.

We finally checked out with two fully loaded carts. Besides dried legumes, we had basmati rice, gluten-free pasta, tofu, unroasted buckwheat for making gluten-free flour, and so many other things. We even got toys for the kids and housewares for the kitchen and bathroom.

When we got back to the apartment, George left right away for the office. The three older boys all came downstairs to help me take everything inside. When I unpacked the toys, five-year-old Andrew was ecstatic about the LEGO Duplo set with a steam locomotive. I spent a long time creating a system for storing all the groceries in our small kitchen.

Later that day, I assembled my desk in our bedroom. By then, I had managed to figure out an innovative arrangement for our bedroom furniture. By pushing one edge of the bed close under the sloping ceiling, I was able to redeem a huge amount of the floor space wasted by the low clearance. This allowed me to move the wardrobe so it wasn't blocking the door anymore. It also made room for my desk, which I placed directly under the skylights. The final effect was a cozy, inviting space, a perfect sanctuary for George and me. There was even just enough room for me to unroll a yoga mat and do a workout.

I surveyed the rest of the apartment with satisfaction. We had almost all the furniture we needed. All we lacked were two benches so everyone could fit around the dining table. There wasn't much storage space, but we had so few things that it wasn't a problem.

For example, one of the wardrobes in the kids' bedroom had six cubbyholes, each roughly a cubic foot. I had assigned one to each child, because the full extent of each boy's collection of clothing could fit inside one cubbyhole. Initially, I considered buying more clothes, but I quickly realized that was impractical, given our space constraints. It was also unnecessary. The apartment washing machine was so small that I had to do laundry every single day just to keep up. Because the clothes we wore one day were washed the next, each member of the family could get by with just two changes of clothing—three, if the weather turned cold and humid and things took longer than a day to air dry. (Clothes dryers are a luxury in Europe, and our apartment didn't have one.) Since we each had at least three changes of weather-appropriate clothes, we truly had everything we needed.

Our apartment was now cozy and fully functional. I really had found a way to make the space work for us. It had taken me nine days.

31

High, Low, Buffalo

Saturday, March 19, 2022: Day 24 of War
Budapest, Hungary

On the first Saturday after we moved into the apartment, George took our kids, Olya and her brother, and Ira and her sons to a huge sports store. George told everyone to pick out whatever they wanted. Money was flowing into our bank account from concerned friends and churches who wanted to ensure we were taken care of, and it only seemed right to share our abundance with our refugee friends.

George and the kids got back after dark, full of things to tell me. After we got the boys settled for the night, George and I took the dog for his evening walk. The war had decimated so many of our routines, but now that Jack was with us again, we could resume this daily ritual.

For several years, George and I had been in the habit of walking the dog every night after the kids were in bed. Conversation was effortless as we strolled. It was the main way we connected, and one of my favorite parts of each day. In the midst of the crazy that was our new reality, this piece of continuity with our old life kept us grounded.

The next day was Sunday, March 20. One of our broken routines was our long-standing habit of gathering for church on Sundays. Both George and I had grown up in church-going families. Regularly getting together with our spiritual family had always been part of the fabric of our lives. It was important to us to pass this heritage on to our children. However, in the weeks since the invasion, I hadn't always known what day of the week it was, let alone where to find a church with a service in a language we could understand.

This was our first Sunday as a newly settled family. We were keeping track of the days of the week again, and George decided to attend the service of a church that was part of our international network. They had English translation but no youth group, so I stayed at the apartment with the kids. I comforted myself with the knowledge that Jon was coming to Budapest that evening to lead another Ukrainian worship service.

That night, George, the kids, and I all attended. It wasn't the same as the Sunday gatherings we had enjoyed in Kyiv with our close-knit circle of friends, but it was still comforting.

The next morning was March 21, the fourth Monday since the start of the war. Mondays used to mean going back to school after the weekend, but that was another habit the war had taken from us.

On the Thursday morning when the full-scale invasion began, Kyivans were jolted awake by explosions. Teachers quickly notified parents not to attempt to bring their children to school. Classes would resume on Monday, March 14. In the meantime, everyone was to stay home, stay safe, and wait for victory. It sounded like a great formula, but I thought they were awfully optimistic to plan to reopen schools in just two and a half weeks.

As the days passed, I monitored the school chat groups for new assignments. I was grateful there hadn't been any, because our life had been too unsettled for homework. But today, Kyiv schools were relaunching, just a week behind schedule. It was impressive, given that the city had been in real danger of falling to Russian forces.

To the amazement of the entire world, the Ukrainian defenders had managed to stop the enemy's advance on their capital. Even ordinary citizens stepped up to repel the invaders. A young man who attended our church sent us a video of him and a group of friends making Molotov cocktails. He said they would attack the

Russians after nightfall. The next morning, we texted him to make sure he was okay. When he didn't reply, I had feared the worst. Hours passed before he finally responded that he was fine.

The Russian army was ultimately forced into a humiliating retreat. Now, with the capital city securely under Ukrainian control, Kyiv schools were starting instruction again. However, because of the constant threat of rocket strikes, classes would be online. COVID had primed everyone for distance learning, and teachers and parents weren't about to let a little thing like a war keep them from educating the next generation of Ukrainians.

Imagining our kids' classmates abandoning their studies to race from their homes to the nearest bomb shelter whenever the sirens went off made me realize how fortunate we were. Budapest was a safe haven—but that didn't mean we always felt safe. I jumped at every loud noise, and I wasn't the only one who did. One day we heard a sharp crack outside the apartment. Five-year-old Andrew ran to me, his forehead furrowed and eyebrows tilted up in the middle.

"Mommy, is the war here in Hungary?"

"No, sweetie." I hugged him. "The war's not here."

"How do you know?"

"I just know. Putin wouldn't attack Hungary."

"Then what was that noise?"

"I don't know, but you don't have to worry. There's no war here." I stroked his back as I held him. I sounded confident, but I was reassuring myself as much as him.

While we didn't have the threat of air raids keeping us from school, we had another problem: we still hadn't connected to the internet in our apartment. The previous tenants had left with the router, and it took about two weeks to convince the internet service provider to connect us again. In the meantime, we had to rely on cellular data for all our internet needs. With George gone at the office all day, the kids and I had only one phone with cellular data. I gave up on the idea of making school happen that first Monday and instead spent the morning organizing the apartment.

By Tuesday, March 22, I realized our life was slowly assuming some order. In the mornings, George would leave to meet with people about relief work and refugee care. I would stay at the apartment with the kids and find useful things for all of us to do. On this day, George had given me the idea of using my phone as a hotspot so the kids could connect to their online lessons.

The four school-aged boys sat around the dining table with all the laptops and devices we had, plus notebooks, pens, and pencils. Their textbooks were available online. I activated my phone's hotspot function and placed it on a windowsill to get a stronger signal from the closest cell tower. Everyone managed to connect from their devices. We were officially back in school.

Then, before anyone got properly started, the internet on my phone stopped working. Other than cell phone calls and SMS through my cellular service provider, we were cut off from the world.

"School's not going to work today," I said. "Let's go to the park!"

"No, not again!" Kiyoshi protested.

"What do you mean? You love the park!" I was confused.

"No, it's stupid, and I don't have any friends."

"Well, the best way to make friends is to go out so you can meet people."

"No."

"Remember when you met Dima and Andriy?"

"Yeah. Why'd they have to move back to Ukraine? It's so dumb."

"I know. I'm so sorry." My heart ached for him.

Though Ukrainian by birth, Dima and Andriy's mom had relinquished her Ukrainian citizenship for an American passport after she married her ex-husband, an American. She lived with her sons in Ukraine, but they had been in Hungary for nearly three months prior to the war. When the invasion started, she had almost exhausted the ninety days she was allowed in the EU without a visa.

As an American citizen, she couldn't apply for refugee status, since the US was not at war. But as a Ukrainian woman, she had no home or relatives to receive her in the US. She did the only thing she could. She took her sons back to the apartment she owned in Ukraine. Our kids became friends just days before she and her boys had to leave Hungary. Kiyoshi and Peter were devastated.

"Maybe you can make new friends," I offered. "There are always Ukrainian kids at the park."

"No."

"C'mon, Kiyoshi. You can't just sit around the apartment all the time."

"No. It'll be boring."

"Take your new rollerblades."

"No, you'll make me wear protective gear. That's so stupid. I'm not gonna fall."

"Kiyoshi."

"No."

I sighed. "Take a sketchpad and draw. That would be fun, right?"

He scoffed and refused to answer.

"Okay . . . well, whether you have fun or not is up to you, but we are going to the park, and you are coming with us."

Everyone else gathered their things, excited to use the new gear George had gotten them at the sports store. Kiyoshi just slumped on the couch. Once everyone was ready, he silently picked himself up, grabbed his sketchpad and pencil, and slouched to the door.

I breathed a sigh of relief. He was taller and heavier than I was, and if he had insisted on isolating himself in his pain, there wasn't much I could have done about it, but that wasn't the kind of existence I wanted for him. I couldn't let him start down that path. We were going to have to find a new normal in Hungary. Moping in the apartment wasn't a good beginning.

Once we got to the park, we ended up at the little skate park. Except for Kiyoshi, all the older boys were on rollerblades. Five-year-old Andrew had a scooter, and three-year-old Isaac had a little balance bike. He quickly got the hang of it and was soon zipping around faster than I could run to keep up. I got out of breath and light-headed, so I took a seat to watch over the kids. Everyone was too busy having fun with their new wheels to think about going to the playground. Kiyoshi positioned himself on a grassy hill to draw.

When we finally headed back to the apartment, we were all happy, even Kiyoshi. For me, the outing had been more tiring than fun, but I was gratified to be establishing a habit of outdoor playtime.

Getting back into a regular cooking schedule was more challenging. That night, I improvised. I made rice, opened some cans of seasoned beans, and put together a salad. It didn't feel like cooking. It felt like cheating—especially after all the nutritionally balanced, made-from-scratch meals I had always prepared in Ukraine. Surprisingly, the food was a huge hit with most of the kids.

"This is so good, Mommy!"

"Yum! What did you put in these beans?"

"I missed salad!"

"Can we have this every week?"

"Yeah, you have to make this again!"

Isaac was the only one who wasn't excited. The baby of the family just wanted to eat plain rice.

George got back before we had finished.

"Hi, Daddy!" all the kids greeted him excitedly.

"Hi." Instead of joining us at the table, George went into our bedroom.

I could hear him moving things around, and the wardrobe door shut noisily.

"Why don't you come eat with us?" I called.

"Not now." He was uncharacteristically terse.

I got up and joined him in our bedroom. "What's wrong?"

"Have you seen my phone charger?"

"No."

"I need it. My phone's about to die."

"Why don't you just plug it into the charging station behind the TV and come eat?"

"I need my phone!"

"George?"

"Yeah?" He stopped his search long enough to shoot me an irritated glance.

"We haven't seen you much. I think it would be better if you just put your phone away when you come home. I mean, of course you can answer it if it rings, but . . . maybe you don't need to have it right next to you 24/7?"

"Okay," he sighed heavily.

I was relieved that he acquiesced so easily. With so many people relying on him, it must have felt risky not to have his phone where he could see the screen at all times, but I was worried about the long-term effect on his mental health and his relationship with our children.

We rejoined the kids. After plugging his phone in behind the TV, George got a plate of food and sat beside me on the couch. The kids were using the apartment's four chairs, step stool, and barstool. That left the couch for George and me. Even though we couldn't all sit around the table, we were sharing a meal. Dinner as a family had been a daily ritual before the war, but I had been struggling to make it happen since our lives had been upended.

The rest of the evening was like a fun family night, another rhythm the war had disrupted. George quickly got into the spirit.

"Hey, guys," he said, "let's do *High, Low, Buffalo*!" This conversation activity had been a weekly staple at our family meals. Everyone shared a recent happy event (high), disappointment (low), and weird experience (buffalo).

After dinner, we revived another family tradition by playing together. Samuel had bought a game when we were staying in Debrecen. For two weeks, he had dreamed of getting all of us to play. It was in Hungarian, but Samuel was familiar with the Ukrainian version and was able to teach us. Soon we were easily differentiating the Hungarian cards—*Gyorstüzelő, Börtön, Nem Talált!*—with the aid of the illustrations. Andrew and Isaac each paired up with an older partner, and we all laughed as we played.

The next morning, Samuel asked to go to the store on his own before we started school. He was secretive about the purpose of his errand, but I was pleased to see his natural confidence and independence back. I happily gave him permission. When he returned, he convinced us to play his game again and surprised us with snacks he had just bought with his own money.

After we finished the game, I sent Andrew and Isaac into the kids' bedroom to play while the older boys did school. My phone's internet connection was working again, and the boys were actually able to get some assignments done using my phone as a hotspot.

It was Wednesday, March 23, day 28 of the war. It still felt like our life was a bag of marbles that had been flung and shattered across a cold, stone floor, but amazingly, our daily existence was already starting to look normal.

32

Regaining Balance

Tuesday, March 22: Day 27 of War
Budapest, Hungary

On the day my cellular data stopped working, cutting me off from the wider world on the internet, I called George to explain the situation.

"I'm supposed to have my first counseling call with Melanie's therapist today," I told him. "But I'm not going to be able to get online for it."

"Dang. That's a bummer! Is there anything I can do?"

"Yeah, could you write Melanie to explain and ask her to contact her therapist and cancel?"

"Okay, sure."

"Thanks. Love you!"

"Love you too."

Later that afternoon, as I was assembling furniture, my phone rang. I was puzzled to see an unfamiliar US number. I answered and was surprised to find Melanie's therapist on the other end.

"Um, you're calling long-distance?" I asked. *How much is this costing her? It can't be cheap. Should I offer to reimburse her?*

"It's okay," she reassured me.

"Oh, well . . . thank you. I don't know what to say."

She gave me a free, hour-long session. Just a few days earlier, I had desperately felt the need for this conversation, but now that it was happening, it was hard to find things to talk about. The anxiety was gone. The mind-bending grief had subsided.

"I don't know why I feel so normal," I finally said. "All that changed is that we moved into an apartment and got our dog back."

I wasn't being ironic. Our lives had been so decimated that permanent housing and being reunited with one of our three pets didn't seem like enough to restore balance.

"Well, research shows that the biggest factor that influences emotional health for refugees is having a stable place to live," the therapist told me.

"Really?"

"Yeah."

"Oh, well, that makes sense now." I recalled being able to breathe normally again after spending our first night in our new place. "But sometimes I feel guilty for feeling so normal. I see other people, and they're totally overwhelmed. They're hardly functional because of all that's going on in Ukraine. I feel bad for not feeling like them."

"How would it help if you did feel that way?"

There was a long pause while I considered her question. "Hmm. Yeah, I see what you mean. It wouldn't help at all. I wouldn't be able to take care of the kids. George wouldn't be able to do what he's doing."

"Right. You're very resilient, and that's a good thing."

The therapist taught me several relaxation and mindfulness exercises. Because I was already so calm, I couldn't tell if they made a difference, but I hoped they'd help me be a more patient, compassionate parent.

The previous day, I had lost my temper and actually yelled at Kiyoshi, who was being extraordinarily rude and disrespectful. Through all the loss and chaos of the last month, the kids had shown amazing resilience. They had helped when asked, had been kind and patient with their little brothers, and had been quick to adapt to all our changing circumstances. It seemed like everyone was weathering the changes well.

But I knew more had to be going on below the surface. The confrontation with Kiyoshi gave me a glimpse of that turmoil, both in my son and myself. Later, I initiated a heart-to-heart conversation with him. I affirmed that he was dealing with a lot and apologized for raising my voice, and he acknowledged that his attitude had been out of line.

The day after the counseling session was a strange one for me. It was March 23, day 28 of the war. For the previous four weeks, I hadn't been sleeping enough, but I had been highly functional, hardly ever feeling drowsy, though I knew my body had to be exhausted. But this day, I was too groggy to keep my eyes open.

While the kids were doing school, I sat down on the couch to monitor them. My eyes felt heavy, and before I realized what was happening, they had slipped shut. My torso slowly folded forward until my shoulders were resting on my knees and my head was hanging down toward the floor between them.

Even in this state, I was aware of what was going on around me. I could hear and understand the kids' conversations, but I couldn't respond. I was trapped in a twilight fog of exhaustion. I lost all track of time.

"Mommy? Mommy? Mommy. Mommy. Mommy. Mommy!" I could sense a child right beside me.

"Shhhh! Mommy's sleeping. Leave her alone," someone else said.

One of my children needed me. I had to come back. With great effort, I willed my eyes to open. I blinked slowly several times, trying to get things in focus. I wiped a bit of drool from the corner of my mouth.

"Huh?" I mumbled groggily.

"Mommy? I'm hungry." Five-year-old Andrew was the child beside me.

"Okay," I sighed. "I'll make lunch."

I dragged myself to the kitchen and improvised a simple meal.

As long as I was on my feet, I was functional, but twice more that day I had the bewildering experience of sitting down and involuntarily folding in half and passing out. Maybe the relaxation techniques the therapist had taught me were allowing me to let down my guard enough to finally experience the accumulated exhaustion of the past four weeks.

Either that, or I'm pregnant, but I knew the latter was nearly impossible.

Thankfully, I didn't have to leave the apartment all day, because I was in no condition to do so. However, we had a stream of people come to us.

First, a pastor from the church George had attended on Sunday stopped by. He brought the church handyman to advise us on repairs, improvements, and home appliance installations that we wanted done. The handyman didn't speak any English, so the pastor accompanied him to interpret. I explained what we needed, and we set a date for him to return.

Later, a man from an internet service provider came to get us connected. But he left without doing anything. I wasn't exactly sure why, since he didn't speak English—the problem had something to do with a "*kábel*."

Right after he left, there was another ring on the apartment intercom that connected to the building entrance. We weren't expecting anyone else. I answered hesitantly, wondering who it was and if I'd be able to understand them and communicate.

"*Allo?*" I said, hoping this was the right way to answer the phone in Hungarian.

"*Helló*," a man said.

Oh, so that's how you answer the phone here, I noted to myself.

"Deleeveri," he continued, in heavily accented English.

I guess he has a delivery for us. "Ah, ah . . . um . . . *jó*," I stumbled over my words, trying to find an appropriate response in Hungarian. I pushed the button on the phone to let him into the building. A few minutes later, he was at our door with a medium-sized box.

"*Köszönöm*," I thanked him in Hungarian before he left.

"What's that?" Kiyoshi asked.

"I think it's the blender Daddy ordered."

"We got a new blender?" James said, his eyes wide with amazement.

This was an exciting moment. Our family had relied heavily on a high-powered blender for the last decade to support our very specific diet. When Kiyoshi was still a baby, George had begun to experience debilitating fatigue that got worse and worse with time. Eventually, when I was pregnant with James, we switched to a raw vegan diet in a desperate bid to find relief for him.

It worked like a miracle.

So for two and a half years we subsisted on salads, nuts and seeds, smoothies, and soups made from blended raw veggies. Ultimately, we figured out that George had celiac disease, the most extreme form of gluten intolerance. After that, we started to eat cooked foods again, but our trusty blender continued to provide the background soundtrack for much of our kitchen work.

I learned to use it to make gluten-free, sourdough batters for all our bread and to grind gluten-free flour for all our other baking. Besides that, smoothies were still a staple, and our three youngest kids especially loved them.

When we found ourselves displaced, I quickly identified the basic tools I needed to feed the family. I bought a decent chef's knife, a serrated paring knife, and a cutting board. The apartment came with a set of pots and pans. We could make do without all the kitchen gadgets we had been used to. It had taken years to acquire them, and there was no way we could replace them right away. Besides, we would be going back to Ukraine soon, so it didn't make sense to buy new things. We would just rough it until we were able to go back home.

George had the opposite mindset. Thanks to the generosity of many churches and friends, we actually did have money to replace anything we wanted. Even though we were telling people we'd only be in Hungary for half a year, George wasn't living like our situation was merely a temporary disruption. He immediately started rebuilding our life in tangible ways. One of the most dramatic was the speed at which he replaced many of the things we had left behind.

Within less than a month of moving into our new apartment, our household would be back up and running the way we were used to with a high-powered blender, a great food processor, and a steam cleaner. The kids would also have new toys to play with to help them cope with the loss of the things they had left in Kyiv.

That evening, George got back at 7 pm. Because of the strange sleeping spells I'd had all day, I still hadn't fed the kids dinner, but George had wonderful news. Our landlord had offered to treat us to a meal from a Mexican restaurant of which he was part owner.

We looked up the menu online, and even George and I were able to find things we could eat. We managed to place a telephone order with someone who spoke a bit of English, and George picked up our food. We all sat down to dinner around 9 pm. It felt like a party, and the food was so good, we decided we had a new favorite Mexican restaurant.

33

What Makes a Refugee?

Thursday, March 24, 2022: Day 29 of War
Budapest, Hungary

"I met one of our neighbors in the elevator this morning." George had just returned to the apartment at the end of the day.

"Oh, really?" I said.

"Yeah, she spoke some English. I introduced myself and told her who we were, and she asked if we'd joined the building's Facebook group yet."

"The building has a Facebook group?"

"Yeah! So I got on it and introduced us. I said we were from Ukraine and posted a picture of our family, that one we took on the steps of our apartment in Kyiv."

"I love that picture."

"And a bunch of people commented to welcome us! Some of them offered help if we need it. One neighbor wants to have you over for coffee, and she invited us to go rock climbing with them on Saturday."

"What? Rock climbing?"

"Yeah."

"I can't believe it! That sounds like fun."

George and I liked adventurous dates. The previous summer we'd done a treetop ropes course, and for Valentine's Day, we'd taken a couple's lesson at an indoor rock-climbing complex. We'd decided to start going regularly, but ten days later, Russia invaded. We hadn't given a thought to rock climbing since, but here it was. It felt like a sign.

We agreed to take our neighbors up on their invitation to go rock climbing in two days at an old quarry just outside Budapest.

The next day was Friday, March 25. While the kids were having lunch, I used Facebook Messenger to contact the neighbor who had invited me over for coffee. Her name was Fruzsi, and she told me I could come over right away and bring all the kids. When I replied that they were eating, she came over to our apartment instead.

She was a slender, active-looking woman, a little taller and a little younger than I. She was bubbly and energetic and spoke excellent English. As soon as Jack heard her voice, he came running from our bedroom, barking. I was embarrassed and apologetic, but our neighbor didn't seem at all alarmed. In fact, she quickly made friends with Jack. After greeting him and me, she engaged with the kids.

"Hey, kids! Are you having lunch? Is it yummy?"

"Hi! My name is Andrew! I'm five. How old are you?"

Fruzsi and I laughed, and to my surprise, instead of deflecting the question, our friendly neighbor happily told Andrew how old she was. "I'm thirty-six."

I liked her immediately.

"Would you like some tea?" I asked.

"Oh, no, thanks! I just came over for a moment to meet you," she smiled. "Come over to our place when you're done eating. We're just down the hall."

"Really? Okay, we'll see you soon!"

When the boys finished lunch, the older ones wanted to work on school assignments, so I only took the three youngest with me.

Fruzsi's apartment was decorated in a clean, modern style. One wall of the living room was made of floor-to-ceiling windows that opened onto a private balcony filled with plants, a living oasis in the middle of the city. Fruzsi introduced us to a tall, athletic-looking man with dark hair. "This is my husband, Viktor."

As Viktor and I exchanged pleasantries, Fruzsi addressed the kids.

"Would you like to play with toys?"

"Yeah!"

"Go in that room," she pointed, "and see if there's anything you like. My kids are still at kindergarten, but you can play with their toys." Hungarian kindergartens educate children for several years before first grade.

I followed Fruzsi into the kitchen. She offered me a drink, and we sat facing each other across the table.

"So, how are you?" she asked. I could tell she wasn't just making conversation. She really wanted to know. Her interest and concern caught me by surprise and connected with my heart.

"It hasn't been easy." I looked down at my glass as I considered my next words. I felt safe with this kind stranger. "The first three weeks we moved around a lot. That was really hard. It's been great having a stable place to live, and we love the park. Budapest is a beautiful city. If it weren't for how we ended up here, we'd love it . . . but we really miss Ukraine."

"Do you have everything you need?"

"Mostly. We've bought a lot of things. But now that the weather's getting warmer, I need to find us some different shoes and clothes. All we have is winter stuff."

"There's a shoe store and a nice used clothing store nearby. I'll send you the links."

"That would be great! I guess I'll need to learn how to use the bus. Where do you buy tickets?"

"You can use Budapest public transport for free since you're refugees."

"Well, we're not really refugees. We're Americans."

"Do you have a home in America?"

"No."

"So, your only home was in Ukraine?"

"Yeah."

"Then you're refugees." Fruzsi's tone implied this should be obvious to anyone.

"But I don't know about riding the bus for free. I don't think that applies to us."

"What do you mean? You're in exactly the same situation as everyone else who came from Ukraine! Do you have any Ukrainian documents?"

"We have our Ukrainian residency cards."

"Just show them that. They'll let you ride for free."

"You really think so?"

"Of course!"

This conversation was the beginning of a long process of finding my identity as an American displaced from Ukraine. I wrestled with the question of what makes one a refugee. Is it your documents, or your heart?

For over two years after we fled Ukraine, I refused to call our family refugees, especially after I heard some Ukrainian friends complaining when an American claimed that status. But when I tried to come up with a different label, it got too complicated. "Displaced American expats who have no other home in the world besides the one they left behind in Ukraine" wasn't easy to say in one breath. Eventually, I realized, while we might not have been refugees on paper, we were refugees in every other way.

I know we are in a different category than Ukrainians. We hold passports to a country that is not at war and have the option of going there. However, the nationality of our documents does not come close to giving the full picture. As a family, we never had a home in the US. In so many ways, our story was identical to the classic refugee experience.

We fled our home and were forced to rebuild our lives wherever we could. In our case, that meant applying for residency in a foreign country, trying to learn a different language, and figuring out a new way to educate our kids, just like all our friends who were "real" refugees. And while I know the emotional anguish we experienced had different nuances from that of our Ukrainian friends, I don't think it was any less profound.

Ukraine may not have been my home by birth, but it was my home by choice. That choice came at an enormous cost. It meant I didn't get to watch my little brother grow up, and I couldn't be there for my college best friend when she was dying. But even though I had to make those sacrifices, I never regretted my decision to live in Ukraine. Though I ached to be closer to my sister and would have liked living near my parents, though I was sad my kids had to grow up without their grandparents, I never doubted Ukraine was where we were supposed to be. Even though for years I felt dehumanized by my inability to communicate in Ukrainian with the same beauty and nuance I used in English, I never once thought of moving back to the US. It wasn't home anymore.

Because the choice to make Ukraine my home was so costly, I was deeply committed. I was there on purpose, and I was passionate about it. I had invested a staggering amount to move my life. The acclimation process was a long, dark, uphill battle through thorns and brambles. Sometimes I collapsed on my face in the rain and the mud, completely demoralized. But I always managed to claw my way forward again until, eventually, the clouds cleared, and I realized I was on top of the mountain. I could see for miles in every direction, and it was breathtaking.

I chose to wrap my heart around Ukraine years before I fell in love with her. After finally achieving my goal of feeling at home, it was like having a limb amputated when I was forced to leave. I don't think I will ever fully recover.

34

A Vacation from Reality

Saturday, March 26, 2022: Day 31 of War
Budapest, Hungary

The next day was the day Viktor and Fruzsi had invited us to go rock climbing. We still had our landlord's car, but it couldn't hold all of us. While George took the other kids, Samuel, James, and I planned to use public transport.

As we left the apartment, I remembered the paralyzing fear I had experienced nineteen years earlier when learning to use public transport in Ukraine. I hadn't been able to speak the language yet, and in that time before smartphones with GPS and language translation apps, I had been terrified of getting lost and being unable to communicate to find my way home.

Besides that, the public transport system was overwhelming. I hadn't even used the bus when I lived in California, and my new home had buses, trolleybuses, trams, subways, and ubiquitous "route taxis"—large vans that followed set routes. Their drivers only stopped when flagged down or when a passenger specifically asked to be let off. The route taxis were the most common and convenient means of transport. Unfortunately, they required both a command of the language and the ability to make oneself heard over the crush of the other passengers. I possessed neither.

Even after I memorized key phrases to tell the driver where to stop, I was helpless if I got pushed to the back of the taxi van. No matter how many times I called out, the driver could never hear me, and the passengers around me never passed my request forward. Sometimes I rode more than a quarter of a mile (400 meters) past my destination, trapped until another passenger bellowed at the driver to pull over for their stop. This experience always traumatized me, and I'd backtrack on foot with tears trickling down my face. It took me over a year to finally master the art of drawing a deep breath and shouting from my diaphragm to be heard from the back of a route taxi, but eventually I could do it like a native Kyivan.

Long before the war started, the government had modernized the route-taxi service, requiring the drivers to stop only at designated bus stops. They started to operate exactly like normal buses. This made riding them far less complicated, but I missed the old days when you could hop on and off wherever you wanted.

All these memories flooded my mind as we set out on public transport that Saturday morning in Budapest, but I knew we'd have no problems. Two decades of technological advancements had transformed the way people navigated. Google Maps had been my trusty companion for the last few years in Ukraine, and it worked just as well in Hungary. I simply entered our destination and selected the public transport option, and the app showed me all the possible subway, bus, tram, and train lines I could take. It even provided maps for the segments I would need to walk.

I selected the fastest route, and Samuel, James, and I walked to the closest subway station. We transferred from the subway to a commuter train for traveling short distances beyond the city limits. As we rode, I watched the little blue dot on my phone that represented us moving along the route. It was so simple. I didn't have to count the number of stops or try to decipher the Hungarian announcements on the loudspeakers.

When we got off the train, George met us and drove us to the quarry. It was a large, flat area filled with trees and surrounded on three sides by sheer cliffs. We saw a number of climbing parties in multiple places along the wall. Viktor and Fruzsi were there with their preschool-aged son and daughter. They had set out a picnic blanket and snacks. Our boys were amusing themselves nearby.

George, Samuel, Peter, and I opted for climbing lessons. Viktor led us to the wall, where we found Fruzsi getting ready. She was wearing a harness with one end of a rope attached to it. The rest of the rope lay coiled at her feet.

Nervously, I noted that there was no safety rope attached to the wall. There was no way we were going to climb without a safety rope. Viktor donned a harness, looped part of Fruzsi's rope through a small metal object, then clipped both the loop of rope and the metal thing to his harness. When he finished, he nodded at Fruzsi. I watched, fascinated. I could see he was preparing to belay—to operate the brake on the safety rope—but I didn't see how the rope was going to help when it was lying on the ground.

Before I could ask, Fruzsi quickly climbed to a spot above our heads. She attached a large carabiner clip to her safety rope and snapped it to a metal ring that had been drilled into the rock. Viktor immediately pulled out most of the slack, leaving just enough for Fruzsi to climb a bit higher to another metal ring, where they repeated the process.

If she lost her grip, she would only fall as far as the highest metal ring below her before the rope caught her. It was a clever way to get the safety line in place, but I wouldn't have wanted to be in her position—she would get some nasty scrapes and bruises if she fell. I was impressed by her confidence.

She had almost reached the top when she stopped. She seemed at a loss. She looked down at us. "I'm scared," she said.

I held my breath. There wasn't anything we could do to help her. After several long moments, she finally found a new set of footholds and handholds. Soon she reached the top, clipped the safety rope to the final metal ring, and rappelled down, removing the clips from all the lower rings as she descended.

Samuel volunteered to go first. Fruzsi helped him put on a harness, instructed him in the necessary safety precautions, and taught him basic climbing technique. He scaled the wall quickly and was soon back on the ground with the rest of us. Peter went second. He had a little difficulty and gave up less than half-way to the top.

I volunteered next. None of us had the proper footwear for rock climbing, but the sneakers I'd gotten at the shoe store Fruzsi had recommended the day before weren't an awful option. I cringed when I saw how my new favorite pair of shoes was getting covered in fine dust, but when I considered that my only other option was a pair of winter boots, I knew I'd made the right choice.

I made quick progress until I got to the spot near the top that had been a problem for Fruzsi. I understood what had troubled her. I found myself clinging, insect-like, to the side of the cliff, unable to advance. Everything I tried to grab was too small for my fingers to grip, and when I tried to push myself up with a new foothold, my feet just scrabbled against the wall, unable to find a divot deep enough to offer support.

There had to be a way. If I kept trying, I'd find it. I was not giving up. I was going all the way to the top. I kept searching for a path across this smoother section of rock, but my muscles were getting tired. It was getting harder and harder to hold on. As much as I hated it, I was going to have to admit defeat.

I looked over my shoulder and down at Fruzsi, who was belaying. "I don't think I can do this. I'm going to come back down."

"Don't give up," she said. "I've got you. Just sit in the harness and rest for a few minutes."

That sounded like cheating, but she was the expert. I let go and let the harness take all my weight. I felt ridiculous hanging in the air above everyone's heads. I should do something useful. I scanned the wall, searching for indentations. After a minute or two, I finally spotted two for my feet and one that could be a handhold. I memorized their positions and rehearsed in my mind the movements I would need to get past this tricky section.

"I'm ready. I'm going to try again," I called down.

"Okay, I've got you!" Fruzsi called up.

I got back into position. Using the moves I had rehearsed and every ounce of my strength and willpower, I was able to climb a little higher and pull myself onto a ledge that could support my whole body.

"I did it!" I whooped. I could hardly believe it.

Compared to what I had just conquered, the rest was easy, and I was soon tapping the top of the cliff in victory and rappelling back down. It was only after I got all the way to the bottom that I realized I'd forgotten to look at the view.

George went next. He barely paused at the difficult section, easily finding the footholds and handholds he needed by stretching his long arms and legs. He was soon back on the ground with the rest of us.

Before leaving, we explored the quarry floor and hiked up to the rim. I finally got to see the view I had forgotten to admire. There was Budapest below us, stretching all the way to the horizon. It was impressive.

Later that night, after the kids were settled, I was stunned to realize that while we were at the quarry, I hadn't thought once about the war in Ukraine or everything that had happened to us. I had been too focused on the immediate physical challenges of climbing and hiking to give a thought to the greater difficulties facing us. It was as if I had been able to relax my grip, take a look around, and inhale huge lungfuls of fresh air.

I wasn't seeking an escape from reality, but after a month of living and breathing the war every waking moment, it had been profoundly therapeutic to experience half a day of freedom, to feel like we were just normal people enjoying a Saturday outdoors with friends, to forget that we were displaced persons with no idea when—or if—we could return home.

While we had been enjoying time unplugged from the broader world, momentous events were taking place. I recorded one in my journal entry that night:

Today was a milestone in what George has been doing. There was a delivery of twenty tons of aid from our warehouse in Krakow . . . to our warehouse in Ternopil . . . using one of our really big trucks. This was the first delivery and shows that the system is working. We anticipate regular shipments now. The plan is for Ukrainian drivers from all across the country to come pick up the aid in Ternopil and distribute it around the country.

More than showing the system was working, this success proved George's efforts were having significant, real-world impact. After weeks of preparation, everything had come together. Now food and hygiene products were on their way to the people who needed them most. It was amazing to think my husband had been one of the main architects behind this project.

In comparison, I felt insignificant. For the last few years, our home had been the hub for much of our missionary work. As the hostess, I got to be right in the middle of it all. Side-by-side, George and I did English clubs, leadership training, and Bible discussion groups. After having worked together so closely before the war, I found it hard to watch from the sidelines now. When

I expressed these feelings, George didn't feel like my role was insignificant at all.

He looked straight into my eyes, his gentle blue eyes intense. "You are the most resilient woman I know. I couldn't have done everything I've done if it weren't for that."

In the coming months, I would replay his words in my mind whenever I felt guilty about not doing enough.

35

WHAT'S WRONG WITH ME?

Friday, March 25, 2022: Day 30 of War
Budapest, Hungary

The night before we went rock climbing, as I was getting ready for bed, I had a nagging feeling something wasn't right in my body. I didn't know what to make of my unease. I paused to reflect, then I picked up my phone and checked my calendar. I was on day thirty-nine of my cycle. My period was over a week late.

I felt an immediate tightness in my stomach and a nervous constriction in my chest. How was this possible? With the chaos of the last month, George and I had only been intimate twice, and we used a contraceptive the one time there was a possibility of my getting pregnant.

The panic I felt wasn't because I didn't love babies. After our sixth child weaned himself, I had longed for a seventh. I had ached to nurse another newborn, to inhale his sweet fragrance, to nuzzle the downy softness of his delicate skin. But I was already forty-one years old, and when I conceived a few months later, I miscarried. I realized the baby-bearing stage of life was behind me. I needed to embrace a new phase.

That had been two years ago. Since then, I truly had moved on. Now the idea that I might have another child growing in my womb brought no joy, only alarm. I was too old for this.

I went into the bedroom to tell George.

"It's been thirty-nine days since my last period."

"Oh, wow."

"I don't know how I could be pregnant. But I've never had such a long cycle."

"Hmm, if you are pregnant, Isaac will be about four and a half when the baby is born."

"How do you feel about this?"

"I'm fine with it."

"Really?" I was surprised. After Isaac had been born, George said he thought six kids was enough.

"Yeah."

"Why?" I asked.

"I don't know. It wouldn't be so bad to have another baby."

I inhaled deeply, held my breath for a moment, and slowly blew it out. "I'm glad you feel that way. It helps me some."

Later, as I lay in bed trying to fall asleep, I talked to God about the situation.

Lord, I thought I was supposed to accept that the baby stage was over. If I really am pregnant, I'll be forty-four by the time the baby is born!

It seems like such awful timing. We've hardly gotten settled. We don't have health coverage here. I have no idea how to find a doctor—and where would we even have the baby? I don't want to give birth in a Hungarian hospital after the stories I've heard. Are there better natural options now?

What are you doing, God? We shouldn't even have been able to get pregnant!

I felt a whisper, the gentlest of mental nudges, and I paused to listen. Everything shifted as a new realization dawned.

But . . . if you planned this when it should have been impossible, you must really want us to have this baby. If that's so, you must have a good reason.

I knew from long experience that God always found a way to give me unexpected blessings from even the most difficult circumstances. *Okay, Jesus, I trust you.* I felt peace settling into my heart, and I inhaled deeply. *Thank you. I love you so much.*

After that, sleep came easily.

The next morning, before we left to go rock climbing, I asked George to buy a pregnancy test. It didn't take him long to find one and return. A few minutes later, I knew I was not pregnant.

I didn't know how to feel. I should have been relieved, but I truly had come to terms with the idea of welcoming a seventh child into our family. I would have been excited about having another baby to nurture. I knew the boys would all have been thrilled about possibly getting a little sister.

But it wasn't to be.

The next day was Sunday, March 27. We still hadn't found a church where we felt at home. The Ukrainian music nights were the closest thing. There was one scheduled for that evening, and we planned to go early for the Bible study beforehand. George's brother Jon would be the preacher.

Things didn't go as planned. By the time we got there, Jon was already speaking. Not wanting to cause a disruption by entering late with six kids, I decided to sit in the foyer instead. I was delighted to see Jon's wife, Stephanie, also there with her youngest kids. We hadn't seen each other since Debrecen. We hugged tightly.

Just as we released each other, a wave of vertigo hit me. I reached out to steady myself against the wall and quickly took a seat before anyone noticed that anything was wrong.

The kids played on the carpet nearby while Stephanie and I talked, sharing what little we knew about our future plans. Their family was suffering from not having a stable place to live. They were considering settling in Krakow, Poland. I didn't say so, but I was keenly disappointed.

I had hoped they would join us in Budapest. My secret dreams—of living within walking distance of each other, of our children having cousins nearby, of doing life with people who understood us—turned to smoke. If Jon and Stephanie moved to Poland, we would be the only members of the extended family to stay in Hungary. David and Deborah were also moving to Krakow so David could manage our aid warehouse. Aaron and Dara still hadn't decided where they were going to live, but Hungary was not on their list.

Grieving over the isolation that awaited us, I focused on breathing calmly and keeping my dismay from showing on my face.

I spent the next week continuing to set up our apartment and getting the kids on track with distance learning. On Wednesday I managed to prepare two hot meals in one day, a first since the war had displaced us. We hadn't been skipping meals, but we'd consumed lots of takeout or convenience foods instead of the nutritionally dense, made-from-scratch meals that had been our normal fare before the war.

The kids gradually adjusted to the new school routine. By the end of the week, they were doing their lessons without much trouble. On Friday night, they got a reward. We had a sleepover with Jon and Stephanie's son, Georgie.

All the kids were ecstatic. Being the only boy among five sisters, Georgie was super excited to spend time with his "brothers," as he affectionately called our boys. They invented an epic version of hide-and-seek that the older ones played through all ten floors of our apartment complex, including the two levels of the underground parking structure.

Throughout that week, I experienced several more attacks of vertigo. They were short, hardly interrupting my activities. Except for me, no one even noticed them. I was used to feeling a little lightheaded from time to time, but these dizzy spells were different, and I wondered what was going on. I was also increasingly finding myself out of breath and easily fatigued. My period still hadn't started, but I had ruled out pregnancy. Anyway, that wasn't an adequate explanation for my growing list of symptoms.

I never considered seeing a doctor because the stress of figuring out how to navigate an unfamiliar medical system seemed far worse than simply putting up with what I was experiencing.

On Saturday, April 2, I took advantage of the break from school to go shopping. There were still so many things we needed to replace. The weather forecast predicted rain, so I bought several umbrellas to keep us dry when taking public transport to church the next day. Meanwhile, George found cumin, which meant I could start making all the savory dishes with beans or lentils that had been our family's favorites before the war.

We still needed numerous things for the kitchen, so George and I took our landlord's car to a kitchen-supply store. I felt empowered when we checked out with all the tools to sprout buckwheat and turn it into sourdough bread. This used to be one of our staples. Besides being gluten-free and high in protein and iron, it was also delicious, and we missed it.

Once we got back to the apartment, I reorganized the kitchen to make space for the new things. As I worked, my fingertips started to tingle, as if they had suddenly gone to sleep. I held my hands up in front of me, rubbing the tips of my fingers with my thumbs in an attempt to bring the feeling back. It didn't help. I shook my hands back and forth, trying to increase the blood flow, but the odd sensation persisted. I examined my fingers closely. They looked normal, but they felt so strange.

With a flash of recognition, I realized I had experienced this before. It had been the previous summer, just before the doctor diagnosed me with anemia.

I knew what was wrong with me—I was anemic again! That would explain all my symptoms, even my late period. I was relieved to have an explanation. Better yet, it was something I knew how to solve.

The first time I was diagnosed with low iron, I was a small child. Ever since, my blood tests usually showed iron levels on the low end of normal. I had spent decades managing this tendency through diet. The iron pills the doctor had prescribed the summer before were in our apartment in Kyiv, but I was confident I could get my level back to normal without them.

Now I was more determined than ever to reestablish our healthy eating habits. We could sprout buckwheat today, and tomorrow I would bake two loaves of iron-rich bread in our new loaf pans. I decided which meals high in iron I would prepare over the next week.

As if it understood my plans, my body relaxed into its regular feminine rhythm before I went to bed.

36

Say Goodbye to Great-Grandpa

Saturday, April 2, 2022: Day 38 of War
Budapest, Hungry

Little Georgie spent the night again. The kids were wild about having another sleepover, and they were hard to put to bed. Despite my love for routines and schedules, I didn't push for an early bedtime. It was a weekend, and they were having so much fun. After everything we'd been through, we needed as much fun as we could get.

All the kids were still wide awake when my phone rang at ten minutes to midnight. Puzzled that anyone would call so late, I checked the caller ID. It was my cousin in Hawaii initiating a video call. My breath caught in excitement as I answered.

"Hi! What's up?" I said.

"Hi, Sharon. I'm here with Grandpa at Life Care Center."

"Oh my goodness, I can't believe it! Thank you!" Without waiting for her to give my grandpa the phone, I ran to the kids' bedroom where all seven boys were hanging out. "Guess what! Great-Grandpa is on the phone!"

"What?"

"Yay!"

"I wanna see!"

They all crowded around me, and I extended my arm as far as I could to give my grandpa the best view of everyone.

"Hi, Great-Grandpa!" several voices chorused.

I looked from their happy faces back to the screen, and my breath lodged in my throat. The last time we had talked to my grandpa had been three and a half months before, on his 101st birthday. He'd had a sparkle in his eye and spoke clearly, interacting playfully with the kids and thoughtfully with me. He hadn't looked a day past 85. Seeing him now, I could easily believe he was 101. I forced a smile onto my face as I struggled to grasp how he had deteriorated so rapidly.

He was trying to say something, but everyone was talking.

"Shhh, kids. I can't hear Great-Grandpa."

They all quieted down, but I still couldn't make out his words. His voice was soft, his syllables slurred.

"I'm sorry, Grandpa. I can't hear you," I said.

He tried again.

"I'm sorry, I don't know what you're saying, but we're so happy to see you!" I decided to fill the awkward silence with our news. I panned my phone across the group of us and stopped to introduce the one face that would be unfamiliar. "This is Georgie, my nephew. He's spending the night. We all had to evacuate from Ukraine because of the war, and we just moved into an apartment in Budapest. And we just got Jack out of Ukraine. George had to leave him behind when he evacuated." I wasn't sure how much my grandpa knew about what we had been through, but I assumed he knew about the war. He had always closely followed world events.

"I got new LEGOs!" five-year-old Andrew chimed in.

"And there's a really cool park by us!" nine-year-old James added.

We were all excited to talk to Great-Grandpa again. Video calls with him had been part of our Saturday-morning routine for as long as most of the kids could remember. Hawaii was on the opposite side of the planet from Ukraine, so our Saturday morning was his Friday night. He had often told us Friday nights with us were the highlight of his week, and it hadn't been unusual for him to prepare something special or comical to show the kids when we called. I was so thankful for the technology that permitted the kids to enjoy a real relationship with my grandpa, even though they only saw him for a week once every three years.

After his hundredth birthday, a persistent, age-related sore had developed on his leg. It required daily medical attention, so he had been placed in the care center where he was now. For a while, we continued our Saturday-morning calls, but his hearing was deteriorating. Soon, he couldn't make out what we were saying, but we still enjoyed the interaction. The kids would show him their latest LEGO creations, and he would tell us stories or make silly faces that set the kids laughing. But then he stopped answering his phone, and I learned it was because he couldn't hear it ringing. I asked my relatives to call us if they ever visited him first thing in the morning, before the kids had gone to bed on our side of the world, but that timing didn't work with their schedules.

Before his birthday, I had contacted the staff at the care center multiple times about facilitating video calls, but the twelve-hour time difference made it impossible for them. Finally, on his 101st birthday, someone made an extra effort, and we got to talk to him. He understood every word, thanks to a special pair of headphones for the hearing-impaired.

On this night in Budapest, we enjoyed a nineteen-minute call. We weren't able to understand anything he said, but I could see the spark of recognition in his eyes, and it was clear he was happy to see us.

When it was time to hang up, I made sure each one of my boys said goodbye before I ended the call. I felt a heaviness inside, and I knew I needed to help the kids prepare for the worst. "Did you boys see how much older Great-Grandpa looked?"

"Yeah."

"Uh-huh."

"What's wrong with him?"

"That's just what happens when people get older. I'm so glad we got to talk to him." I paused, choosing my words. "This might have been the last time we ever get to talk to him." Tears formed in my eyes.

"You mean he might die?" nine-year-old James asked.

"Yeah. But we'll get to see him again in heaven."

The kids were sober and quiet.

It was just under two weeks later, on Friday, April 15, when I got the call from my sister. Our grandpa had left this world. Because of his age, I had been anticipating this loss for over a decade, but it was still a heavy blow. This man and his wife had generously given themselves to help my dad raise me and my sister after our mother died when we were small children. Losing him felt more like losing a parent.

At the same time, I was comforted imagining him reunited with my grandma, his wife of sixty-seven years. He'd missed her every day since she'd passed twelve years earlier. I gathered the kids to tell them the news.

"Great-Grandpa is with Jesus now," I said.

"He died?" five-year-old Andrew asked, his brow furrowed and eyebrows tilted up in the middle.

"Yes, he did." I gave Andrew a hug.

The kids absorbed the news. They were thoughtful and sad, but they didn't seem surprised or traumatized. I was glad I had prepared them.

The next day we met with an American film team sent by a Christian nonprofit organization to get stories about the situation in Ukraine. They were planning a trip into Ukraine with George as their guide.

In the course of our conversation, it came out that my grandpa had died the day before. I said we were considering sending me to the memorial service alone, since it would be too expensive to take the whole family.

The leader of the team, who was sitting directly across from me, asked, "Did the kids have a relationship with him?"

"Yeah, they did," I answered, describing the weekly video calls we had enjoyed for so many years.

The man looked me straight in the eye and said, "My wife and I would like to pay for your whole family to go to the memorial service."

I was stunned. Did he have any idea how much money he was talking about? And we had just met him—how could he afford to be so generous to strangers? The first response that came to mind was, *Thank you, but that's not necessary*. But I was too moved to speak. Instead of trying to refuse the gift, I simply looked down at my lap and started to cry.

He continued, "I was a missionary kid in Papua New Guinea. To get to where we lived, first you had to get to Papua New Guinea, then you had to have a bush pilot fly you inland, then you had to take a day-long trip up a river in a canoe, and then you had to hike up the side of a mountain. So when my grandpa died, my dad was the only one who went back for the funeral. That always bothered me. I don't want your boys to have to experience that too."

I looked up, tears trickling down my cheeks, emotion clogging my throat. "Thank you," I whispered.

My grandpa's remains were cremated, and my relatives planned his service for May 21, giving us over a month to prepare for the trip. Our sponsor told us to feel free to book a multi-city itinerary, so we planned a two-month trip with stops to visit people in eight different US states.

We were stunned by God's provision. Visits to the United States usually happened once every three years. We had just made one the previous summer. Despite all the trauma we'd experienced, we hadn't considered a trip to the US. Even if we'd had the money, it wouldn't have seemed like the right way to use it when so many pressing needs surrounded us. But this lavish gift would make it possible for our family to get a little distance from the hard realities of our life. Maybe we could begin to process our hurt and recover.

37

George Returns to Ukraine

Saturday, April 16, 2022: Day 52 of War
Budapest, Hungry

In the meantime, George had a trip to make into Ukraine. It would be his first time back since evacuating, and I had mixed feelings. Getting our whole family out had felt like a major accomplishment. The situation in Ukraine continued to be unstable, and I had been relieved that George had shown no inclination to cross the border.

We knew people who were coming and going, some on errands of mercy, others to retrieve people or things. Our friend Anya actually went all the way back to Kyiv in early April to get some of her belongings, and while she was there, she visited our apartment and filled a small suitcase with items we requested.

Our friends Olya and Imre made a number of trips. Imre was practically running a non-stop shuttle service from Ukraine to Budapest in his minivan, and Olya always accompanied him to translate for the Ukrainian women and children they picked up. On one of those trips in April, they brought back Ivory and Ebony, our two pet rats. With their arrival, it finally felt like our family was complete again.

By contrast, George hadn't been needed in Ukraine. His main work was connecting Western donors with Ukrainian pastors and chaplains. His most powerful tool was his smartphone, paired with a stable internet connection. Because of the possibility of Russia targeting civilian infrastructure, seamless access to the internet wasn't a given in Ukraine, so it didn't make sense for George to go there.

All that changed when the film team came to Budapest. They wanted to travel to Bucha to interview people who had survived the Bucha Massacre. They needed a guide and interpreter, and George, with his extensive connections, knowledge of Ukraine, and fluency in both the Ukrainian and Russian languages, was the perfect choice.

I wanted this project to succeed, to raise awareness about the situation in Ukraine, but I was worried about George's safety. As we discussed the plans with the film team, I had questions I didn't know how to voice. What kinds of risks were they going to take? What if the situation deteriorated suddenly, and they became trapped in a dangerous area?

The head of the film team seemed to read my mind. He looked straight into my eyes, his gaze intense.

"I promise you we will not take your husband anywhere unsafe. And if something does go wrong, I have people on speed dial who can make things happen."

I nodded, somewhat reassured. He had an air of authority, like he knew what he was talking about, and I was a little in awe that he seemed to have powerful connections. Who was this guy? I later learned he was a retired US Special Forces Marine and had been involved in privately organized, crowd-funded evacuations from Afghanistan.

Later that day, my sister-in-law Melanie called. I felt a surge of joy when I heard her voice. We hadn't talked in the month since she, her husband Paul, and their kids had left Hungary.

"It's amazing that Paul and George are both going to be in Ukraine at the same time!" she said.

"Wait—what?"

"Oh, you didn't know? Paul's going into Ukraine, and he asked George to go with him to meet with the head chaplain after George gets done with the film team."

"Uh, where are they meeting?"

"They're going to travel to the chaplain's city. He said he's too busy right now to make a trip to Kyiv."

I felt like I had a rock in the middle of my chest. The head chaplain lived south of Kyiv, about halfway between the capital city and the southern front line of the war. I had accepted the idea of George going as far as Kyiv, but I was not okay with him getting any closer to the fighting than that. Even if he didn't get too close to a combat zone, I was worried about landmines. Ukraine is now the most mined country in the world, and even that early in the war, mines were already a major problem.

"How are they going to avoid mines?" I asked Melanie.

"They're getting their routes from the chaplain's network," Melanie reassured me. "In our experience, their intel is always good. They know the safe routes. They know the situation on the ground."

Since returning home, Melanie had been heavily involved in coordinating getting aid into Ukraine and smuggling people out of Russian-occupied territory. Her efforts had recently resulted in 100,000 euros of insulin being taken into Ukraine and distributed all over the country. When she said things like "intel" and "situation on the ground," I knew she wasn't just trying to sound impressive. She'd been living and breathing this stuff for days.

The chaplain Paul wanted to meet was the head of the group that trained George before the invasion. These chaplains were a crucial part of the pipeline connecting our aid warehouse in Western Ukraine to the hot spots where the aid was needed. Paul felt George's presence at the meeting would be invaluable, and I knew he was right.

I worried for the father of my children, but I appreciated that George could change the outcome of the trip. His catalytic personality both generated and fueled ideas, and he could jump-start projects by easily connecting the right people. I didn't want to stand in the way of something that could save thousands of lives, so I set my fears aside and gave him my blessing to go.

George left that evening. Since Ukraine was a war zone, it was impossible to fly into the country. He and the film team drove across the border. Our teammate Ira accompanied them. The film crew wanted to help her reunite with her husband Kolya, whom she hadn't seen for seven weeks, since the night they were separated while evacuating from Bucha.

They were gone for five days. George's chaplain connections allowed the film crew to gain access to Bucha, where they collected stories and footage that became a powerful miniature documentary.[1] As they interviewed Bucha residents, many said the film crew needed to talk to a man named Vasyl. When they met him, Ira gave a cry of joy and ran and threw her arms around his neck. He had been her sons' karate teacher.

Scan to watch documentary.

On the first day of the war, Vasyl had taken his family and 150 of his neighbors and hidden them in the basement of his martial arts studio. As the Russian soldiers terrorized everyone above, he kept these people, mostly women and children, safe. Daily, Vasyl and a few other men would collect water from a nearby lake and search for food to feed everyone.

One day the invaders discovered the entrance to the basement. They pounded on the door. "Open up!"

Some of the women and children cried out in fear, but Vasyl immediately quieted them. He knew the soldiers could easily break down the door if they suspected anyone was hiding. Vasyl and his neighbors cowered in terror and suspense. Finally, the banging and shouting stopped. The soldiers had left.

Eventually, Vasyl managed to evacuate everyone safely, except for one man. He was a husband and father who had been risking his life to bring food and water to the people sheltering in the basement. The Russians caught him and shot him—once in the eye and three times in the heart. As Vasyl was telling the story, this stoic man, whom friends had nicknamed "Ironman," was so overcome with emotion that he had to ask the cameraman to stop filming.

---

1. *Watch documentary: SharonTMarkey.com/documentary*

Vasyl also lost several neighbors. They had turned down his offer of shelter, and the Russian soldiers murdered them. One of the victims was an old man whom they dragged from his home and shot for sport with an anti-tank rocket.

Ira and her husband were able to spend a few days together before Ira had to return to Budapest to take care of their children. In the meantime, George headed south with Paul to visit the head chaplain. It was a significant meeting. As they talked, the chaplain shared an idea. Instead of transporting food from Europe to provide relief for war-affected Ukrainians, he wanted to source it locally. Agricultural exports normally comprised a huge part of Ukraine's GNP, but the Russian blockade of Ukraine's Black Sea ports was preventing farmers from selling their crops on the international market. He had a dream to buy their surplus, package it, and distribute it around the country.

The plan was genius. Not only would it cost far less than transporting food into Ukraine, but it would also support Ukraine's crippled farming sector and war-shattered economy. The chaplain had already done the research on logistics and cost; he just needed funding.

George connected him with the same Christian nonprofit that had sent the film team, and within months, the chaplains were delivering Ukrainian-sourced grocery boxes all over the hardest-hit parts of the country. Each box contained staples to support a family of four for a week and cost only $20 to produce. This project continued for over a year.

When George got back to Budapest, we celebrated his safe return. I was grateful for the amazing things he had accomplished, but I hoped it would be the last trip he'd have to make into Ukraine before we were all able to safely move home again.

38

Craving Connection

Spring 2022
Budapest, Hungary

That spring we swallowed pain by the tumblerful. In the early weeks after we evacuated, we'd been surrounded by loved ones. At the peak, there were twenty-eight members of George's family in Hungary, and that wasn't counting the eight members of our immediate family. It was a painful time, but a precious one as well. It couldn't last forever.

Those who came to support the displaced families had to return to their lives in other countries. And of those who had been displaced, our family was the only one to settle in Hungary. David and Deborah and their four kids moved to Krakow, Poland, on March 30. Just a week later, Jon and Stephanie and their six kids followed. Another week passed, and we said goodbye to Aaron and Dara and their two kids. They had a scheduled trip to the US, and then they planned to return to Ukraine.

Budapest felt gray and dead after they all moved on. In Kyiv, we had shared our lives with a circle of dear people. We all lived in the same neighborhood and saw each other frequently. Some were part of our church; some were the families of our kids' good friends; some were people we had simply met at parks or our favorite coffee shop.

We'd always had a constant stream of visitors. We ate and played and laughed and shared hours of conversation over endless cups of tea. Of all the losses the war had occasioned, being torn away from those people was the most painful. Once we were established in our own place, we began to ache for companionship and meaningful connections.

We had a number of friends from Ukraine who had ended up in Budapest. On April 10, George and I launched Sunday morning Bible studies at our apartment and invited all our Ukrainian friends, both old and new. We were hopeful that we could create a circle of friends like the one we'd had in Kyiv.

We were disappointed when no one showed up that first week. We continued to try, inviting friends over to the park or to our cramped apartment as often as we could, for any pretext. While we had some success getting people together, the sense of community we craved wasn't there.

As we searched for connection with people in our new context, we also tried to maintain old ties. On Friday, May 6, we had a video conference call with our former team from Podil. It was the first time we had all connected since the war had started. Everyone shared where they were and what they had been doing.

The three single ladies who had been on our team were all in Budapest and had joined our new team. The other four members of our old team were two married couples, and they were still in Ukraine, since the husbands weren't allowed to leave the country. Neither couple had children to worry about. The four of them had resettled in a city on the Ukrainian border with Slovakia, where they had been pleased to find a decent apartment for a good price. They happily signed a rental contract.

Shortly after they moved in, a wave of displaced people inundated the city. Rent prices skyrocketed. Our friends hadn't even been in their new apartment for a month when their landlord informed them they had to move out. He showed up with several police officers to evict them, in violation of their contract. Our friends were worried the husbands might be conscripted into the army on the spot if they protested. Their fear was so great that they simply grabbed their things and cleared out as quickly as they could. Not wanting to draw attention to themselves with a draft underway, they never pursued legal action against the landlord.

After that, the two couples parted ways. One couple, the owners of the cat that Olya had brought to Hungary when she evacuated during the early days of the war, moved on to another city. They were settling in and had managed to get their pet back.

The other couple had gotten a van through donations George had raised, and they lived like vagabonds for weeks, transporting people and aid wherever needed. After it was clear that Kyiv was not under imminent threat of Russian occupation, they moved back to the capital and took up residence in our old apartment. They gathered a new team, who all moved in with them. Together, they continued the work we had been doing before the war. Their goal was to create a church that was available 24/7 to empower Ukrainian youth and to meet the physical, emotional, and spiritual needs around them in the midst of war. Our old apartment was once again a hub of friendship and life.

I still believed that as soon as the war was over, we would all go back to Kyiv and pick up where we left off. The experience of being displaced was just a temporary interruption. Soon we would be back together in our beloved Podil, doing life with the same community of people we'd had before the war. But that conference call forced me to face the fact that things would never be the same. Even if our family could return to Kyiv and live in our old apartment, so much would be different.

For one thing, these dear friends might not all choose to return with us. Even if they did, it wouldn't be the way it was before. The war was altering all of us. Those who fled were lacerated with grief and homesickness and tormented by guilt. Those who stayed were living under a level of stress and trauma that defied comprehension.

The separate wounds we suffered were making us into different people—different from who we were before the war and also different from each other. Even though we wanted to remain close, I feared our radically disparate experiences would drive a wedge between us.

Besides that, Podil wasn't the same. So many of the people from our neighborhood were scattered, and who knew if they would all return? I had loved our life, and the knowledge that it was gone forever gouged a cavernous hole in my chest that defied the possibility of ever being filled.

On May 11, we said goodbye to Anya, one of our teammates from Kyiv and our kids' favorite babysitter. She was moving back to Ukraine—not to Kyiv, but to a safer city in Western Ukraine where her parents lived. As we hugged her goodbye on the eve of her departure, it felt like the fledgling community we were trying to cultivate in Budapest was wilting before it could even take root.

On Sunday, May 15, we had another video conference call with our team from Podil. It was even more emotional than the first one. The nine of us talked for two hours, and the conversation had several of us in tears, myself included. I hadn't shared much during the first call, but I opened up this time, finding the words in Ukrainian to bare my heart to these dear friends. I felt like I'd deserted some of them in their time of need by not being in touch since we'd all been displaced.

"It's been so hard for me just to take care of my family. I haven't been able to even think about taking care of my other relationships." I paused and swallowed. "Forgive me." My voice was shaky. I took a deep breath. "And I feel like even the things I am doing, I'm not doing ideally, the way I'd like."

Everyone shared from the heart, and by the end of the conversation, it felt like we were all taking leave of each other.

"It feels like we're saying goodbye for good," someone observed. All the women were crying. One of the men might have had tears in his eyes too.

Another one of the men reassured us. "We'll still keep in touch and be there for each other." His words brought me no comfort. They only highlighted the fact that things were changing—they had already changed—and we were all going our separate ways.

Something rare and beautiful had died. It felt like my cup of pain couldn't get any fuller.

39

INVISIBLE SUFFERING

May–July 2022
Hawaii, USA

A few days later, our family left for the United States. We always started our visits to the US in the American Midwest, where we had many friends, relatives, and supporting churches. Then we'd travel to see my immediate family in California, and from there we'd make the five-hour flight to Hawaii. This time, we went straight to Hawaii from Europe, traveling almost half-way around the planet in about twenty-four hours. We had never gone so far, so fast.

When we landed at the little airport in Kailua-Kona, we picked up our eight-seat rental van and checked into guest rooms at the campus of a Christian university not far from the airport. My grandpa's memorial service would take place in two days on the opposite side of the island.

The next morning we went to the campus cafeteria for breakfast. The dining area was outdoors on an enormous, covered patio. It was open on one side to lovely sea breezes and a panorama of the ocean. The opposite side had a dramatic view of mountains that made up the interior of the island.

I was stunned by the beautiful setting, but I didn't have the leisure to enjoy it. The little kids needed help, and the older ones were rowdy and required supervision. While George minded the children, I hurried back and forth across the expansive dining area like a waitress on a busy Friday night. Finally, all the boys finished eating, and the older ones went off to explore the campus.

George looked at me, and I saw understanding and sympathy in his gentle blue eyes. "I'm going to take the little guys to the playground. Why don't you just stay here and get some rest?"

"That sounds nice," I said. "Thanks."

The dining area was nearly deserted. I sat alone at an empty table, enjoying the silence and solitude. The only sounds were the trilling of exotic birds. Though the afternoon promised to be hot and muggy, the morning was the perfect temperature. I recognized the familiar caress of moist, tropical air on my skin, and I felt at home. Here, literally half a world away, the drama unfolding in Ukraine seemed distant. For a brief moment, I was at peace.

However, the pain in my heart was never far off, ready to overwhelm as soon as I had nothing else to distract. I felt it coming, and for once, I did nothing to avoid it. Instead, I surrendered. I accepted this agony of loss as my new baseline. Rather than blinking away the tears, I opened my eyes wide and bathed in the sadness. Would I never feel whole again?

Involuntarily, my gaze turned to the mountains that dominated the inland view. Behind the campus rose a volcano that culminated in a peak towering against the sky. Lush, green vegetation studded with bright tropical blossoms surrounded me and carpeted the slope. The sun was preparing to rise from behind the mountain, and the sky was a glorious halo of pinks and yellows around its summit.

I drank in the beauty like a parched wanderer dying of thirst. As I did, my eyebrows lifted in surprise, because I felt an unexpected opening in my chest and a lightness in my heart. I breathed deeply of the fresh island air and whispered a prayer of gratitude to God for the gift of all this loveliness. I let it soak into the dry places of my soul, bringing refreshment and comfort. I had never experienced the healing power of beauty before.

That evening we made the ninety-minute drive across the interior of the island to reach the city of Hilo on the opposite side. The funeral took place the next day at the church my grandpa had attended. Family members shared tributes, and the pastor spoke about the eternal life that awaits followers of Jesus. Almost all the guests wore brightly colored Hawaiian prints in tribute to my grandpa, who had often worn aloha shirts. At the reception afterwards, people shared memories and reconnected with each other while eating local delicacies. As I nibbled sushi and sweet Hawaiian pineapple, I watched the guests interacting. I knew my outgoing and friendly grandpa—who never turned down a chance to eat something tasty—would have approved of the cheerful gathering.

I will always be grateful that our family was able to attend my grandpa's memorial service. He had meant so much to all of us, and not getting to be part of the celebration of his life would have been a painful blow. At the same time, it wasn't a comfortable experience.

All the guests were united in sadness over the passing of this special man, but I felt isolated in private grief over the traumatic changes in our life because of Russia's full-scale invasion of Ukraine. My grandpa's memorial service didn't seem like the time or place to go into detail about our experiences, but as I socialized, people invariably asked how George and I and the kids were. It felt dishonest to respond without some acknowledgment of the difficulties we were facing.

This tension between being honest and being socially appropriate continued over the next two months as we leapfrogged our way across North America and back to Eastern Europe. We interacted with hundreds of people in a variety of settings, and it never got easy to navigate how much to share and how much to keep back. I felt like I was living in a parallel reality. The people around us were preoccupied with such normal things. I, on the other hand, often knew what day of the war it was, but not what day of the month.

Just before our trip, I had finally realized that even if the war were to end tomorrow, it would be impossible to get back the life we had before. Still reeling from that realization while we were in the US, I decided to take time to grieve over all that had been stolen from us. My sorrow was deliberate and calculated. I listed our losses and honored them by allowing myself to sit unapologetically in the middle of my pain and mourn each one.

A quaint neighborhood we adored.

A rhythm of life we loved.

A close-knit community of friends who were always in and out of our apartment.

Our stability.

Our sense of security.

Our children's innocence.

I was deeply sad for days on end. Tears leaked out of me like fluid from a festering lesion. It was intensive care for the soul, more demanding than being in the ICU. My pain was as real and present as a physical wound, but it was harder to bear. I needed as much care as someone with a bleeding gash across her forehead, but no one could see the source of my suffering, and so I often passed by, unnoticed. Sometimes I wished I could just wear a name tag or a sandwich board with the pertinent details of our recent experience:

I am a refugee from the Russian invasion of Ukraine.

My family and I fled to Hungary last February.

We don't know when or if we will ever return home.

I knew it might make people uncomfortable, but at least the truth would be visible. Some might choose to avoid me, but at least I could feel comfortable being open with those who did engage me, because they would know what they were getting into.

I longed for someone who was asking for an honest response when they said, "How are you?" I knew that if I answered that question candidly, it would cause awkward moments. The person talking to me might feel inconvenienced by the spilling of my story, so I rarely took that path. However, I believed it would have been life-giving for both of us. We were created to live in community, but too often we settle for being in proximity.

I wasn't looking for anyone to say something profound that would solve my problems or absolve my pain. I just wanted someone compassionate who would take the time to stop and listen and be a safe place where I could process my grief. I wanted someone who would resist the urge to hijack the conversation by talking about how they had gone through something similar. I just wanted a listening ear and a simple affirmation:

"That must have been really difficult."

"I'm so sorry that happened to you."

"Can I give you a hug?"

Sometimes I couldn't help myself, and the need to be known pushed me into sharing our story in wildly inappropriate contexts. But one day this social faux pas led me to someone who understood how to honor my grief and help me take another step toward healing.

We had reached the state of Indiana, where we were officially residents, and we made appointments for the kids to get checkups at a pediatric dentist. Amazingly, the dentist's office was able to accommodate all six of them at the same time. When we arrived, there was a sign on the door that no one was allowed entry without a face mask.

From my purse, I produced a zip-lock bag with masks, and everyone donned one before we went inside. When the receptionist called the boys' names, we followed her to an area with multiple examination tables side-by-side. Each of my kids lay or sat on one of these while we waited for the dentist. She was a soft-spoken Asian woman who knew just how to put each child at ease as she examined his teeth. She even managed to get the worried expression off Andrew's face and make him giggle.

She informed me that some of the kids required further treatment. Since we wouldn't be in Indiana long, I had to explain why I wanted all the dental work done as soon as possible. While it would have sufficed to say we lived in Europe and needed appointments before we returned there, I found myself giving this stranger a thumbnail sketch of our recent experiences.

"We live in Budapest. We're trying to get the kids' dental work taken care of before we go back, since we have medical coverage here. We're Americans, but we lived in Ukraine for many years, and we evacuated to Budapest when the war started."

The dentist immediately gave me her full attention. Though her face mask hid her expression, her eyes connected deeply with mine, communicating compassion.

"I'm sorry. That sounds like it must have been really difficult," she said.

I nodded, and then the tears came. "Thank you," I sobbed.

"What's wrong? Can I get you something?" she asked, taken aback by my sudden emotion.

"No, it's okay," I assured her. "It just makes me cry when people are so kind. Thank you."

I was learning that compassion had the power to release pent-up grief. That release was good, and I knew I needed it. I also knew that if we were going to recover as a family, we all needed to grieve, no matter how uncomfortable it was. How could I help the kids do this? I had tried several times to give them space and encouragement to talk through their feelings, but they hadn't had much to say.

40

"I Live in Budapest"

July 2022
Indiana, USA

A few days later, the eight of us were in a borrowed van on the road to yet another state to visit one of our supporting churches. My phone chimed, and I noticed activity in the chat group for our old team from Podil. Some of the ladies were sharing memories of our life together and sending sentimental greetings. The grief welled up again, and tears trickled down my cheeks.

Just then, one of the kids asked me something. I twisted around in the front passenger seat to answer. I had barely started crying, so I didn't think my eyes would be red, and I didn't expect the kids to be able to see the tear tracks on my face from several feet away. Their eyesight was sharper than I'd anticipated.

"Mommy, what's wrong?"

"Yeah, why are you crying?"

"I miss Podil," I answered. "Don't you miss it?"

"Yeah."

"What do you miss the most?" I asked.

"Friends," Peter said.

Kiyoshi said, "I miss being able to talk to people."

"I miss Luka! When am I going to see him again, Mommy?" Andrew asked.

While tears continued to drip down my face, everyone shared, even George. I saw a few moist eyes as we all allowed ourselves to acknowledge and honor our pain.

After two months of living out of suitcases, relocating every few days, and staying in borrowed spaces, we were finally getting ready to return to Budapest. We were looking forward to going *home*.

It felt odd to use that word. Before our trip to the United States, I had never once called Budapest home. In fact, I didn't even tell people I lived there. I couldn't say the sentence, "I live in Budapest." I said, "We live in Kyiv, but right now we're in Budapest."

At some point, I realized my perception was wildly at odds with the way things actually were. We were renting an apartment in Budapest. Other people were living in our old apartment. We had replaced most of our household goods. Our three pets had made the move. We had found meaningful work to do in Hungary. Even if our hearts were still in Kyiv, our lives were firmly in Budapest.

Fearing I was going to give myself a complex if I continued to insist on a nonexistent reality, I practiced saying the hated phrase, "I live in Budapest." I forced myself to form the words and voice them daily until they felt less jarring and untrue.

Now, after two months of unrooted living, the prospect of returning to the one place on earth where we had a home to welcome us sounded wonderful. There was one complication. We did not have Hungarian residency yet.

As Americans, we were allowed to visit the EU for ninety days without a visa. If we wanted to stay longer, we needed to apply for residency. Otherwise, we would have to leave the EU for ninety days or get visas before we could return. Our understanding was that we had until day ninety to start the residency application process.

Before we left for the United States, we were told that if our residency cards weren't ready before our departure, we could be denied reentry to the EU. The Budapest immigration office was swamped with applications from thousands of people who had fled Ukraine, so processing times were much longer than usual. Since we would not exhaust our ninety days before our flight to the US, we decided to wait to submit all our documents to the immigration office after we returned.

When we left on our two-month trip, we were secure in the knowledge that we'd have over a week to apply once we got back. We had already begun preparing the necessary documents, to avoid last-minute scrambling. However, just a few weeks before our scheduled return, we received a message from a Hungarian friend who was helping us navigate the application process. She had heard a rumor that the immigration office was refusing applicants who had less than two weeks left of their ninety days, but she couldn't get confirmation. Just to be safe, she recommended we get Hungarian visas before returning, but she promised to keep calling the immigration office until someone picked up the phone and gave her an answer.

I called the Hungarian Consulate in Chicago and was dismayed to learn we couldn't get visa appointments until September. And, if we were approved, it could still take months to receive our visas.

My pulse was racing. My breath came in shallow gasps as I contemplated having to wait in the US until the New Year or longer. Where would we stay for that length of time? Would the people who were caring for our pets be okay keeping them that long? And what about our team in Budapest? They were doing amazing work connecting with Ukrainian refugees all over Hungary, but we felt a responsibility to be with them. We didn't want them to feel abandoned.

When George and I discussed our options, we realized if we couldn't return to Hungary as planned, we should simply extend our trip another month. If we stayed out of the EU for ninety days, we would automatically be granted another ninety days when we reentered. However, before paying the equivalent of multiple months' rent to change eight airline tickets, we wanted to know for sure that our residency applications would be rejected if we returned on schedule. Our Hungarian friend had helped scores of foreigners through the process and had never heard of this happening. We convinced ourselves the rumor was probably unfounded.

As our departure date approached, our friend still hadn't gotten an answer from the immigration office. We prepared for the return flight. Twenty-four hours before departure, George checked us in online, as he always did. That was when our friend finally got confirmation. The rumor was true.

We quickly shifted to Plan B. George contacted the airline through the chat feature on their website. He gave all our ticket details and requested a new departure date a month later. Everything went smoothly, and the chat responded that George would receive an email with the new itinerary, but it could take a while to arrive.

We were disappointed not to be leaving the next day, but we weren't devastated. We'd known this might happen. We unpacked our bags and transitioned from travel mode to extended vacation mode. It could have been worse.

The next day, two hours before our original departure time, I received an alert on my phone. It was from the airline, reminding me we should be at the airport. I felt a surge of adrenaline, and my heart started to race. Why did their system still think we were flying today?

I was with the kids at the house where we were staying, church-owned lodging for missionaries. George was running errands. I immediately called him.

"Did you ever get the confirmation email about our ticket change?" I asked.

"No, not yet. Why?"

"I just got an alert from KLM that we're supposed to be at the airport! I don't think the ticket change went through."

"Oh, no! Do you want me to contact them?"

"No, I'm going to call customer service. Just pray that I don't have to wait too long to talk to an agent!"

Thankfully, I was on the line with an agent in less than twenty minutes. She told me the ticket change had not gone through because we'd already checked in for the flight. We needed to cancel our check-in through the KLM app—then she could reissue our tickets.

This proved impossible because the first flight on our itinerary was operated by Delta. We needed to cancel our check-in through their system, and the Delta app didn't have that functionality. I hung up and called Delta.

As I waited to speak to an agent, I paced back and forth, checking my watch frequently. If I couldn't get our check-in canceled and we didn't show up at the airport, we would lose our tickets. But even if all eight of our suitcases were already packed, all our things loaded in the van, and we left for the airport immediately, it was too late to get there before our gate closed.

"Breathe, Sharon, breathe," I kept saying aloud.

Finally, the Delta agent answered. I quickly explained our predicament. The agent informed me that only a desk agent at the airport had the authority to do what I needed.

"Okay, can you please give me the phone number for the Delta desk at the Indianapolis Airport?"

"I'm sorry, ma'am. I can't do that."

"Why not?"

"We're not allowed to give that number out."

"Can you connect me then?"

"No, I'm sorry; I can't."

"What am I supposed to do?"

"Ma'am, you can go to the airport and talk to a desk agent."

"But I won't get there in time."

"I'm really sorry, ma'am, but there's nothing I can do."

I heaved a huge sigh. "I understand. Thank you. Goodbye."

I quickly wrote in our family chat, describing the situation and asking everyone to pray. Then I did an internet search for the phone number of the Indianapolis Delta desk. All I could find was the information number for the Indianapolis Airport. I called and asked for the number to the Delta desk. The operator told me that information was unavailable.

I hung up. I was out of options.

"God, help me," I prayed aloud. "I don't know what to do. You knew this would happen . . . I guess if we lose the tickets, you can give us the money to buy new ones." That perspective settled my nerves.

Within seconds, my phone rang. It was Pam. She had seen my message on the family chat. She was a Delta frequent flyer and had the cell phone number for a Delta desk agent who had once helped her out. I couldn't believe it.

I called the number, but no one answered. In desperation, I texted and explained the problem. I got an immediate response. The man said he was not at his computer—he was in a secure zone at the airport getting his annual security clearance renewal. That's why he'd been unable to answer my call. He said he'd try to contact one of his colleagues to cancel our check-in. I thanked him—with several exclamation points—and thanked God.

Then I waited.

I had hoped for a quick response that all was well, but minutes passed with no news. I couldn't focus on anything besides the hands of my watch as they steadily moved toward our departure time. My fingers itched to text the man to ask what was happening, but I knew that wouldn't change the outcome. I determined to wait until he contacted me.

I had stopped pacing by now, and I ended up kneeling on the floor, my forehead resting on the carpet in front of my knees. I focused on breathing calmly while I prayed.

I glanced at my watch. Our gate had shut. If our check-in hadn't been canceled, we had just lost our tickets. I imagined all the passengers aboard, stowing their luggage, buckling their seat belts, and listening to the safety presentation. I continued praying, face down on the floor.

Now our plane was taking off. I hoped against hope that somehow the agent had been able to cancel our check-in, but with our plane airborne, I was pretty sure it didn't make any difference. Since we hadn't rebooked before takeoff, we'd probably lost our tickets either way.

About forty minutes later, my phone finally rang. It was the Delta agent.

"My colleague was able to cancel your check-in. You can contact KLM now to rebook."

"Really? We didn't lose our tickets?"

"No, everything should be good."

"Oh, my goodness! Oh, wow! Thank you so much!" In my excitement, I could hardly form a coherent sentence.

As he said, everything was good; we easily rebooked with KLM. Now we just had to figure out what to do with all the free time we suddenly had.

41

I Will Not Let You Steal Our Friendships Too

August 2022
USA

For two months, our family had maintained a mind-numbing schedule. It was always this way when we visited the United States. Our loved ones and supporting churches were spread from Hawaii to the East Coast. Cramming all those visits into nine weeks required meticulous planning and a high tolerance for upheaval. We sometimes grew weary of the pace, but we all agreed it was worth it to reconnect with everyone.

When we changed our return date, suddenly we had a whole month with nothing scheduled. It sounded heavenly. I looked forward to relaxed family time and visiting people we'd been too rushed to see. I also hoped we could all experience more healing.

I was relieved we had all started grieving, but grief takes years, and it's unpredictable. It can be a tsunami or a gentle spring rain, and you never know which form it will take today—or if it will skip a day and let you enjoy the sun.

As we continued to navigate that watery wasteland, two things emerged as the greatest challenges for me. Prior to being displaced from our home, I was highly competent, effectively managing multiple responsibilities without breaking under the strain. But now I felt fragile and scatterbrained, as if the experience had altered my brain architecture, severing neural connections I'd relied on for decades. It was unnerving and frustrating. Sometimes this stress-induced mental handicap made it difficult to manage our large family. I would neglect to buy obvious groceries, or lose track of important items, or forget things I'd promised to do. I had to learn to show myself grace, take things slower, and say no to added responsibilities.

But by far the most difficult thing was being separated from all our pre-war friends. The hardest separations to accept were not those with people who were still in Ukraine. Seeing them again felt realistic, because we still hoped to move back one day. But the rest of our friends had ended up scattered across Europe and North America. While it was theoretically possible that we could visit them all, it was wildly unlikely. Even if we did visit, the sad reality was those relationships would never grow into what they would have been if we hadn't been torn away from each other. Each arrested friendship felt like yet another casualty of the war.

One day during our extra month in the United States, Andrew, who had recently turned six, approached me, his brow furrowed and eyebrows tilted up in the middle. "Mommy? When am I going to see Luka again?" Luka had been his favorite play buddy in our neighborhood in Kyiv. This wasn't the first time Andrew had asked about him since we had evacuated from Ukraine.

When I didn't answer right away, Andrew continued. "Can I share this candy with him when I see him?" He held up an open package of Sour Patch Kids. "And he told me that they don't usually have chips at their house, so maybe I could give him my chips," he added hopefully, rummaging in his backpack and producing a snack-size bag of potato chips that he had been saving for a special occasion.

I finally found my voice. "I don't know where Luka and his family are," I repeated for what seemed like the dozenth time, "and I don't know when we're going to see them again." The crushing reality was I didn't know *if* we were going to see them again, but I couldn't bring myself to say that to my six-year-old.

As I told my little boy these things, I felt tears starting to rise again, crowding the breath out of my throat. He should not have been forced to leave his friends without warning or a chance to say goodbye. It was wrong and unnatural and something that no little kid should ever have to endure.

At that point, I had been grieving intentionally for two months. Suddenly, I felt a new emotion. I was angry. For too long, I had felt powerless, pushed around by the swirling currents of chaotic events, and now I was finally ready to rise up. On February 24, 2022, I became a passive observer of my own life. Now I wanted to become an active participant again. I had been the victim, but now I would become the victor.

So much had been taken from us, but on that day I resolved that Putin's war would not steal our friendships as well. I would find a way—despite separation, different time zones, and uncertain futures—to keep those relationships alive.

I started by asking George to track down Luka's parents, and then we set up a video call so Andrew could reconnect with him. I watched as Andrew's characteristic worried expression dissolved into one of joy and wonder. He held George's phone in front of him with both hands and spoke with his long-lost friend. He walked all over the house where we were staying, giving Luka a virtual tour and telling him about the projects he'd created from LEGOs, the playground nearby, and the trip we'd made to the Indianapolis Children's Museum. He was animated and engaged, and despite all that had changed in our life, he only had positive things to say to his friend.

As I watched him, I knew I had found a key to helping our children recover and thrive. Going forward, I would prioritize giving the kids time to interact online with their friends and cousins. Despite my dislike of video games, I even encouraged them to meet up online with their friends to play web-based multiplayer games.

I remember one day when Kiyoshi, Peter, and James got online with two friends in Belgium and one friend in Poland. We had all lived within walking distance of each other before the war. The six kids formed a team and spent an hour facing off against other teams online. The friends all joined a conference call to plan their strategy. We put it on speakerphone in our living room. They laughed and whooped and called out encouragement and instructions to each other. The house was filled with the happy sounds of their play. It almost felt like they were all together again.

Samuel started having conference calls with his three closest friends. One had evacuated to France; the other two were still living in Kyiv. Whenever I saw a report that their district of the city had been hit by a rocket (which happened frequently), I made sure Samuel contacted them to check if they were okay.

Finally, after three months, the day came when we could return to Hungary. It was bittersweet for me because we would be the only members of George's family in the EU. While we had been in the US, all three of George's brothers who had been displaced by the war had relocated. Aaron and Dara and their two kids had returned to Ternopil, Ukraine. Jon and Stephanie and their six kids had flown to Florida, where Stephanie's mom was in the final stages of a battle with cancer. David and Deborah had spent four months with their kids in Krakow, Poland, overseeing the aid warehouse. That project was not needed after organizations like the UN and Samaritan's Purse got their huge aid-distribution programs up and running in Ukraine, and the family had moved to Tbilisi, Georgia in early August.

It would have been so much better to be returning to Ukraine like Aaron and Dara, or even to be joining other relatives in Tbilisi, as David and Deborah had done. But I was still happy to be going back to Budapest. We would get to see our Budapest friends and resume a normal routine. The kids talked excitedly about being reunited with their toys and our pets. As I pictured our cozy little apartment, I felt at ease, knowing we had a place to call home.

42

Next Year

Fall–Winter 2022
Budapest, Hungary

Having to spend ninety days in the United States was a pivotal experience for me. The forced time away from Hungary changed my perspective on living there. When all I could compare it to was our settled, happy experiences in Ukraine, life in Hungary had felt transient and unwelcome. But after two months living like vagabonds in the US, I longed to return to the relative stability of Budapest. When I couldn't, suddenly Hungary became a desired haven. Once we were finally allowed to return, I felt as if I were going home.

When we arrived back in Hungary, my outlook was radically different from what it had been during the spring. I had fully accepted that we lived in Budapest, but I could tell something was still lacking in my mindset. As the months passed, I realized what was missing was the ability—or the willingness—to embrace our new life. In my mind, it was still a temporary arrangement. I was holding out for a future where we moved back to Ukraine.

Coming to terms with our reality was even more difficult when Jon and Stephanie and their kids moved back to Ternopil in October 2022 after the passing of Stephanie's mom. It hadn't been as hard for me to accept when Aaron and Dara moved back. Dara was Ukrainian, and she wanted to be near her mom, who was staying in Ukraine because her husband was serving in the Ukrainian Army.

But Jon and Stephanie were just like us—two Americans with six kids who had grown up in Ukraine. If they could go back home, why couldn't we? I knew the answer: their home city, Ternopil, was relatively safe, while ours was not. But that didn't make it easier to accept our lot.

George and I had agreed we wouldn't move back to Kyiv until there was no risk of bombing, and currently there were frequent missile and drone attacks on the capital city. Besides, other people were living in our apartment. They assured us the place was still ours whenever we wanted to return, but we didn't want to disrupt the important work they were doing. And we had important work of our own in Hungary. As much as my heart longed for Ukraine, I had to admit moving back didn't make sense yet.

That left us in Hungary for the foreseeable future, settling into Budapest life. It should have been comforting to create new traditions, to get to know the rhythms of the place, to put down roots. Up until being displaced, I had always enjoyed that part of moving. But I wasn't carefully transplanted to Budapest. I was violently uprooted and tossed. Part of my root structure hadn't made it and was still buried somewhere in a war-torn country.

I knew if I was not fully present, I would sabotage my joy and my effectiveness. But I was still trying to figure out how to be present. Certain things were obvious, and I had taken all the practical steps I knew.

I'd put much time and energy into transforming our apartment into a comfortable space for our family. I learned how to use Budapest public transport and started exploring. I began learning the Hungarian language, and I was even making friends with some of the locals. But the hope of returning to Ukraine was keeping me from putting down roots.

Even as I tried to become fully present in our new life, I found myself reluctant to do anything that could create long-term ties. It would have felt disloyal to Ukraine, the country into which I had poured two decades of my life. And it would have felt incredibly risky to put down roots that could just be ripped out again.

In December 2022, I took Samuel, my eldest son, to a Christmas concert performed by a gospel choir. The hall was packed when we arrived. We were meeting friends, and they'd saved spots for us. We threaded our way to them through the aisles, squeezed past a few people, and slid into the two empty seats. Before long, the house lights dimmed, and the choir filed onstage.

Each member was wearing a black skirt or black slacks with a solid-colored shirt. No two shirts were alike, and the effect was a joyful riot of color onstage. The singers swayed and even clapped as they sang, obviously enjoying themselves. Their enthusiasm was infectious.

Between two of the songs, the director faced the audience to say they were an amateur choir—they accepted anyone, even people who couldn't sing. Then he motioned to the choir, and they launched into a lively number. As I moved to the beat, thoroughly enjoying the music, I had an idea. I glanced at Samuel, a music lover who had been in a choir in Ukraine, and I started to lean over to say something in his ear. I gasped and stopped myself. I sat perfectly still, my eyes wide in shock at my own thoughts.

I had been about to say, "You could join this choir and perform in this concert next year!"

I was drawn up short by those last two words.

Next year.

Heat burned my face and coursed through my veins. How could I have so casually assumed we would still be in Budapest next year? What about Ukraine? Had I given up on moving back? How could I turn my back on the place I'd called home for so many years? Had the joy of the evening caused me to let down my guard and forget where I really belonged?

I wasn't enjoying the performance anymore. I wanted to cry. I wanted to hide.

I knew if we were still—God forbid—living in Budapest in December 2023, we would probably attend this concert again. Part of me looked forward to the possibility of hearing this choir next year, but part of me still didn't know how to manage the disconnect between my dream of moving back to Ukraine and the real trajectory our life was on.

By that point, nearly ten months into the war, George and his team of displaced Ukrainians were regularly traveling to Ukrainian refugees all over Hungary. They delivered humanitarian aid and organized activities to foster a sense of community among the Ukrainians in each of the Hungarian cities they visited.

Many of these refugees came from areas now under Russian occupation or from towns so badly destroyed that returning wasn't an option. Even if the building where they had lived was still standing, the city infrastructure no longer existed, making life untenable. Stores, schools, and hospitals no longer functioned. In the words of our army chaplain friend, entire cities had been "wiped off the face of the map."

For many of these refugees, Hungary was likely to be their final stop. Their children were getting established in their new lives, attending Hungarian schools and making friends. By the time the war ended, it might be more traumatic to uproot them and return to Ukraine than to remain in Hungary, especially since they had nowhere to go in Ukraine.

The focus of our lives was on helping these people. The longer the war continued, and the more invested in them we became, the more likely it was we would also remain in Hungary long term. While I accepted this on a theoretical level, I was fighting it in my heart. I was stuck between what I wanted and the direction our life was taking.

43

I Don't Want to Move

Winter 2022–2023
Budapest, Hungary

While I was emotionally stuck, our family was physically stuck. At the time of year when everyone celebrates coziness and cheer, our little apartment was starting to feel cramped instead of cozy. We barely had enough room to accommodate the people and pets in our household, let alone a Christmas tree. Instead, I decorated a small, imitation, tabletop version and placed it on a bookshelf. We hung tinsel garlands and lights around the apartment to compensate, but I could sense tempers flaring as we approached our first Christmas as displaced people living in close quarters.

Back in the spring, when I had seen how much the lack of privacy bothered my second-born Kiyoshi, we had bought a small set of patio furniture and placed it on the balcony beside our apartment door. I encouraged him to spend as much time out there as he needed. Sometimes he would sit outside alone and draw. Sometimes he would take the dog or his brother Peter and just hang out. It was like having an extra room. But once the weather turned cold, he stopped using the balcony. I dug his ski pants out of storage and hung them by the front door with his coat.

He seemed to like my idea of bundling up to use the balcony through the winter, but I don't remember him ever doing it. Instead, he demanded that everyone adapt to his need for silence and space.

One day, as I was journaling in my bedroom and the older boys were working on school lessons, I heard Kiyoshi explode at Andrew and Isaac, who were playing in the living room. "Oh my gosh!

You're so noisy! How many times do I have to tell you? Stay in the bedroom!"

He'd had a growth spurt and started puberty since we'd evacuated from Ukraine, and the angry tones of his deep, masculine voice filled every corner of the apartment. I cringed. Hopefully, our neighbors wouldn't mistake the sound of his voice for the father of the family yelling at his kids. George would never do that.

The commotion drew me into the living room. "Andrew and Isaac, go play in your bedroom. Kiyoshi is doing school."

I went up to Kiyoshi, where he was sitting at the computer in the living room. "Kiyoshi, I need to talk to you."

"What?" he snapped, barely glancing at me.

"Kiyoshi," I took a deep breath, "I understand they can be irritating, but I won't let you treat your brothers that way. It's not okay to be mean to them."

He hung his head. "I know."

"You have amazing self-control. I've seen it. Can you please promise me you'll try to be patient with them?"

"Okay."

"Thank you." I squeezed his shoulder.

I understood how he felt.

I had begun to experience a sort of social claustrophobia because there wasn't a single space in our apartment where I could be alone. Even our small bedroom doubled as a schoolroom, and we only had one bathroom for eight people, so hiding there wasn't an option. Even when I was using it legitimately, I was likely to be interrupted by someone who needed it.

In one of our previous small apartments, I had discovered there was just enough room for me to sit in the space we used as a linen closet. When I was desperate for some alone time or needed a quiet place to talk on the phone, I'd go there. But the wardrobes in our current apartment were too cramped for me to fit inside. There was no relief from the constant company of other people.

We had spent nearly a year in a holding pattern, waiting to see what was going to happen in Ukraine. Initially, we had been willing to put up with the inconvenience of a tiny apartment because of the amazing park nearby—and because, in our minds, it wasn't long term. We were going back home soon. But as the war neared its first anniversary with no end in sight, I was beginning to realize this arrangement was no longer temporary.

In early February 2023, I received a text message from Anna, the Budapest friend who had offered to let us stay with her if war broke out in Ukraine. She was sharing a link to the listing for an apartment available for rent: **If you know anyone who's looking for a large apartment, this one is in your neighborhood. It's a great price for the location.**

I couldn't think of anyone who needed a large apartment, so I thanked her, closed the message, and dismissed it.

George had a different reaction. When he got home, he wanted to talk about it. "Did you see that message from Anna?"

"The one about the apartment?"

"Yeah."

"Yeah, I did."

"We should go look at it!" George sounded excited.

"Why?"

"For us."

"For us?" I asked, confused. We'd never talked about moving.

"Yeah, this place is too small."

"I don't want to move."

"But we need more space."

"I hate moving. I don't want to move again."

"Let's just look at it. We don't have to move if you don't want to."

"I don't know. What's the point of looking if we're not going to move?"

"It can't hurt just to look."

"Okay, I guess."

We took the three youngest kids to look at the apartment. We thought we lived close to the park, but this place was even closer. It had four bedrooms, a living room, and a large storage room that I could see becoming a LEGO workshop. One bedroom even had a disco ball with colored lights and a loft with a climbing rope. The boys were agog.

The apartment also had two full bathrooms. We had been making do with one for so long that the inconvenience now seemed normal, but I couldn't deny the allure of a life where we didn't need to keep a bucket on hand as a back-up toilet or leave the bathroom door unlocked while showering.

Despite my reluctance to move, I had to admit I loved the spacious kitchen. It reminded me of the homey kitchen in our Kyiv apartment where we had entertained a constant stream of friends. Could this apartment possibly be the answer to recreating that aspect of our life? Despite months of trying, we still did not have people gathering regularly in our Budapest apartment.

I went through all the rooms, taking a video to show the older boys, then we thanked the landlady and left.

"I think we should take it!" George said.

"Can we even afford it?" I asked. "It's more than double what we pay now."

"I think so. People have been really generous with us since the war."

"I still don't know about moving."

"We need to move."

"I need to pray about it."

When we talked to the kids, they had mixed reactions. Samuel, our eldest, was excited by the possibility.

"C'mon guys, let's move!" he said to his brothers.

"No," fourteen-year-old Kiyoshi said, categorically.

"Meh, I don't wanna," said twelve-year-old Peter.

"I don't want to move," six-year-old Andrew looked up at me with his worried little face.

"Move? Why?" nine-year-old James opened his expressive eyes wide in confusion.

Four-year-old Isaac didn't like the idea either.

If we moved, it would disrupt their lives all over again.

44

Good Advice

February–March 2023
Budapest, Hungary

The thought of moving paralyzed me. The tiny apartment where we all lived on top of each other was a safe, cozy space. It wasn't our real home, but it was our little cocoon, where we were recovering from the trauma of being displaced.

Our location was so convenient; why would we want to relocate? We had a grocery store and an indoor farmer's market right across the street. I had finally learned to shop there for almost everything we needed. I had it down to an art: stocking up once a week and hauling everything home in an oversized backpack and two large, reusable shopping bags. I knew exactly where to find everything and how much I could put in the cart and still be able to carry all the groceries on my own. I'd never be able to transport a week's worth of food all the way to the new apartment.

We had a parking space in the basement. Where would we park if we moved? We had great neighbors—some had even become friends. How could we say goodbye? We were safe here. Why would we upend our lives with another move?

For days the pain twisted inside me, as if someone were wringing the last drops of moisture from an overused rag. Every time I thought about moving, I curled around the hollow ache in my chest, and I wept. We couldn't do this. I couldn't do this. *Not again. Oh God, please, not again.*

I had managed to hold it together through seven moves in less than a month, and we were settled now. This was asking too much.

It was one thing to be strong when we had no choice, but we had a choice now. We did not have to put ourselves through this again.

Little by little, as I wrestled with God over this question, my perspective shifted. I was able to recognize my emotional response for what it was: an irrational reflex due to past trauma. In other words, a trigger for post-traumatic stress disorder (PTSD). There was nothing inherently threatening about moving. The danger was in my mind. I didn't have to be afraid.

I had a choice. I could let fear control me, insulate myself from the world, and hide from new experiences. Or I could break out of my fears, pursue life, and seize fresh opportunities. Seen in that light, the choice was simple. I knew moving was right.

I also realized it was a step I must take to set an example for my kids. I did not want to negatively influence them with my reluctance to take root where God chose to plant us. Even if I were okay living a stunted life while I waited to return to our "real" life in Ukraine, that was not what I wanted for my children. When it came to them, I would be satisfied with nothing less than their thriving here and now. But how could I help them achieve that if I was unwilling to pursue growth and fruitfulness myself?

During the first eight years of my life in Ukraine, I always lived in terms of the next move. We stayed in eight different apartments in the first four and a half years. Most of those relocations were forced on us by things beyond our control, so at some point I accepted that we would never live anywhere long-term. Rather than unpack and repack every few months, I bought a bunch of clear plastic storage bins to hold most of our belongings. I stacked them in closets or out-of-the-way corners, and when the time came, we just picked them up and took them to the next place. During that stage, I didn't decorate our living spaces. What was the point when I had no idea how long we'd be staying?

I remember the day I finally started to turn our rented spaces into homes by daring to settle in and even decorate. It was transformational, and I wondered why I'd waited so many years. Now I realized it was time to dare again. We needed to settle in, this time, in Hungary. Among other things, that would mean getting a larger apartment.

Our apartment may have felt like a safe cocoon, but like a cocoon, it had become too constricting. We had been growing and changing over the past year, and now it was time to emerge. God had given us wings. It was time to learn to use them.

The five younger kids were still resistant to the idea of moving. I realized I needed to help them see the good things that could come with a move, but I wasn't sure how. Andrew unknowingly provided the needed inspiration. Seeking ways to make the kids feel more at home in Hungary, I asked them what they missed about our apartment in Kyiv.

Andrew didn't even have to think about his answer. "I miss our LEGOs."

We'd had a huge plastic bin, the kind for storing things under a bed, filled with thousands of LEGO pieces collected over the course of a decade of raising boys.

Andrew's words gave me a sudden flash of inspiration. "I'm sorry you miss your LEGOs, buddy. But where would we put them?"

"In our room."

"But it's too small. If we put the LEGO bin in your room, it would take up the whole play area, and you'd have to stand in the bin to get in the closet!"

"But that's okay."

"No, we couldn't live that way. But you know what? If we moved to the bigger apartment, Daddy could go to Kyiv and get your LEGOs. Remember that storage room in the apartment we looked at? There'd be plenty of space to put your LEGOs there!"

Andrew looked thoughtful. I didn't say anything else, but I hoped this tactic would change his opinion about moving. It seemed a little manipulative, and I tried not to feel guilty.

A few days later, my sister called. I told her about the possible move and the kids' resistance to it.

"You know," she said, "when people experience trauma, the imagination center of the brain shuts off, because when you're running from a tiger, your imagination isn't going to help you survive. So when you're traumatized, you can't imagine that things could be different than they are—or that they could be better. You need to help the boys imagine how the new apartment could be better."

After that, I no longer felt manipulative as I looked for opportunities to help the kids imagine the benefits of more space. The next time Kiyoshi got upset with his brothers about being too loud, I pointed out that the new apartment would have enough rooms for him to have privacy when he needed it. When Peter was trying to record sound files in the kitchen for a song he was producing, I told him about the little bedroom at the bigger apartment where he would be able to record in a quieter environment.

Little by little, I chipped away at the kids' resistance. After a few weeks, everyone came around. We let the owner of the big apartment know we'd made up our minds. The current tenants had a contract through the spring. After some renovation, we would be able to move in July 2023.

In helping the kids reimagine our situation, I had awakened the imagination center in my own brain. I was looking forward to the move as a new beginning.

There was another significant beginning around the same time, but this one was not hopeful. On February 24, 2023, the full-scale war in Ukraine began its second year. That day was jarring for me. It was not just the anniversary of the war: it also marked the twentieth anniversary of my move to Ukraine from the United States.

I had looked forward to that milestone for a decade. I had assumed I would still be living in Ukraine, anticipating many more years of fulfilling work. I expected to celebrate in Ukraine with a huge party, a reunion with friends from all the different stages of my life there. Instead, I found myself exiled from my adopted home. Along with everything else the war had stolen from me, it had also taken that milestone.

Now, when we introduce ourselves, George says that before the war, he and I lived in Ukraine for thirty years and twenty years, respectively. I always wince. I want to interrupt to point out that, while he left Ukraine only four months shy of reaching that impressive thirty-year mark, I lived there just nineteen years to the day before fleeing. I have no right to claim two decades in my adopted home.

I once asked him about it privately, and he said he was rounding up. I pointed out that while he had every right to round up, I couldn't. Nineteen years and zero months doesn't round anywhere. It's just nineteen. But he keeps telling the same story every time we meet someone new. And I keep wincing and biting my tongue.

Maybe he's right. Who am I to tell him how to round numbers? He's the one with the master's degree in applied mathematics. Maybe the story he tells is the true one. But it feels like a lie to me, for my heart tells a different story: I dreamed of the day I could say I had lived in Ukraine for twenty years, but now I can only say I lived there for nineteen.

In light of the bigger picture of the war, this is a trivial loss. But it was a pain that cut me keenly, and as such, I believe it worth recognizing.

Even if I had been in Ukraine on that day, I'm sure I would not have felt like celebrating. February 24th is no longer my day. Just as Osama bin Laden's attack on the Twin Towers made the date September 11th synonymous with death and carnage in the minds of all Americans, Putin's invasion of Ukraine imbued the date February 24th with enough infamy to last Ukrainians for several generations. Now, no one who loves Ukraine can hear that date without feeling anger and pain. It would have been wrong to celebrate anything on that day.

As spring arrived, we thanked God that Ukraine had survived not just the first year of the war, but also the winter. Russia had attempted to break the spirit of the Ukrainian people by destroying the country's electricity and heating infrastructure during the coldest months of the year. The plan backfired. Putin's tactic of causing widespread civilian suffering only made Ukrainians angry—and strengthened their resolve to win.

During the fall and winter months, we raised money to send generators and satellite internet devices to Ukraine. The government initiated a program to help people cope with the rolling blackouts and lack of heating. Any place with a generator and satellite internet could register as a Point of Invincibility. Throughout that long, dark winter, the Points of Invincibility gave people locations to warm up, charge their phones and laptops, and get online. Several of the Ukrainian churches in our network served their communities in this way. Our old apartment in Podil even became a Point of Invincibility.

Spring 2023 brought new life to me. The adjustment process was still slow, but it was far less painful than during the previous year. I was in a new stage, with more groundedness, purpose, and satisfaction.

Despite these encouraging changes, throughout that spring I had a recurring, perplexing experience. It could strike anytime I was relaxed and enjoying the moment—perhaps while strolling in the park, raising my face to the sun, and inhaling the fresh air. Or while hanging out at a friend's home, smiling at the banter among a group of people we had met after coming to Budapest. I might glance around the room at the happy faces of new friends, then suddenly be yanked out of the moment. I would feel disconnected from what was going on around me, trapped in a bewildering maze of confusing sentiments. I could fight my way back to the positivity of the moment, but the episodes kept happening until they forced me to pay attention. What was my heart saying?

For a year, I had been in survival mode. Each day I simply did the next thing to care for our kids and reestablish our family. As a result, we now had a full life, complete with new routines and relationships. The shock and pain of being displaced began to fade. As they did, I started to experience things differently.

I finally came to myself after a year of hurt and lostness. I awoke to a life with all the pieces arranged—and I did not recognize it. *What is this place? How did we get here? Who are these people? Is this really our life now?*

The disorienting feelings would intrude into normal moments without warning. It was unnerving and uncomfortable. I became hesitant to relax and enjoy anything. If I kept my guard up at all times, I couldn't be ambushed. Maybe then I could avoid being off balance and uncertain. But constant vigilance was exhausting and joyless, and it made me feel neurotic. Eventually, I stopped repressing the unwelcome feelings and accepted them as a necessary part of the path to healing.

One day I was walking near our apartment, and I ran into a neighbor who was coming home after picking up her two kids from kindergarten. Like me, she was a foreigner, but she'd been living in Hungary longer than I'd been in Ukraine. She seemed right at home. She spoke several languages, including English and Hungarian. After Viktor and Fruzsi, she had been one of the first neighbors to welcome us after we moved into our building.

"Hi, how are you?" I greeted her.

"Hello! We are well. We are grateful for all the beautiful things in our life." She paused after that philosophical pronouncement and peered deeply into my eyes. "How are you?"

I realized she wasn't expecting or wanting me to say I was fine, unless I truly meant it.

"We're actually doing well," I answered thoughtfully. "Last week was the anniversary of the start of the war, and that was hard. We didn't think we'd be here this long. And it was also the twentieth anniversary of my moving to Ukraine, so it was hard not to be there to celebrate. But we've realized we need to stop living like we're only here temporarily. We recently signed a contract for a larger apartment near the park."

"I'm really happy for you!" She paused. "We fled Serbia twenty years ago with nothing. You just have to move forward." She shrugged and smiled gently, looking a little sheepish. "That's my very simple advice."

I was stunned to learn that this kind and caring woman who seemed like a Budapest native had arrived as a refugee. I hadn't known her backstory. I couldn't imagine we would still be in Hungary in twenty years, but if we were, maybe there was hope I, too, could learn to feel at home and find the same level of peace and contentment she modeled.

45

Trapped in Grief and Guilt

March 2023
Budapest, Hungary

Despite the upheaval and change that had characterized our life for the past thirteen months, George was thriving. After he fled Ukraine in the wee hours of the war's third day, reuniting with the kids and me, he went to bed utterly exhausted. But he only slept a few hours, and upon awaking, found himself surrounded by amazing opportunities to do enormous good. Without pausing to take a breath or missing a beat, he jumped into a swirl of activities and new partnerships. These resulted in hundreds of evacuations in the war's critical early weeks, aid worth millions of dollars, and ongoing help for refugees in Hungary and elsewhere in Europe. I had rarely seen him more alive.

On one of our nighttime walks with our dog in March 2023, I found myself wrestling with the disparity between our separate experiences of being displaced. While I had spent months unable even to pronounce the sentence, "I live in Budapest," George hadn't had any trouble moving forward into the new life God had given us. In fact, he embraced it.

While we usually used the time walking Jack to debrief about the day, on this particular night, we were silent as we walked, absorbed in our own thoughts. Mine were heavy. Grief over the loss of our old life had resurfaced. The cycle was relentless. Would I ever feel normal again?

For months, I had waited for George to begin the grieving process, but he seemed completely fine. I was grateful he was balanced and able to do so much good. At the same time, I felt alone in my pain and wished for his companionship. I couldn't understand how he could be so unaffected by the catastrophe that had shattered our world. As we walked, I wanted to break the silence by asking, "Do you even miss Ukraine?" I held the words on the tip of my tongue for half a block, wanting so badly to say them, but sensing they were somehow wrong.

As I reflected, I had to admit it was a horrible question. It wouldn't invite any conversation, it might put George on the defensive, and it was almost certainly unfair. My husband had spent thirty of his forty-seven years of life in Ukraine—he had to miss it. So I sorted through my feelings and tried to come up with a better question.

After we crossed a street and started down another block, I finally asked him, "What do you miss about Ukraine?"

He hardly had to pause to think before answering. "I miss the people . . . friends . . . and I miss being able to go up to anyone and just start a conversation."

He spoke thoughtfully and softly, but without any apparent emotion. Even so, it was comforting to hear his heart and know that, despite seeming unaffected, my partner in life also shared in the loss I felt so keenly. I carried this knowledge into the coming days, a quiet reassurance that I was not alone.

A few days later, George and I were on our way to a meeting, struggling through Budapest morning traffic. I had forgotten to put on my watch, so I leaned over to read George's. We were an hour behind schedule! How in the world had that happened? I frantically drew George's attention to the time, and he calmly explained that his watch was set to Kyiv time, which is an hour ahead of Budapest's.

My immediate relief that we weren't running late quickly gave way to curiosity. Why was his watch set to Kyiv time? Had he simply forgotten to change it after his most recent trip back to Ukraine? I asked questions, and the truth came out.

He never reset it after evacuating.

Even through the three months we spent in the United States over the summer (where the time difference would have been much less easy to calculate), he clung to that one last connection to our former life. Unlike me, he never had any trouble saying we lived in Budapest, but all the while, his watch face showed where his heart truly was.

By contrast, my watch had stopped working soon after we left Ukraine. Maybe it was out of protest when I reset it to match our new time zone.

As far as I could tell, George never struggled with any sense of guilt over leaving Ukraine. I did. From survivor's guilt, to regret over the cascade of decisions that ultimately led to evacuating, to types of guilt for which I didn't have names—I experienced it. At one point I was even torturing myself with the accusation that, when it came right down to it, I hadn't loved Ukraine enough to stay when things got dangerous. Though trusted advisors told me flat-out this was a lie, I found it difficult to believe them. In the midst of all the pain from external forces, I was actively shredding my own heart to ribbons.

I think the reason George didn't have to deal with guilt is that while I was mostly isolated at home with the kids, hurting and grieving, he was out in the thick of things, being and doing. And everything he was doing was having a positive impact on Ukrainians. Even from my vantage point, it wasn't hard to see that God had put us in Hungary to fill a crucial role few others could. I would tell myself we had been uniquely prepared for this moment in history, we were doing important work, and we were exactly where we were supposed to be. I believed it—but for many months, I didn't feel it. I would simply repeat this mantra to assuage the pain and guilt I felt over not being in Ukraine. It didn't work.

My greatest source of guilt was one I refused to talk about. Though it was my habit to talk to God about everything that troubled me, I made this topic off-limits even with him. I first felt this guilt after we got settled in Budapest. Once my trauma-induced brain fog cleared a little, I remembered the psalm I had read before the full-scale invasion. I recalled that I had been certain God was telling me we were not to be afraid, that we were to trust him and stay in Kyiv.

But we hadn't.

Instead, we followed the advice of a friend, and the kids and I left Kyiv. We didn't even pause to ask God about this step. Then I gave in to fear and fled Ukraine without George, and he'd been forced to follow us to Hungary. Now our whole family was living outside Ukraine, and *it was all my fault*. I felt like I had disobeyed God and led my husband and kids astray as well.

I had spent my entire life enjoying the exquisite beauty of a life lived close to Jesus. I had basked in his love, listened for his voice, and followed wherever he led. I didn't know how to handle this perceived breach. I was devastated by my failure.

Moving back to Ukraine seemed out of the question. We had too many refugees in Hungary depending on us. I simply needed to receive God's forgiveness and move on. But I was too ashamed. How could I ask God to forgive me? Wasn't I living in rebellion to his instructions to stay in Kyiv? It would be hypocritical to ask for forgiveness when I had no intention of obeying. And didn't God hate religious hypocrisy? My thoughts spiraled from guilt into suffocating self-condemnation.

At the same time, I had to admit I didn't sense God was displeased with us. On the contrary, it seemed he had meant for us to come to Hungary to serve refugees and be a bridge between war-affected Ukrainians and those in the West with the means to help. The refugees George and his team visited told them no one was doing what we were doing. There were plenty of aid organizations with distribution points in Budapest, but the people we visited in cities all over Hungary said we were the only ones who came to them and cared for them.

A little over half a year after our team started making these trips to support displaced Ukrainians, a lady named Natalia told us something that would reshape much of what we were doing. Most of the refugees were women and children, since men between the ages of eighteen and sixty weren't allowed to leave Ukraine. Though Ukrainians are among the most highly educated people in the world, many of these women had been forced to take low-paying, factory jobs and were living in crowded shelters where they shared one room with their kids and used communal bathroom and kitchen facilities. Even if they had husbands in Ukraine, these women were essentially single mothers.

Despite these conditions, when we visited Natalia's city to distribute aid shortly before Christmas, she told us, "You don't have to bring us anything. Just come and talk with us. Our greatest needs are emotional and spiritual."

Partly in response to this appeal, Olya, our teammate and former apartment mate, created a course on emotional health for refugee women. A singer and songwriter, Olya had a natural ability to clearly communicate profound truths. The full-scale invasion froze her budding music career by ruining the long-anticipated launch of her debut album, but she turned her talents in another direction. She compiled all the research and strategies that helped her cope with being forcibly displaced and shared them with women in small discussion groups.

Olya partnered with a graphic design artist on our team to create beautiful worksheets that we printed in full color and gifted to the women. These pages highlighted all the important information Olya presented and gave them a place to process their feelings and record the action steps they would take to move forward with their lives.

The ladies were deeply grateful for everything we did. As a result of our actions and conversations with George and his team, many of the women were starting to understand God's special love for them. It seemed obvious that God wanted us in Hungary.

This realization brought me little comfort. Instead, it gave me another reason to feel guilty. If God had wanted us to come to Hungary, then he couldn't have told me to stay in Kyiv. That meant I had imagined he was speaking to me when he hadn't actually been saying anything.

I had thought I knew how it felt when God whispered to my heart. I had been certain I heard him. That I could have been so mistaken was as painful as the idea that I had disobeyed him.

I could see only two logical options: either I was a rebellious daughter—or I was a daughter who knew her Father so little that she couldn't even recognize his voice. I had no idea which was true, but both shook me to my core.

I had experienced the lavish grace of God in the past. I knew sweet forgiveness was mine for the asking. I understood that Jesus became human for that reason—to die as the scapegoat for everything wrong I'd ever do. If I had disobeyed him, God would forgive me freely, because Jesus had already been punished in my place. All I had to do was ask. But I didn't. I was locked in a prison of guilt.

In my shame, I withdrew from everyone, even George. We never kept things from each other, but I didn't know how to share this. Knowing I was hiding a dark secret, I gradually became less open, afraid George would realize something was wrong if I let him get too close.

This went on for six months or more. I don't know where this downward spiral would have taken me. Thankfully, God loved me too much to let me find out. He gave me Olya. He gave me George. And he gave me Jack.

Olya devoted an entire lesson in her emotional health course to the topic of survivor's guilt and emailed it to me. I had an "aha" moment as I read her explanation for the complicated emotions that assail people who survive traumatic incidents. I was intimately acquainted with the feelings she described, and I wept as I read her words on how to cope with my guilt over leaving Ukraine when others had stayed.

Remember who is actually guilty in this situation—it's not your fault. The guilty party is the aggressor who attacked our land and is forcing everyone to suffer. ~ Don't take responsibility for factors that were beyond your control. ~ Be kind to yourself: there's no guidebook for how to live or make decisions in the context of war—you did what was best for you and your family under the circumstances. ~ Think about all the people who love you and want you to be safe.

The words were balm to my lacerated heart.

That night when George and I took Jack for his evening walk, I shared how Olya's course was helping me. I told George how much I was suffering from survivor's guilt. I felt a loosening of tension as I opened up to him. I hadn't planned to talk about the deeper guilt plaguing me, but as we continued to stroll with our dog, I realized I wanted to come clean.

"I've been feeling guilty about something else, too."

"Oh? What is it?"

I took a deep breath to settle my nerves, then I shared my feelings about leaving Kyiv when I thought God had told me to stay. I ended with, "Either I'm a disobedient daughter, or I'm a daughter who can't recognize her Father's voice." I blinked, and tears trickled down my cheeks.

George looked at me, took my hand, and squeezed it. "Or—God just wanted to give you the gift of choice."

I didn't understand what he meant. I mulled it over while we continued to walk. "Wait . . . you mean maybe God was speaking to me through that psalm, but he wasn't telling me that we had to stay—he was just saying that if we chose to stay, he would protect us? . . . That we had the option to stay, but we could do what we wanted?"

"Yeah."

It was as if the heavens parted, and I glimpsed the mysteries of the universe. I drew a quick breath as my eyes opened wide in wonder. "That makes a lot more sense. That matches what I know of God. Wow . . . thank you."

"You're welcome." George chuckled.

I squeezed his hand and glanced sideways up at him. "You're pretty wise—you know that?"

"That's why you married me, right?" He grinned, released my hand, pulled me close, and kissed the top of my head. The wall I'd been building between us dissolved, and I melted into his embrace.

I dismantled the wall I had been constructing between myself and God. It took a while for my emotions to get in line with my new understanding, but I no longer tried to hide my feelings from my Creator. I talked to him about every nuance, even the recurring guilt. I ranted in prayer about my confusion and pain. I asked him to forgive me for allowing fear to influence my decisions instead of calmly trusting him. And I knew, in the deepest way I could know anything, that he was right beside me, cheering me on.

46

I MISS MY HOME

April 2023
Kyiv, Ukraine

As months passed with our kids still separated from their friends, George and I discussed having the older ones visit Kyiv with George the next time he went. By that point, he had made several trips to Ukraine.

I was nervous about George's safety when he was in Ukraine, but he always promised to heed the air-raid sirens and take shelter, even if the locals didn't. The sirens had become a normal part of existence, so by that point, many people had started to ignore them. Life hadn't stopped for the war, and running back and forth to the closest makeshift bomb shelter several times a day was a huge disruption to one's daily routine.

When we announced the plan for George to take Samuel, Kiyoshi, and Peter to Kyiv to see their friends, ten-year-old James shot a reproachful look at George and me.

"I want to see my friends too!"

"Which friends?" I asked, puzzled, because all the friends his age had left Ukraine.

"You know, Illia, Reveka, Ira . . ." his voice trailed off as he listed adults who had been part of our community. My throat constricted. I had underestimated how much being displaced had affected my fourth son.

"What about me?" six-year-old Andrew interrupted. "I want to go to Kyiv too!"

"You want to go to Kyiv? Why?"

"To see our apartment!"

"Me too!" four-year-old Isaac chimed in cheerfully, his large, brown eyes sparkling.

We decided to make a trip to Ukraine as a family. Kyiv had been "quiet" for a bit. That was the new Ukrainian euphemism for days without aerial attacks. We seized the opportunity and scheduled a quick visit.

On April 14, 2023, we drove from Budapest to Ternopil, retracing our evacuation route of over a year ago. When we reached the border, the first effect of the war I noticed was the presence of female guards at the Ukrainian checkpoint. George explained that they were women who had enlisted in the army and were given these less dangerous jobs to free up more men to fight.

A male guard dressed in army fatigues checked our van while his female colleague looked on. She was wearing a matching uniform and a stern expression, and she held an automatic weapon slanted across the front of her body. There were always armed guards at the border, but usually their weapons were slung across their backs, not held at the ready. The war had everyone on a heightened sense of alert.

The male guard was shocked that a family of Americans was crossing into Ukraine. He was also surprised that we could speak Ukrainian.

"We lived in Kyiv before the full-scale invasion," George explained. "We're taking the kids back to see friends."

The guard nodded sympathetically and handed back our documents.

"Glory to Ukraine!" George used the patriotic expression that had become the country's rallying cry in the face of Russian aggression.

"Glory to the heroes!" The guard answered with the standard response and waved us through.

Without the long lines of evacuees at the border and at military checkpoints, the entire trip only took about ten hours. Friends and family in Ternopil were expecting us. They had organized a simple evening reception in our honor. It was already dark when we arrived. People were genuinely happy to see us, but the atmosphere was subdued.

Though Ternopil had been spared most of the violence of war, the town had absorbed a huge number of displaced people. This church had done an amazing amount of work from day one of the war to house them, feed them, and provide for their needs while they got back on their feet. The demands were never-ending, and the church members were exhausted.

We talked in small groups or one-on-one, picking up the threads of old friendships, trying to relate to what these dear people were living through. The time was over all too soon, and we said goodbye and checked into the apartment we had reserved for the night. We met for breakfast with George's brothers Jon and Aaron and their families.

The morning with family went by too quickly, but we couldn't linger. Kiyoshi's best friend was leaving Kyiv the next day to visit his dad, who had a few days' leave from military service. We needed to make it to Kyiv early enough for Kiyoshi to have time with his friend before he caught his train the next morning. We said our goodbyes and got back on the road for the six-hour drive.

As we approached the outskirts of the capital city, ten-year-old James spoke up. "What happened to that building?"

"What building?" I asked, looking back over my shoulder at him.

"That one back there." He pointed.

"I'm sorry. I didn't see it."

Fourteen-year-old Kiyoshi never missed anything. He turned his dark, pensive eyes toward me. "It's from the war."

"What?" Twelve-year-old Peter was suddenly sitting up straight and staring out the window.

Before long, we saw more damaged buildings. I had known they were there—George had shown me pictures after his first trip back to Kyiv—but it hadn't prepared me for seeing them firsthand.

My mouth felt suddenly dry, and there was a heavy feeling in the pit of my stomach. I couldn't stop staring at the bombed buildings, even though it felt inappropriate to gawk. Broken rooflines. Metal beams bent and twisted. A huge complex with all its metal siding blown out and crumpled as if made from something no more substantial than cardboard. Each new evidence of Russia's aggression held my gaze. Involuntarily, I found myself twisting around in my seat and watching until it was out of sight.

The war had never felt so close. This caught me by surprise. I hadn't thought about seeing the destruction on this drive, and I hadn't done anything to prepare the kids. I wanted to help them process what they were seeing, but I couldn't think of anything to say. I had static in my brain.

We made it to our old neighborhood just before the curfew started. We dropped Samuel, Peter, and James off where they would be staying: the home of Peter's best friend, Misha.

Shortly after the war started, Misha and his mom had evacuated to Poland. The previous April, our family had driven to Poland and spent a day and a half with them. It was clear that the refugee experience was crushing their spirits. By the end of summer, Misha and his mom were tired of living apart from their father and husband. They decided to go home.

Misha's dad worried for his family's safety and would have preferred they stay in Poland, but Kyiv seemed safe, so they returned. A few weeks later, a wave of missiles rained down on Kyiv and other targets around the country, announcing a new phase of the war: throughout the fall and winter of 2022-2023, Russia relentlessly and systematically targeted civilian infrastructure all over the country. Thanks to advanced air-defense systems, Kyiv was well protected compared to the rest of the country, but even the falling debris from intercepted missiles damaged buildings, ignited fires, and killed people. Kyivans called days like these "noisy."

Since Peter didn't have his own phone, he and Misha communicated with each other using one of the messaging apps on my phone. Whenever I saw that Misha had written, I'd hand my phone to Peter so he could respond. One morning I saw this message: *Good morning! But it's not a good morning for me. I'm scared.*

Tears obscured my vision as I took my phone to Peter. I pictured sweet Misha, with his quiet manners and innocent blue eyes, cowering in fear at the blasts overhead. My free hand clenched into a fist, and I wanted to pound something. For one of the first times in my life, I actually had no words to express my feelings.

I thanked God our children did not have to live with that kind of stress and trauma. They faced trauma of another sort, but I hoped being displaced would turn out to be the lesser of two evils. They just needed to find healthy ways to process their feelings.

One way Peter coped with his pain was by writing and recording a song. He finished it shortly before our trip to Kyiv. When I heard it, I knew we'd made the right choice to take the kids back to visit.

I Miss My Home

Verse 1:

I never thought that I'd leave Ukraine,
But now I've been gone such a long, long time.
Sometimes I can't stand the pain,
But sometimes I feel just fine.

Chorus:

It makes me sad—why did everything change?
But I'll fight my tears and hide the pain.
It breaks my heart—why can't I be at home?
But I'll push right through it, even when I'm alone.

Verse 2:

Now it has been almost one year,
Since the last time I saw my best friend.
Every day I wish he could be here—
Will we have a happy end?

Chorus

Verse 3:

I hope and pray that Ukraine will win.
I believe that the tide will turn.
When it's over, Ukraine will rise again,
And then all her children can return!

Chorus Variation:

It makes me sad—this is not what I want,
But I trust God if I go home or not.
It breaks my heart—why can't we all be free?
But I know God knows what's best for me.[1]

Scan to watch song.

---

1. *Watch Peter's music video: SharonTMarkey.com/song*

He'd consulted with me for help with the rhymes, but the heart behind the song was all Peter's. He wrote the chorus variation entirely on his own, and the first time I heard it, I was stunned by the depth of faith in my little boy. Now God had answered the cry of his heart and was allowing him to see his best friend again.

After leaving the three boys at Misha's apartment, we dropped Kiyoshi off to spend the night with his friend. I had reserved a private room in a nearby hostel for George and me and the two youngest kids. When we entered, I noticed signs pointing the way to the bomb shelter, which was simply the building's basement. It was a sobering reminder of the risk we were taking by visiting Kyiv.

47

Seeing Ghosts

April 2023
Kyiv, Ukraine

The next day, we went to our old apartment. We parked by the curb and walked under the arch into the familiar courtyard outside the apartment's entrance. The grapevines on the building were covered in lush greenery, with clusters of immature grapes already peeking through. Breathless with excitement, I paused to inhale deeply. The cool air smelled of damp earth and growing things. It felt like coming home.

Illia and Reveka, our friends and former teammates who now lived there with their new team, ran out to greet us with excited exclamations. We all hugged long and hard. I had tears in my eyes, and I wasn't the only one.

As soon as we stepped through the door of the apartment, four-year-old Isaac gave a gleeful cry and ran to the stairs. I heard his little feet thumping down the wooden steps to the basement, where we'd had our family room and playroom. Before long, I heard his excited footfalls coming back up. Without pausing, he ran up the stairs to the second floor as if we still lived there.

I realized I should have prepared him by explaining this was other people's home now. We couldn't barge into all the rooms. It was too late for that, because I couldn't stop him in front of our friends. With typical Ukrainian forbearance for children's antics, they would just tell me it was fine for him to go wherever he wanted. Maybe it was better that way. I was happy for his sake that I hadn't thought to say anything ahead of time that would have put a damper on his joy.

Over the next two days, I spent hours in the apartment. My goal was to sort through all the things we had left behind and decide what we would get rid of, donate, or take back to Budapest. We didn't want our belongings to be a burden to the apartment's new tenants, and if the landlords decided to sell, we didn't want to be stuck scrambling to move our things in a hurry.

It was a huge undertaking: our large family had accumulated a lot of stuff over the years. When they moved in, Illia and Reveka had graciously taken on the job of packing what they couldn't use into a few storage spaces in the huge apartment. I started in the basement, in a closet under the stairs.

Like a real-life game of Tetris, furniture, boxes, and random items filled all the available nooks and crannies. The physical work of excavating them was exhausting. The emotions were unspeakably worse.

Soon, I was surrounded by echoes of our old life. It was like seeing ghosts. I just wanted to sit on the floor, hug my knees to my chest, put my head down, and sob until I had no tears left, but that would take precious minutes I couldn't afford. I forced myself to keep my eyes dry and my hands busy.

Once again, knowing the reality beforehand did nothing to prepare me for the experience. This apartment was home to other people now; they were living here and using our things. I was happy for our friends to benefit, but seeing our belongings made it hard to accept that this was no longer our home. Everywhere I looked, I saw something that had been part of our life for years, things we had used over and over again during happier days.

There was our green couch where we'd entertained so many friends, our four-poster bed with its graceful metal headboard and footboard and memory-foam mattress, the dishes we'd chosen together early in our marriage, beautiful artwork that had come to us as gifts, and so much more. I couldn't enter a room without seeing something that reminded me of our life before the war. I hadn't thought of many of these items for over a year, but as soon as I saw them, memories came flooding back, an overwhelming onslaught of nostalgia and grief.

At the same time, not everything was the same. Furniture had been moved; rooms had been repurposed. It didn't look like our home anymore, and the combination of familiar objects and a changed environment created a jarring dissonance.

Reveka approached me partway through that first day to ask how I was doing. It was awkward because she was clearly so happy to see me, but my distress was caused in part because she was living in my home. I was tempted to say I was fine, but I decided to tell the truth, searching for just the right words in Ukrainian to express my discomfort.

"To be honest, it's hard for me to be here. I feel like I'm at home, but I know I'm not. Other people live here now. But I see all our stuff, and it feels so familiar—but then other things are different . . . it's really hard." I sniffled and brushed tears off my cheeks.

She gave me a long, comforting hug.

"Thank you," I said.

"You know, if you want to take anything, don't worry about it. These are your things. Take whatever you want."

I was amazed at her perceptiveness. I had been wrestling with precisely this problem. As soon as I saw many of the treasures we'd left behind, I had a longing to pack them up and take them back to Budapest to incorporate into our new life. But I didn't know if I could bring myself to steal them away from the people who had been enjoying them in our absence. It would have felt too selfish.

Reveka's words gave me a great gift: the freedom to take bits of our old life back with us. Besides the things from the basement closet that I decided to keep, I also packed two cozy fleece blankets that my sister had given us, a pair of laundry baskets with a lovely wicker design, a reprint of a sunset painting, and a glass jar filled with beautiful seashells.

I worked for hours in the basement over the course of two days. I felt like I was being buried alive under the growing piles of things I was sorting. Despite my best efforts, I wasn't able to finish going through everything in the short time we had. The rest would have to wait for another visit.

While I was working, Andrew and Isaac played with forgotten toys they'd discovered. I kept my two youngest children close by, reassured that if there was an air-raid siren, we would already be underground. Their happy chatter filled the basement, a stark contrast to my heaviness.

George and the older kids took advantage of the time to reconnect with people. I didn't have much time for socializing, but I made the most of the few hours I could spare. Since I had to eat anyway, I shared most of my meals with different friends. We also invited everyone we knew to an evening reception, which allowed us to see many more people than we had the time to visit individually.

One afternoon George watched the little boys while I traveled across the city to a dear friend's apartment. She met me just outside the subway station, and we threw our arms around each other.

As we walked to her home, she pointed out a huge crater on the far side of a large playing field.

"See that? A rocket hit in the middle of the day. Normally, there would have been lots of people on this path going to and from the subway, or going from the dorms to the university. Praise God, no one was hurt."

"Wow! How is that possible?"

"It was during an air-raid siren, so most people were inside. The kids and I were at home." She pointed to a building on the far edge of the field. It seemed to be made entirely of glass and steel. "See that building? All the windows on both sides were blown out. It was so loud. My son wouldn't talk for an hour afterwards. I can tell he's still traumatized."

We reached her apartment building. My friend made tea, and we took seats opposite each other at the kitchen table. It felt cozy and homey, but I was on edge. What was the right way to approach this conversation? I had to make it count. There was no time for small talk.

I dived right into the deep end. "What has it been like? How are you managing?"

My friend stared into her mug for a moment. "Oh, how can I describe it to you?" She sighed. "There's an underground parking lot across from our building, but we don't go there anymore when there's a siren. There's nowhere to sit, and the air-raid alert can last for hours, and you're just standing down there in the cold. Now we just follow the two-wall rule."

"The what?"

"You know, the two-wall rule." Her tone indicated that everyone knew what that was.

Feeling a little foolish because of my ignorance, I admitted, "I don't know what that is."

"It means there needs to be two walls between you and the outside."

"Oh, I see." My mouth went dry as I grasped the significance. Two walls to stand between you and an incoming bomb.

"So we just sit in our hallway. We put the kids to bed at night, and the sirens usually go off between 11 pm and 1 am. So we get them up and all move into the hallway. It can be four o'clock in the morning before the all-clear sounds. The kids fall asleep in the hallway before then, but my husband and I can't sleep until we go back to bed. And then you have to get up in the morning and go through your day like normal. And when you read the news, you see who was hit. You're relieved that you 'got lucky,'" she made air quotes with her fingers, "but then you feel guilty that your home is still intact when others got hit during the night."

"I can't even imagine living like that. I'm so sorry." My Ukrainian words felt inadequate. I wished for better ones to convey the depth of my empathy, but if I found them, wouldn't they make a mockery of her experience? What did I know of her suffering? I had fled on the second day of the war and had only returned for this brief visit. Sitting across from her at that table, I was ashamed to say anything about my own pain or the challenges we had faced. I didn't feel I had the right to speak in the presence of one who had endured the real hardships of war.

The time went by far too quickly, and soon I had to say goodbye. We embraced tightly. It wasn't enough. I had no idea when we would see each other again. We were now separated by more than just hundreds of miles of terrain and an international border. The complications of traversing a nation at war and the vast differences between our respective experiences since the beginning of the full-scale invasion added to the distance between us.

On one of my breaks from sorting through things in our former apartment, I took a walk around our old neighborhood. I loved this part of Kyiv more than just about anywhere else in the world. My steps took me to the Dnipro River, and I walked along the bank, surveying the water and the historic buildings across from it. It was beautifully picturesque, almost as I remembered it. These streets were unscarred by the war. But they were not completely unmarked.

I was confused to see odd metal structures clustered at various points along the sidewalk. Three long metal beams attached in the middle, they looked like mammoth versions of the six-pronged metal pieces from the children's game Jacks. With a quickening of my pulse, I realized what they were. Tank obstacles. They must have been hurriedly constructed during the battle for Kyiv and strategically placed to impede the progress of enemy tanks, should the Russian army break through the city's outer defenses. Now that Kyiv was no longer in immediate danger of being overrun, the structures had been moved to the side of the road. Their presence was a sobering reminder of just how close the capital—and our own neighborhood—had come to falling.

On April 18, 2023, we packed our van with all the things we were taking back to Budapest and tearfully hugged our friends goodbye. As we passed through the familiar streets of our old neighborhood one last time, I could hardly breathe past the strangled feeling in my throat. I pinched my lips together and blinked rapidly in an effort to maintain control, but my will broke. I opened my lips, and silent, breathy sobs escaped my mouth.

We would most likely return to visit this beloved city, but I was realizing it was unlikely we would ever return here to live—and my heart was breaking all over again.

While we drove, George debriefed the kids. "How was it being back in Kyiv again?"

"It was cool," Kiyoshi said.

"I'm mad there were no bombs," Samuel said.

"What?" I twisted around and stared at Samuel. "How in the world can you say that?" I knew my sixteen-year-old liked to make ludicrous statements purely for their shock value, but this seemed too insensitive, even for him.

"It would have been cool to experience." Samuel's clear, gray eyes steadily met my gaze. He seemed sincere.

I realized I felt something similar when it came to the horrendous winter Ukrainians had just endured. Russia's precision attacks on Ukraine's civilian infrastructure throughout the fall and winter resulted in a serious energy crisis. When I heard people's stories of the rolling blackouts and how they planned their whole lives around the few hours a day when their building was scheduled to have power, part of me wished I had been there for those dark months. Since the hours of electricity didn't always happen during daylight, people had tales of getting up in the middle of the night to charge all their devices, do laundry, and cook all the meals for the next day.

Families found new ways to pass the long winter evenings, playing card games by battery-operated light or watching movies they downloaded to laptops they charged during their allotted hours of electricity. The experience had unified the country. I was thankful my children hadn't suffered through frigid nights without heat, but part of me was sad we hadn't been there for that historic winter—to test our mettle against the difficult conditions and come out stronger, to suffer side-by-side with the people we loved.

"Well," I said to Samuel, "I'm glad there weren't any sirens. I was praying there wouldn't be."

"I wanted there to be sirens and rockets," twelve-year-old Peter said, "to know what it's like for Misha."

I glanced at George. His blue eyes were serious as he met my gaze. He briefly raised his heavy, dark eyebrows at me, and with that one look, we comprehended each other's thoughts. Our son was wrestling with deep issues.

"You wanted to be able to understand what Misha's going through?" George asked Peter.

"Yeah, I wanted to sit with him in his hallway during the siren and hear the explosions. Then, when he writes that there's a siren, I'll know what it's like."

The city had been quiet for the entirety of our visit, but that night, just hours after we got safely away, the sirens began to wail. Missiles were headed for Kyiv again.

48

It's Not All Bad

April 22–23, 2023
Vienna, Austria

The next morning, we were relieved to learn that none of our friends had been hurt by the previous night's aerial attack on Kyiv. A few days later, we were back in Budapest, the harsh realities of life in Ukraine still fresh in our minds. It was surreal to cross a border and immediately be in a place where people felt safe and life was normal. How could everyone go about their business as if nothing was wrong when, just next door, there was a country where people lived with the daily threat of sudden death from the skies? It was difficult not to feel guilty about resuming our peaceful life when our friends did not have that option. At the same time, we couldn't just sit around and feel sad. We had plans to keep and obligations to fulfill.

The day after we returned from Ukraine, Samuel and I got on a train from Budapest to Vienna. Samuel was running his first marathon, the full 26.2 miles (40.2 kilometers). Whatever happened the next day at the race, just getting to this point was a major victory.

During the October before Russia's February 2022 invasion of Ukraine, Samuel had run his first race. It was a 10K charity event (6.2 miles/10 kilometers). Other participants and bystanders were amazed that a fourteen-year-old was running that distance. George and I were stunned by how quickly Samuel had turned his body into a distance-running machine.

What began as a whim at a kids' camp that summer had quickly become a passion. As soon as we realized he was serious, we bought him a pair of high-end running shoes, and Samuel trained daily, sometimes on his own, sometimes with Aron, the father of the Ethiopian family with whom we were friends. To augment his training, Samuel devoured information on running technique and training routines and watched YouTube videos about the world's top distance runners.

When we evacuated, Samuel lost both his running partner and his interest in the sport. Even after his uncle and aunt bought him new running shoes to replace the ones he'd forgotten in Ternopil, he only ran a few times. After we resettled in Budapest, I knew I had to help him recover his passion.

For several weeks, I encouraged him to go running at the park. It had a 1.25-mile (2-kilometer) running path covered in a rubberized, springy surface. Samuel wasn't interested.

"Why not, Samuel?"

"I don't want to."

"Then why did you ask Daddy to buy you those expensive running clothes when he took you all to the sports store?"

"I dunno."

"C'mon, Samuel. You asked for those, and now you're not even using them."

"Why are you pushing me?"

"Because you used to love running. It makes me sad that you've lost that."

I was sure that if he got back into a running routine, it would rekindle his love for the sport. I insisted he run at least one lap around the park most days. I called it his P.E. requirement. It was a challenge to get him out the door, and I got tired of the struggle. Could I find a better way?

Remembering how he'd run with Melanie after she and Paul bought him the shoes, I wondered if he just needed a running partner. I disliked running, but I kept myself reasonably fit with home workouts. Jogging more than a mile didn't sound pleasant, but I was pretty sure I could do it without embarrassing myself. The question was whether I was willing to put myself through it. Looking at my eldest son, I knew it would be worth the sacrifice.

"Samuel, would it help if I went running with you?"

"I dunno. Maybe."

"What if I ran with you twice a week, and you could train on your own the other days?"

"I guess. We could try," he mumbled.

I'd hoped for a more enthusiastic response, but I was glad he was at least open to the idea. "Okay, shall we start tomorrow then?"

"Okay, I guess."

The next morning was a sunny spring day. To my Hawaii-born, California-raised sensibilities, there was a slight nip in the air, but I could tell the afternoon would be warm. Samuel and I walked to the park together. He wore the running clothes George had bought him during the shopping spree at the sports store: dark leggings and a coordinating top made from a special sweat-wicking fabric.

I was wearing my pajamas.

I felt indecent and exposed, but the worn-out gray cotton leggings and t-shirt I used for sleeping were the only things I had suitable for running. I'd left all my workout clothes behind in Kyiv. *No one can tell these are pajamas. Plenty of people run in leggings and a t-shirt. You'll fit right in on the running path*, I told myself.

Once we got to the park, we stretched on the grass. When we were ready to run, Samuel told me to set the pace, and he'd match me. I picked the fastest speed I felt I could maintain for the complete loop. Samuel jogged easily beside me, making conversation. The sun was bright, the air was fresh, and we chatted cheerfully.

After we'd run about a quarter of the distance, I didn't feel like talking anymore: I was too focused on maintaining an even cadence and breathing properly. I was worried about tiring too soon and being a poor workout partner. Besides that, I didn't want to look like a weakling in front of my son.

Samuel kept up a steady stream of commentary and questions. I kept my answers short to conserve my breath. As we approached the half-way point and I felt my leg muscles beginning to tire, I pushed myself to run faster than was comfortable. I was relieved when we finished the loop. I stretched in the grass, panting slightly.

"Good job, Mommy! You almost kept the same pace the whole time!"

This encouraging coach persona was a new side to my son. It was sweet and warmed my heart. "Thanks, Samuel. It was probably way too slow for you, yeah?"

"No, it was fine. I was actually surprised what a fast pace you set."

"You're kidding, right?"

"No, I mean it."

I laughed. "You just thought your mom was too old to run."

"No, Mommy, c'mon! You did a good job."

"Okay, thanks." I realized he was sincere. "Did it help to have me run with you?"

"I think so."

"Is it worth it for me to keep doing it?"

"Yeah."

"Are you gonna run some more right now?" I tried to sound nonchalant, but I felt like a lot was riding on his answer. Would he continue on his own? Would he reconnect with his inner runner?

"No," he said.

I was disappointed, but I didn't push.

Before we were able to run together again, we flew to Hawaii for my grandpa's memorial service. We didn't manage to run while in Hawaii, but the next week we stayed with my sister in Northern California. Samuel asked if a group of us would go running with him. He was insistent, and despite the oppressive summer heat, my sister, her two daughters, and I agreed to jog to the park and back. However, we were too slow for Samuel, and he ran ahead. I was pleased to see him taking the initiative with his running again.

Our next stop was Colorado to visit a church that supported us. Two of the pastors were avid runners and invited Samuel to join them. To my joy, he eagerly accepted. Though he struggled with the workout at high altitude, he enjoyed it. The experience flipped a switch inside him. After we left Colorado, he began to run daily on his own. We relocated every few days, but despite our hectic schedule and changing locations, he managed to stay consistent with his runs.

Soon Samuel got interested in competing again. He pored over US race schedules online to find events that coincided with our crazy itinerary. In July, he ran a 5K race (3.1miles/5 kilometers) while we were in Indiana, and in August, he ran another 5K race while we were visiting my parents in Southern California. He also connected with a boy his age who was a nationally ranked runner.

This new friendship turbo-charged Samuel's growing enthusiasm for the sport.

In September, after we returned to Budapest, Samuel ran two 10K races (6.2 miles/10 kilometers). In October, he ran a 10K/5K, back-to-back combo. Along the way, he even got nine-year-old James into running, and James competed in shorter races at three of Samuel's events.

After Samuel's October race, he set his sights on the marathon distance. He was determined to earn the distinction of running a marathon at the age of sixteen. Most European marathons do not permit minors to run, but the Vienna City Marathon allowed Samuel to enter after we signed a parental waiver form. We bought him a training plan, a heart monitor, and a running watch to keep track of his distance and pace. He began a rigorous schedule of training runs and strength workouts. For months, his life revolved around his running. Then, a month before the race, he got sick.

He was on his back for several days, and even after he was feeling better, it took over a week before he felt strong enough to resume running. The experience interrupted his training schedule at the critical phase when he was supposed to be doing the longest, hardest runs. By the time he made a full recovery, the plan was calling for shorter distances to allow his body to rest so it could be in peak shape on race day. Samuel was tempted to do the hard runs he had missed while sick, but a veteran marathoner advised him to follow the plan. Otherwise, he risked being too worn out to compete well.

Samuel and I traveled to Vienna the day before the race. George stayed in Budapest to take care of the rest of the kids. On race morning, Samuel and I took public transport to the starting line. Over 33,000 people were running. There were crowds everywhere we went. Samuel stretched then found the segment of runners where he was supposed to start. I gave him a hug and wished him luck.

Thanks to the chip in his race bib, I could track his progress on my phone. I wanted to cheer him on from the sidelines, so I picked a spot about one-third of the way along the route and traveled there on the subway. When I came above ground, I checked Samuel's progress. I was shocked to see that he was almost at my position. I'd miscalculated. I tried to rush from the subway to the race route, but the crowds were so thick, I had trouble moving quickly. Beautiful, historic buildings lined the road, but I barely glanced at them. Instead, I looked for openings between people and darted through to speed up my progress. But it was all for nothing. I watched helplessly as the moving dot showing Samuel's location passed my position. I was too far from the curb to see him or shout encouragement.

I struggled through the crowds back to the subway station and picked another spot farther along the route. But once again the crowds were too thick, and Samuel was moving too fast for me. At this rate, I was going to be late to the finish line, and that was not an option. I got back on the subway and headed straight to the end of the course. I arrived in plenty of time, but the compact mass of people between me and the curb made it impossible to see anything. After failing to cheer Samuel on from the sidelines, I was determined to take a video of him crossing the finish line.

There were trees enclosed in tall metal railings lining the road. Some spectators had climbed up on the railings to get a better view. There weren't any free perches that I could see, but I moved close to one of the trees and prayed for an opening. After a few minutes, several people climbed down. I quickly hoisted myself up, gaining a clear view of the final stretch.

When Samuel came into sight, he was running strong, his lanky frame moving easily. As he passed me, his posture was straight, and the end of his rattail bounced in time to his stride.

I whooped and shouted like a college girl at a football game. "Go, Samuel! C'mon, Samuel!"

I glanced at the digital race clock above the finish line. He'd finished in three hours and forty minutes. I knew he'd be disappointed: his goal had been three hours and thirty minutes. I climbed down from the railing and went in search of him.

"Good job, Samuel! How do you feel?" I gave him a hug.

"I have a lot of energy."

"Ha ha. Yeah, right. Suuure." I chuckled and shook my head at his joke.

"No, really, I mean it. I paced myself too slow."

"Oh! You mean you held back too much?"

"Yeah. I didn't know how much energy I needed to save. I could've run it in three-thirty."

"That's a bummer! I'm sorry, Samuel."

"Yeah."

"But you did it! You ran a marathon at the age of sixteen! That's amazing!"

"I guess."

"What do you mean, 'You guess'? How many other sixteen-year-olds do you think have done that?"

"It was easy."

"Well, okay . . . that just shows how amazing you are! *No one* says that when they finish a marathon!"

To celebrate, I took him out for a nice meal at an Italian restaurant before we caught our three-hour train back to Budapest. I would never have chosen to be displaced by war, but I couldn't deny that traveling to Vienna, one of Europe's most famous cities, to cheer my eldest son on at a big race, had been an unforgettable experience. We probably would never have considered doing this if we were still in Ukraine. When we lived in Kyiv, we had felt too far away from the rest of the world to consider jaunting around Europe. I had to admit not all the changes in our life had been bad.

49

Taking Back Control

Spring–Summer 2023
Budapest, Hungary

As we became more established in Budapest, I experienced a troublesome side-effect of being displaced. I had unpacked the things we recovered from Kyiv and was overjoyed to have all my favorite sweaters again. One day I donned a lovely green turtleneck that had been a gift from my sister. Wearing it felt like receiving a warm hug from her. I surveyed my reflection in the mirror, smiling at myself in the familiar garment.

But something was missing.

I stared at my reflection, struggling to remember. Then it came to me. I had always worn this sweater with a long, purple-bead necklace my sister had made for me. The green and purple complemented each other perfectly, and the beads added my favorite color to the outfit.

I pulled out the basket that held the jewelry I had brought with me when we evacuated. Since my jewelry box was still in Kyiv, I had organized my necklaces into an empty candy box. Everything was right where I expected, except for the purple beads. I searched, shifting the contents of the basket, peering under things and into corners. The beads were missing.

What had I done with them? When did I last wear them?

Suddenly, I realized I couldn't recall having used them—or even having seen them—since before the start of the full-scale war. They must still be in Kyiv, buried somewhere among the things I hadn't had time to sort through during our short visit.

Why had I been so certain I had them? What was wrong with my mind? Was I headed toward early dementia? I felt like I was losing control.

The more established we got, the more frequent this sort of confusion became. Though frustrating, I eventually realized it was a positive sign of how comfortable I was becoming with our new life. We had everything we needed, and we felt settled. Our current experience had many similarities to our former life. We had retrieved possessions from Kyiv, we had the same three pets, and even some of the same friends. The familiar things surrounding me lulled me into believing that everything from before the war should be at my fingertips now.

I realized as soon as we moved into the larger apartment, we were going to feel even more settled. Would that help me feel more in control?

Moving day finally arrived. With almost no furniture, it was one of our easiest moves. Pre-war moves had involved transporting lots of furniture and a piano. Although we missed our belongings in Ukraine, having fewer things to move was wonderful.

After the five younger boys and I overcame our initial resistance to moving, we had embraced the plan. We were taking back control of our lives. When we finally claimed the apartment keys, we'd been dreaming about the apartment for so long that it already felt like home.

The kids were ecstatic about all the extra space. The four youngest boys played together excitedly, climbing up and down from the loft in the kids' bedroom and running back and forth—until the neighbors downstairs complained about the noise. After that, no more running was allowed in the apartment.

We got to know our new location. The park was close, a bus stop was just outside the building, and a tiny grocery store stood around the corner. The store was the setting for a major milestone in my adjustment to living in Hungary.

One evening, I ran out of salt. Rather than ride my bicycle to the larger grocery store across from our old apartment building, I decided to try the little shop. I'd never been inside, but I was confident they would carry a simple staple like salt. It was getting dark, and I hurried down the sidewalk, unsure if the store would be open this late. To my relief, it was.

I pushed open the glass door and heard a bell attached to it ding once. The interior was a tiny, cramped space, presided over by a grim-faced woman standing behind a counter with her arms crossed. I nodded to her and started looking for the salt.

To maximize the small area, the shelves displayed only a few items of each available product. I scanned them. There was soap and toothpaste, tomato paste and pasta, bread and crackers, water, soda, beer, and whiskey, but no salt. Unwilling to give up, I searched the shelves again, slower this time, certain salt had to be somewhere. If it was, I couldn't find it.

What should I do? The middle-aged shopkeeper didn't seem like someone who would be able to speak English. In my experience, English-speaking clerks tended to be younger and friendlier. I briefly contemplated trying to communicate my need with hand motions. An expat friend once told me she pantomimed a chicken laying an egg to ask where the eggs were in a large grocery store, but I had no idea how to act out the word *salt*.

Then, with a flash of recognition, I realized I actually knew how to say, "Where is the salt?" in Hungarian. I was so surprised that I didn't immediately do anything.

Up to that point, all my hours studying Hungarian using language-learning apps on my phone had not given me the ability to say many useful things. I could parrot my favorite sentence perfectly, but I had yet to find a context where "I wash dishes, and I sing" was a helpful thing to say. I certainly had never created my own sentence to serve in a specific situation.

But I had learned to say, "Where is the bus?" and I knew the Hungarian word for salt. I mentally rehearsed my sentence, then I gathered my courage, approached the clerk, and carefully enunciated, "*Hol van a só?*"

She answered with a lot of detail that I didn't understand, but I caught one word. Ott. "There." And I noted the direction she was pointing.

"*Kőszőnőm.*" I thanked her and went where she indicated. On the bottom shelf, in plain sight beside the rolled oats, were bags of salt. How had I missed them? I grabbed a bag, paid, and left the store.

I forced myself to walk calmly down the sidewalk, but I wanted to skip, leap, twirl, pump my fist, and whoop. After a year and a half of linguistic helplessness, it was powerful to know precisely what to say. One of the most demoralizing experiences of my life had been leaving Ukraine just when I was finally able to communicate with conviction and nuance. Having spent nineteen years mastering one language, the idea of starting from scratch with a new one made me feel like quitting. But here was hope that I could regain control over this aspect of my life also.

The salt had barely cost anything, but it felt like a weighty treasure as I carried it home.

A few weeks after moving into the new apartment, we made our second trip back to Ukraine. This time, we didn't go all the way to Kyiv. Instead, we stayed in Ternopil. The four older boys were attending a kids' camp with cousins and friends, and George and I looked forward to reconnecting with people we barely had time to see during our rushed spring visit.

Though Ternopil had only been targeted a few times since the beginning of the full-scale war, there were frequent air-raid sirens. The chilling wail triggered memories of the first time I heard it, along with the shock, fear, and heartache of the war's onset. No matter how long I live, it will remain one of the most mournful sounds I have ever heard. It was impossible to feel indifferent. It made me want to clamp my hands over my ears, or weep—or both.

The locals ignored the sirens, and if your apartment was far from downtown, you couldn't even hear them. The apartment we'd rented was close to the siren speakers, but just to be safe, I also downloaded an air-alert app for my phone. The siren and my app both startled me awake the first night.

I shook George, sprang out of bed, and rushed to wake all the kids. The older boys hadn't left for camp yet. Expecting George to resist going to a bomb shelter in a city unlikely to be targeted, I chose to follow the two-wall rule instead. Like our Kyiv friends, we went into the apartment hallway. I shut the doors to every room as a precaution against flying glass or shrapnel, and then the eight of us sat on the floor with our backs to the walls. I made sure everyone avoided the less protected areas near the doors.

"Mommy!" Seven-year-old Andrew's normally worried expression had escalated to one of terror. "What's going to happen?"

I darted across the doorway between him and me and sat on the floor beside him, wrapping my arms around him and pulling him onto my lap. Five-year-old Isaac snuggled against me, and I put an arm around him too.

"Probably nothing, sweetie. The siren is just to warn people. Ternopil almost never gets hit."

"I'm scared!" Andrew sounded like he was about to cry.

Sixteen-year-old Samuel spoke up from the far end of the hallway. "C'mon, Andrew, what are you scared of?"

"Yeah," fourteen-year-old Kiyoshi added, "even if a rocket came here, there're so many buildings. Do you even realize how small the odds are that it would hit this one? And if it did, it wouldn't hit this apartment."

I felt Andrew stiffen.

"Okay, boys, that's not helping Andrew feel better," George said.

"Let's pray," I said. "Who'd like to pray for us?"

"I will," Kiyoshi said. "Dear God, please help Andrew not to be scared. Please help the rockets not to come to Ternopil. And . . . thank you that we got to come here. Amen."

Later that day, George's brother Jon explained that most of the air-raid alerts in Ternopil were caused by a specific type of military plane taking off somewhere in the Russian Federation. Because it could launch long-range missiles, whenever one was airborne, every region in Ukraine was under an air-raid alert until it landed. Often one would take off, cruise around for twenty minutes, then land without launching any missiles—sometimes several times per day. I heard people joke that the Russians were just doing it to annoy their neighbors.

To me, it was no joking matter. All it would take was one time when the pilot had orders to fire. Those who let down their guard could be hurt or killed. Jon showed me how to look up the reasons for ongoing alerts and monitor incoming threats, in case we didn't want to shelter every time a warplane took off in Russia. I thanked him, but I couldn't imagine ignoring the sirens—not when I had small children in my care.

That night, Andrew didn't want to sleep in his room. His older brothers had left for camp, and he felt vulnerable.

"I want to sleep in the hall." His eyebrows tilted up in the middle as he looked at me.

"No, sweetie, you can't sleep in the hallway."

"But what if there's a siren?"

"If there's a siren, I'll hear it, and I'll move you into the hallway."

"Are you sure?"

"Yes! Look—I'll make a bed on the floor for you with this comforter, and then I can just pull you right into the hallway." I demonstrated, pulling the improvised bed across the slick laminate floor with him on it. His worried expression relaxed, and he giggled.

"You promise?" he asked.

"Yes, I promise."

"You pull me too?" Little Isaac's enormous brown eyes looked up at me expectantly. He didn't seem worried, but apparently he didn't want to miss out on the action.

"Yes, I'll pull you too." I smiled at him.

Before George and I went to bed, I propped a twin mattress against the hallway wall. If we ended up sheltering there again, at least we would be comfortable.

A few hours later, I was jolted awake by the wail of the siren. I quickly pulled the sleeping boys into the hallway without disturbing them, and George and I cuddled on the mattress until the all-clear sounded. This happened nearly every night. George and I would go back to bed afterward, but we'd leave the boys undisturbed till morning. Andrew and Isaac got used to falling asleep in their bedroom and waking up in the hallway with no memory of the nocturnal siren.

When the sirens woke me on Saturday night, I went through the normal routine, pulling Andrew and Isaac into the hallway and putting the mattress on the floor. George was still asleep. I checked my phone to see the cause of the alert, expecting it to be just another warplane cruising around in Russian airspace.

It was not. A missile was headed toward Ternopil. My mouth went dry, and I felt lightheaded. I dashed back into our bedroom and shook George awake. I couldn't understand how he was able to sleep through the sirens.

"Do we really have to go into the hall?" he said.

I thrust my phone in his face and jabbed my finger at the announcement that a missile was headed our way. "Yes, we do!"

He still didn't seem worried, but he followed me back to the hallway. Wanting the kids as far from the bedroom doors as possible, I laid little Isaac on a comforter in the narrow space between the mattress and the inner wall, and I placed Andrew on the mattress beside me. Neither boy awoke. Lying on the other side of me, George dozed off within seconds, but I was on high alert. Sandwiched between George and Andrew, every muscle tense, I strained my ears in the darkness. I kept checking my phone for updates.

The missile had entered the Ternopil region.

Now it was in the air right over the city of Ternopil.

I couldn't believe what was happening. Ternopil was supposed to be safe. How could an instrument of death and destruction be right above our heads? I wanted to hide my dear ones, to stretch a canopy of protection over all of us. The two walls between us and the potential point of impact seemed flimsy, inadequate. I wanted to do something, but it was too late to go to a bomb shelter. The missile could strike at any moment. There was nothing I could do except pray and wait. I was grateful that the older boys were safely outside the city. Their remote camp was unlikely to attract any air strikes.

Please, God, please let it pass us by. Let it pass us by. Don't let it hit here.

I immediately felt guilty. I was essentially asking God to let the missile hit other people. How could I do that? I changed my approach.

God, please protect everyone.

I waited in the darkness, praying until the all-clear sounded. *Oh, thank you, Jesus!* I crept back to bed for the few remaining hours before my alarm would go off. The sky was already brightening. George and the boys were sound asleep. I left them in the hall.

It was a Sunday, and after we got up, we headed for church. There we learned some people had actually heard the roar of the rocket passing overhead. The pastor, who lived on the top floor of his apartment building, said the vibrations had rattled his windows.

The rocket had struck a neighboring region. Thankfully, no loss of life was reported. God had answered the collective prayers of everyone who engaged in the spiritual battle to defend Ukraine that night.

Sirens went off during daylight hours just as often as they did at night. One day I was watching Andrew and Isaac and two of their young cousins at our apartment when I heard the familiar wail. It started out low, then it steadily gained volume as the pitch rose, lingered, then fell again. I hurried to the living room, where the children were playing.

"Okay, kids," I said calmly, "let's go sit in the hallway on the mattress."

Isaac giggled. "Mommy, it's Andrew!"

"What?" I noticed the siren had stopped already.

"I was making the noise," Andrew said. "Listen." He started again.

My mouth dropped open. He was pitch-perfect. It was eerie.

From that point on, Andrew seemed much less frightened. After we returned to Budapest, Andrew and Isaac went through a phase when one of their favorite activities was to mimic the air-raid siren. I tried to get used to it. Though the wail made me want to clutch my heart each time they started, I didn't discourage their play.

One day, the quality of the sound was different. Was this the real thing? But it couldn't be. I'd been through this debate with myself before. Hungary was practically the last place Putin would attack. Curious, trying not to worry, I walked through the apartment looking for Andrew and Isaac. I found them in the living room. Andrew was holding an empty metal can, wailing into the open end. The reverberations amplified the noise and added a metallic edge that defied my ability to distinguish this sound from the real deal.

For eighteen months, I had been trying to help my boys come to terms with the war and everything we had experienced. I got them to talk on a few occasions, but a therapist told me kids usually do not process through speech. They lack the vocabulary and self-awareness. For many children, play is the best outlet. Our second trip to Ukraine had an unintended effect. It allowed our two youngest kids to take control of the war through play.

50

A Homecoming

Thanksgiving 2023
Budapest, Hungary

Throughout the spring and summer of 2023, we took advantage of the warm weather to connect with Ukrainians at the park. We rented the miniature soccer field on Sunday afternoons and invited Ukrainian kids to play. We brought food to share and encouraged the other parents to do the same. That began a tradition of Sunday afternoon picnics, and our children made new friends. Often we'd hang out until dinner time—or until late-afternoon thundershowers chased us all home.

After our move, we finally gained traction in our efforts to start a Ukrainian church in our home. Old and new friends joined us in our larger apartment each week to discuss the Bible. As the months passed, we moved beyond small talk to communicate on a deeper level. We shared our highs and lows, triumphs and disappointments, joys and fears. A community was forming around our spiritual discussions. We helped each other, prayed together, played together, ate together, and celebrated.

The group cheered my efforts to write this book. We followed the job search of a man who was providing for his displaced mother. We encouraged an entrepreneurial couple who were starting over after losing everything they'd built in Ukraine. We prayed with a couple whose son insisted on returning to Ukraine after his eighteenth birthday, despite the risk of being drafted into the army. We supported a doctoral student who abandoned Russia in protest over the war and was experiencing a crisis of identity over the evil deeds of her country.

We also said goodbyes: one woman realized she couldn't put her life on hold any longer. Despite the risks, she moved back to Ukraine to marry her fiancé and have children. Another member of our community, a Ukrainian seaman, was only with us for a few months between two ocean voyages. After these friends left, they remained in our hearts, and we cherished the thought of future reunions.

Thanksgiving 2023 found us in a better place. The previous November had us in a cramped apartment, living with a refugee mindset, missing home, and mourning the loss of friendships we had enjoyed in Ukraine.

We hadn't invited anyone to share our Thanksgiving meal in 2022. In Ukraine, we usually had friends join us, but that first year in Hungary, I felt too homesick and heartsick to entertain. In the end, we'd attended a Thanksgiving potluck at a conference near Budapest.

As we approached our second Thanksgiving outside Ukraine, our family circle had grown by two, because a Ukrainian couple with nowhere else to go was living in the guest room in our new apartment. Besides that, friends and acquaintances frequently came to our home to eat, hang out, and have fun. We had embraced a mindset of abundance and were enjoying the people in our lives.

As Thanksgiving approached, I wasn't sure how I wanted to celebrate. Should it be a private affair for the ten people living in our apartment? Or should we share the day with a larger circle? In the end, my desire for friends and community won out over my love for calm and quiet.

Samuel volunteered to make half of the traditional dishes. A few months after achieving his dream of running a marathon, he pivoted from one passion to another. He took up cooking again, something for which he'd shown an interest and aptitude since the age of five. He loved creating elaborate meals and jumped at the chance to experiment with new Thanksgiving recipes. I prepared our traditional favorites and asked all our guests to contribute something. We rearranged the kitchen and set up extra tables.

Samuel and I were still working when our first friend arrived, a woman who was part of our team of displaced people serving Ukrainian refugees all over Hungary. Like any self-respecting Ukrainian, she immediately washed her hands and joined us in putting the finishing touches on the meal. As each guest arrived, the celebratory atmosphere increased. Soon we had many helping hands, and lively conversation and laughter filled the kitchen. It felt like old times in the kitchen of our large Kyiv apartment. This is what I had been pining for. More than anything else since being displaced, I had longed for this sense of community.

We crowded around the tables, shoulder-to-shoulder, until everyone had a seat. George said a simple prayer of thanksgiving, then Samuel and I served the food. Everyone exclaimed about how delicious it was.

As we finished the meal, George asked what we were most thankful for.

Everyone had gone through incredible difficulties over the previous twenty-one months. We had all been displaced. Some had been forced to roam city streets at night, seeking shelter. One woman had lost her husband, a Ukrainian serviceman who died in a military-related auto accident. All of us were far from home and separated from loved ones.

But as each person shared their answer to George's question, everyone sounded sincerely grateful. Light and love filled the room, banishing the darkness and pain that once threatened to overpower us all.

Long before it was my turn, I knew my answer. I was thankful for all these friends celebrating with us in our home.

Perhaps my response sounded hasty and superficial, as if I'd grasped at the most obvious thing without taking time to reflect. The opposite was true.

As I gazed at the happy faces filling the room, I was amazed. Many were new friends. Had we stayed in Ukraine, our paths would never have crossed. This was not our old life transplanted—this was a new life. It had been growing slowly, now blossoming into this beautiful expression of love and friendship around a shared meal.

How had we gotten here from the anguish and devastation of the previous year? Had that desolate Thanksgiving been only twelve months ago? How had we discovered this fullness and joy so far from home? Questions swirled, then suddenly they gave way to a dazzling realization.

I *was* home.

Just as I'd chosen to build a life in Ukraine two decades ago, I'd finally made a similar choice in Hungary. It had crept up on me. I couldn't remember a specific moment when I said, *Okay, Budapest is my home now. I choose to be fully present, to be happy and content.* And yet, there I was: happy and content, enjoying a sense of home.

Thinking in those terms brought a pang. Ukraine still felt like home. If not for the danger of life in the capital city and the importance of our work in Hungary, I would have returned to Kyiv's Podil district in a heartbeat.

I swallowed and blinked to stop the tears that threatened to spoil the moment. Was I doomed always to feel torn? Could we hope for a full existence after everything we had experienced? But separate from the questions and the sadness, something sweet and tender was growing within me. I was determined to water it and help it thrive. I owed it to myself and my family to clear away the wreckage of my dreams and create space for this new life.

I inhaled deeply and opened my heart to embrace a surprising truth. I had fought it. I had denied it. Now I accepted it.

Home is anywhere you have the courage to put down roots.

Epilogue

Daring to Dream

February 24, 2025
Budapest, Hungary

Three years ago today, our world was shattered. Our life before the full-scale Russian invasion was a beautiful dream. Every time I walked the streets around the converted old mansion that housed our apartment in downtown Kyiv, I couldn't help but thank God. That charming neighborhood—filled with historic buildings, trendy cafés, interesting restaurants, and unique shops—felt like a gift. We had a close-knit church family who all lived within walking distance and a wider community of friends who were in and out of our home on a regular basis. To top it all off, our new landlords told us we could stay at least five years, and we planned to do precisely that. After fourteen moves in eighteen years of marriage, we were finally settled. I was profoundly content.

I never imagined the dream would only last nine months, or that we would end up more unsettled than ever, relocating seven times in just three and a half chaotic weeks. When we finally landed somewhere we could stay long-term, we found ourselves in Budapest.

Once I had time to reflect, I worried we'd moved to Budapest too haphazardly. Normally, relocating to another country would be deliberate, involving research and prayer. We would only proceed once we were sure God was leading us. But this time, we had been leaves in a turbulent stream, tumbled about until the current smacked us up against the muddy riverbank somewhere. What if we were not supposed to be in Budapest at all—or Hungary, for that matter? What if God had intended us to go elsewhere?

As I wrestled with those thoughts, I felt the gentle presence of God whispering to my soul: *Who controls the current of the stream?*

And I knew. He did. He always had.

That meant we were exactly where we were supposed to be. Though still traumatized by the route, I was finally at peace with the destination.

Friends from our life before the war ended up in Budapest also, and we see them regularly. Our circle has expanded to include new friends as well. In many respects, you could say we are still living a beautiful dream. Sometimes it feels more like a nightmare, but increasingly, the pain of the past fades into a distant background behind a present joy. More and more, I can forget that we didn't choose this life, that we are only here because a life we loved was stolen.

Even so, sometimes I am overcome by a sharp longing for home—not a homesickness for Ukraine, but something more profound. It is a deep yearning for my true home, for something just beyond my reach, a sweetness of friendship yet untasted, a sense of belonging still impossible to achieve.

After moving abroad as a missionary, I learned to appreciate the unsettled feeling of not fitting in a foreign place. It was a constant reminder that my true home is elsewhere. It helped me keep my priorities in order and my heart focused on my eternal home with Jesus and the family of all God's people. Over time, I began to appreciate living in this tension. I considered it a privilege to be unable to get so comfortable that I forgot this reality.

Now, displaced both by calling and war, I experience this strain even more acutely. I will never truly feel at home until the day Jesus restores creation to its original blueprint: a paradise where humans work together in perfect harmony. Scarcity, disease, and suffering will be distant memories, nearly forgotten under the beauty of God's good world. Can I be thankful for this more painful reminder of that glorious future? I am learning to be grateful even for this.

While editing this book, I experienced a revelation. I was transiting through an airport, and as I walked down the jetway toward the terminal, I eyed a series of advertising messages posted on the wall. The words on one literally stopped me in my tracks.

Is home where you're from or where you're going?

It was like the sign was calling to me—singling me out of the flow of people rushing past—to pose this arresting question. This poster suddenly laid bare the problem that had plagued me ever since the day I took my children and fled Ukraine in February 2022.

After we resettled in Hungary, when people asked me, "Where are you from?" I would usually say, "I'm American, but I'm from Ukraine." I ached to go back because it was where I was *from*. For months and months, I couldn't conceive of feeling any other way. But that ad in the airport forced me to confront the truth that I hadn't always been from Ukraine, and I hadn't always called it home. When I moved there twenty-two years ago, I would have said I was from the United States. But though I still felt like the US was home, I was already anticipating the time when Ukraine would become home.

There was a tectonic shift in my outlook between when I moved to Ukraine and when I moved to Hungary. Twenty-two years ago, my parents dropped George and me off at Los Angeles International Airport and hugged us goodbye. We were newlyweds, and I was headed to Ukraine to join George in a life he already had well established. I knew where I was going, and I had chosen it. I was focused on the destination, and I was excited about the future. I started to call Ukraine home years before it felt that way. Back then, I definitely would have said home was where I was going, not where I was from.

But somewhere between fleeing Kyiv by train and spending a sleepless night in a basement in Western Ukraine because of air-raid sirens, I lost this sense of adventure. When I got into the van that evacuated us to Hungary, I was hardly focused on the destination. My only thought was to get my kids to safety. Unlike that day in 2003 when my parents dropped me off at the LA Airport, I didn't know where I was going, and I felt like I had no choice in the matter.

I have spent so much of the last three years mourning the fact that we had to leave home. I was focused on where we were from. I knew I needed to move forward, but it was hard to stop looking backward. The pull of home was so strong. I was missing it too much to turn my face away. But it's hard to make progress when you're looking over your shoulder all the time.

Little by little, my focus has changed. Unexpectedly, I started to enjoy Budapest. I began to form new friendships in this foreign place, and I started to put down roots, despite myself. One day I realized: *I have a life here.* I'm not merely existing anymore, waiting for the day the war is over so we can return to our real lives in Ukraine. I am active and invested in things going on around me. I'm not looking backward nearly as much. My focus is on the present and the future.

I am recovering my sense of adventure. For a while it felt like the experience of being displaced had eviscerated that brave young woman who moved to Ukraine without a backward glance. Why was relocating so hard this time? I felt like a different person, as if that woman was no longer a part of me. But now I sense she's still there. She's been bloodied and traumatized, but she's still breathing, and her pulse is stable again. In fact, it's gaining strength.

Today I can say once again that home is where I'm going, not where I'm from. Given the uncertainty of current events, I can't say I know for sure where that is, but I know I'm on my way.

Before You Go...

Dear Reader,

I'm on a mission to get 500 reviews to raise awareness about the plight of Ukrainians. If *Finding Home Again* touched something in you, would you please help more people discover it by leaving a review?

Even a single sentence makes a difference. Just share what you liked best about the book:

SharonTMarkey.com/finding-home-again

Thank you so much! Self-published authors rely on reviews to spread the word about their work.

Read more of my writing, join my community, and download a free seven-day devotional at: SharonTMarkey.com

Scan to leave review.

Acknowledgements

I owe a huge of debt of gratitude to everyone at The Write Practice and 100 Day Book. Your direction and feedback took what started as a series of blog posts and turned it into my first book. Special thanks to Joe Bunting, Sarah Gribble, Sandy Juker, Evelyn Puerto, Elizabeth Nettleton, Sally Husch Dean, Peggy Fish-Oliver, and Robert Harrell.

Thank you to the Pensives—Lynn Bunting, Joanna Medawar, and Suzanne Ruiter—my own Inklings. Your questions, insights, prayers, and support have been invaluable. Discussing these chapters with you has drawn out feelings and ruminations I didn't know I needed to express. This book is so much better because of you.

Joy Vee, your friendship, encouragement, and guidance always came at just the right time. Thank you for being perpetually ready to pray and share your professional experience.

Thank you to my editor, Jessi Rita Hoffman. I deeply appreciate your generosity and interest. Your expert advice alerted me to problems in the book that others had missed and gave me a compelling book description.

Rolf Vetter, thank you for believing in me and my book enough to fund this project. It's amazing to have a patron!

To the talented Sarah Janisse Brown, thank you for helping capture the suffering and hope in this story with your beautiful artwork.

Thank you to my six sons—Samuel, Kiyoshi, Peter, James, Andrew, and Isaac—for your patience and support as I worked to polish draft after draft.

George, thank you for never giving up on my dream of writing a book, even though it took over two decades to become reality.

Without your regular encouragement, I might have let the dream die.

And finally, to you, Jesus, I give my eternal gratitude for always being my true Home.

About the Author

Sharon T. Markey is an American-born author who spent nearly two decades living in Ukraine with her husband and six children, helping plant churches and build faith communities. In 2022, the Russian invasion abruptly ended their life there, forcing their family to flee the country they called home and begin again as refugees in Hungary.

A graduate of California State University at Long Beach with a BA in creative writing, Sharon writes true stories drawn from lived experience. A missionary, mother of six sons, and displaced person, she is especially drawn to stories of hope and redemption in the midst of suffering. *Finding Home Again* was birthed out of her family's journey through war, exile, and the search for belonging.

Scan to visit Sharon's website.

You can find her online at:
www.SharonTMarkey.com

About BridgeUA

Within the first month of Russia's full-scale war against Ukraine, Sharon's husband, George Markey, found himself surrounded by an astonishing number of opportunities to get involved in the global effort to help Ukraine. George's knack for seeing the big picture and connecting the right people had a tremendous impact: from funding grass-roots humanitarian missions to advising professional evacuation operations and facilitating the delivery of millions of dollars of military-grade protective gear.

Realizing that their work had grown beyond its pre-war, church-planting focus, in the spring of 2022, George and Sharon and their team nicknamed their ministry BridgeUA. (UA is the international abbreviation for Ukraine.) In 2023, BridgeUA became an official non-profit with a mission to meet the physical, emotional, and spiritual needs of war-affected Ukrainians by connecting them with God and with caring people all over the world.

George and Sharon have a dream that no Ukrainian would have to feel alone, but that each would have the opportunity to become part of a vibrant community of people who love and follow Jesus.

Learn more and get involved at:
www.BridgeUA.org

Scan to visit the BridgeUA website.

www.ingramcontent.com/pod-product-compliance
Lightning Source LLC
LaVergne TN
LVHW091108080826
845145LV00008B/1852

* 9 7 8 1 9 7 1 0 1 2 0 1 8 *